SUBMARINE COMMAND

In the first desperate year of World War II, the names of two ships were constantly in the headlines—one was H.M.S. *Sealion* and the other H.M.S. *Safari;* both were "S" class submarines and both achieved their greatest successes under the command of Rear-Admiral Ben Bryant.

He took part in the grim Norwegian campaign, surviving the hazards of depth-charging. He landed and retrieved agents in occupied Europe. He went on Mediterranean patrols, preying on Rommel's supply lines to North Africa. He survived more patrols than any other submarine commander, torpedoing or destroying by gunfire thirty-two enemy ships and damaging many more.

His was an exciting, adventurous career; he was one of Great Britain's most distinguished submarine aces.

THE BANTAM WAR BOOK SERIES

This series of books is about a world on fire.

The carefully chosen volumes in the Bantam War Book Series cover the full dramatic sweep of World War II. Many are eyewitness accounts by the men who fought in a global conflict as the world's future hung in the balance. Fighter pilots, tank commanders and infantry captains, among many others, recount exploits of individual courage. They present vivid portraits of brave men, true stories of gallantry, moving sagas of survival and stark tragedies of untimely death.

In 1933 Nazi Germany marched to become an empire that was to last a thousand years. In only twelve years that empire was destroyed, and ever since, the country has been bisected by her conquerors. Italy relinquished her colonial lands, as did Japan. These were the losers. The winners also lost the empires they had so painfully seized over the centuries. And one, Russia, lost over twenty million dead.

Those wartime 1940s were a simple, even a hopeful time. Hats came in only two colors, white and black, and after an initial battering the Allied nations started on a long and laborious march toward victory. It was a time when sane men believed the world would evolve into a decent place, but, as with all futures, there was no one then who could really forecast the world that we know now.

There are many ways to think about that war. It has always been hard to understand the motivations and braveries of Axis soldiers fighting to enslave and dominate their neighbors. Yet it is impossible to know the hammer without the anvil, and to comprehend ourselves we must know the people we fought against.

Through these books we can discover what it was like to take part in the war that was a final experience for nearly fifty million human beings. In so doing we may discover the strength to make a world as good as the one contained in those dreams and aspirations once believed by heroic men. We must understand our past as an honor to those dead who can no longer choose. They exchanged their lives in a hope for this future that we now inhabit. Though the fight took place many years ago, each of us remains as a living part of it.

SUBMARINE COMMANDER

REAR ADMIRAL BEN BRYANT

BANTAM BOOKS
NEW YORK • TORONTO • LONDON • SYDNEY • AUCKLAND

*This edition contains the complete text
of the original hardcover edition.
NOT ONE WORD HAS BEEN OMITTED.*

SUBMARINE COMMANDER
*A Bantam Book / published by arrangement with
William Kimber & Company, Ltd.*

PRINTING HISTORY
*First published in Great Britain in
1958 by William Kimber & Company, Ltd.
This book was originally published in Great Britain under
the title One Man Band.
Bantam edition / August 1980
2 printings through May 1989*

*Drawings by Greg Beecham.
Maps by Alan McKnight.*

ISBN 0-553-28266-2

Published simultaneously in the United States and Canada

PRINTED IN THE UNITED STATES OF AMERICA

KR   11 10 9 8 7 6 5 4 3 2

Submarine Commander Ben Bryant

CONTENTS

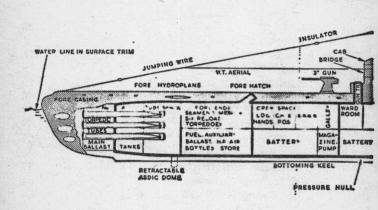

WATER LINE IN SURFACE TRIM

JUMPING WIRE

INSULATOR

W.T. AERIAL

CAB
BRIDGE

3" GUN

GUN TR

FORE HYDROPLANE

FORE HATCH

FORE CASING

FORE ENDS
SEAMENS MESS
S.A RELOAD
TORPEDOES

CREW SPACE
LDG. Cr. & P.O.S.
HANDS. POS.

WARD
ROOM

TORPEDO
TUBES

FUEL, AUXILIARY
BALLAST, H.P. AIR
BOTTLES, STORE

GALLEY

MAIN
BALLAST

TANKS

BATTERY

MAGA-
ZINE.
PUMP

BATTERY

RETRACTABLE
ASDIC DOME

BOTTOMING KEEL

PRESSURE HULL

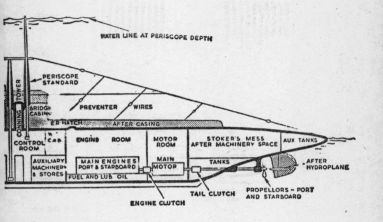

WATER LINE AT PERISCOPE DEPTH

PERISCOPE
STANDARD

CONNING TOWER

BRIDGE
CASING

PREVENTER WIRES

2 B HATCH

AFTER CASING

CONTROL
ROOM

W
C&B

ENGINE ROOM

MOTOR
ROOM

STOKER'S MESS
AFTER MACHINERY SPACE

AUX TANKS

AUXILIARY
MACHINERY
8 STORES

MAIN ENGINES
PORT & STARBOARD

MAIN
MOTOR

TANKS

AFTER
HYDROPLANE

FUEL AND LUB OIL

ENGINE CLUTCH

TAIL CLUTCH

PROPELLORS - PORT
AND STARBOARD

"S" CLASS SUBMARINE HMS SEALION

FOREWORD

It had been my intention in writing these reminiscences to mention no names except for a few senior officers whose identity was self evident.

So many served with me, some for short periods, some for long, that to mention all would be impractical. Although, in the event, a few names have crept in, these are fortuitous because they have happened to be concerned with the particular incident being described. It has been my object to avoid this book becoming a catalogue of names, either of men or ships.

If any of those who served with me read this book they will recognize the part they played. A submarine depended upon every single member of the crew and to all those who helped me to bring *Sealion* and *Safari* through those stirring times I dedicate this book.

The sort of things I have recounted in these chapters are the sort of things which happened in many other boats. But in one respect, for the submarine C.O., it was the end of an era. British submarines in 1939/43 had scarcely any electronic equipment. The boat was still fought practically entirely by eye, and in action the C.O. alone, at the periscope, could see or have any idea of what was going on. He had no time to take advice, it was a game for the individualist. But for the transformation of his appreciations into action, the C.O. relied entirely upon his crew; together they were an integrated fighting team. The development of electronics and vastly improved torpedo control systems have since revolutionized submarine warfare.

I am indebted to the Admiralty for allowing me to refresh my memory from my old patrol reports, and to Flag Officer, Submarines, for other aids to memory.

1

TRAINING CLASS

A familiar roughening of the rugged suspension of the old Hispano proclaimed the worst. Another back tire had gone. With both spares already expended, there was nothing for it but to set to by the side of the road and mend the best one, an occupation rendered the more unpleasant because it was now dark and had started to rain, and we had been up dancing nearly the whole of the night before.

It was the autumn of 1927, and Marjorie and I had been over to Belgium to spend my summer leave with my people. We had set out from Dorset three weeks before for Dover, allowing ourselves a 40 m.p.h. average, and, having tarried by the way, had ended up by putting more miles into the last hour than I have ever done before or since in a car on English roads. The Hispano was hard on tires and a sub-lieutenant's income did not lend itself to their renewal. They were usually near the canvas and that last dash to Dover had been too much for them, only the two on the front wheels were fit for further service. It was obvious that we must revise our plans.

I cannot remember if we were engaged or not at that time in our own minds; but we certainly were not in the eyes of my future in-laws. I was supposed to be driving Majorie from Dover to their house in the New Forest and then going back to H.M.S. *Dolphin*, the Submarine Base at Fort Blockhouse, Gosport, to join for my submarine training class. The tires might just get me to Gosport, the odds against their completing the extra eighty miles were infinite. The choice lay between incurring further parental disfavor, or a risk of being adrift for joining my new ship.

1

As always in the Service, domestic affairs have no precedence and when we limped into Fareham we holed up in
the local hotel. We had some difficulty in persuading a
suspicious proprietress, annoyed at being routed out of bed,
that all was above board, but she eventually produced a
room. So I left Marjorie there to make her own way back
next day and produce her own explanations to her parents,
and drove on the last few miles to Blockhouse. It was well
past midnight and this was to be my first day in the
submarine service; for Marjorie it was a prelude to the
knockabout life of a submariner's wife.

As I crossed the old drawbridge, long since disappeared, and passed through the archway under the battlements, I had no thought that twenty-one years later I
should be flying my broad pendant from those same
battlements as Commodore Submarines. I was just a very
anxious sub-lieutenant, wondering where to go.

A dance was just ending in the mess. Blockhouse
dances had a reputation; submariners got six shillings a
day extra pay, nearly half as much again as the 1925 rate
of pay for a lieutenant in general service, and were
comparatively wealthy young men; they did things well. I
hung back in the shadows and looked at the officers in
their mess dress, blue, gold and white. I suppose there
were women as well, but my eyes were on the men, to
whom Fort Blockhouse was home. I noted that some of
them, against all the uniform regulations, had flowers in
their buttonholes, but then submariners had a reputation
for being a bit of a law unto themselves, and the older
lieutenants and the lieutenant-commanders had medals.
They would have served in submarines in the 1914/18
war, hoary-headed veterans in their late twenties or thirties. They all seemed very sure of themselves and I tried to
fancy myself also as a submarine officer.

In the meantime I was feeling particularly unsure of
myself and wondering whom to consult. The matter was
solved by the hall porter, who had spotted me by the door.
Hall porters at all the old established schools which are the
headquarters of the various branches of the Navy are an
institution, and those at Blockhouse were no exception.
They, and Mr. Cawte, the Mess Secretary, seemed ageless;
as the years rolled by one could return to Blockhouse from
a foreign commission, from wanderings in general service,

perhaps for a reunion of old submariners, and always at
the hall porter's desk one would find a familiar face to
greet one. The hall porter had a list of the new training
class and when I gave him my name he told me the
number of my cabin and escorted me to it.

The training class in those days lived in a leaking old
hulk which was the name ship of the establishment,
H.M.S. *Dolphin*. She did not actually leak through the
bottom, but she did through the top. I found that I was to
have the dignity of a cabin—sometimes members of the
training class had to live a communal life on one of the
dim old mess decks. As far as I can remember at this time,
no one but the training class lived in H.M.S. *Dolphin*, the
remainder of the hulk being given over to offices—including that of Rear-Admiral Submarines, workshops and store
rooms.

H.M.S. *Dolphi*n had been known by many names.
Originally a merchant ship, she had been converted into a
submarine depot ship as H.M.S. *Pandora* and in her
declining years had been brought up Blockhouse creek and
secured alongside a jetty. She was badly in need of refit,
touching the mud at low water, and most of her cabins had
been condemned as unfit for human habitation, which
meant that they were suitable only for sub-lieutenants. I
had got used to living in the crowded squalor of the
midshipman's chest flat of a "Royal Sovereign" class battleship and, never having been one of those who claim to
like sleeping in a hammock, a cabin to myself, even if it
was small and smelling of damp wood, was sheer luxury.
Poor old *Dolphin*, re-fitted and patched up, continued to
prop up the jetty in Blockhouse creek till 1939. When the
war started, with all ships at a premium, she was towed
away to be used as a depot ship at Blyth. But she was
weary of wars, her aged bottom yearned for the support of
the Blockhouse mud and she settled to the bottom off the
east coast. She was typical of the submarine service, the
Cinderella of the Royal Navy, which somehow contrived
to remain efficient, with a morale and faith in itself
knowing no bounds; but, when it came to funds for
equipment, had all too often to rely upon ingenuity to
adapt to its own use things designed for other purposes.
However in the matter of depot ships a new era was
dawning and some very fine ships specifically designed to

ENGLISH CHANNEL

MILES
0   50   100   150

14 Fathom Line

service submarines and accommodate their crews were on the way.

At 09.00 next morning the training class, wearing frock coats and swords in accordance with tradition when joining a new ship, were introduced to the captain. Then we went off to our classroom outside the moat and the officer in charge of submarine training started the first lecture. He was called away in the middle, and thereafter we were turned over to Chief Petty-Officer Blake, a submarine torpedo gunman's mate of great experience. Blake and another T.G.M. in turn were for a number of years responsible for the instruction of the officers' training class. He taught us practically everything except engineering and wireless. Engineering was taught by Engineer Lieutenant Housego, an officer, like most of the submarine engineers of that era, who had come up the hard way. I cannot remember him without a pipe in his mouth and his lectures seemed mostly composed of the reasons why the various bits of mechanism of a submarine "fell over for a pastime."

I think it fair to say that at this time the reliability of a submarine engine was assessed not so much on the infrequency of a breakdown, as on the frequency of its recurrence. The shortcomings in the design of the early diesels were accentuated by the fact that they were condemned to operate mounted on a flexible structure. A popular little ditty in early submarine days started: *"Rock-a-bye diesel on the tank top."* As a result of this the bolts which held the cylinder head down, known for some reason as breech-end studs, used to fracture with such regularity that their replacement under way was a routine operation. When a cylinder, for some reason or other, failed to respond further to the efforts of strong men with crow bars, the practice was to "hang" the piston, that is to disconnect it from the crank shaft and secure it out of the way at the top of its stroke; special facilities were included in the design for this defeatist operation, and the engine then continued on the remaining cylinders. In this way the engine could keep going till it ran out of cylinders. Old-time submarine engineers would vie with each other in tales of how few pistons remained in action whilst they coaxed their boats home. With this background it was

logical that the training class should be as familiar with the
reasons for the equipment's failure to work as with its
workings when in good health.

But, compared with the far more elaborate training
program and the increased staff of officers and instructors,
which started building up shortly afterwards, the Blake/
Housego team had much to recommend it. We sub-lieutenants, having recently completed our technical courses,
were saturated with book learning. Our instructors, with
their great fund of practical experience, could give us the
knowledge we really needed. Equipment was pretty simple
in those days; the executive submarine officer was supposed to have a practical knowledge of all its working and
the aura of black magic with which technicians now invest
simple and complicated machines alike had not yet been
developed.

Blake was not only a man of ability, but of great
patience and understanding, for sub-lieutenants are not
particularly docile students. In the mornings we would
have lectures and in the afternoons go and actually work
the things we had heard about, in the boats along side; on
Fridays we would usually go to sea for the day in one of
the training boats. By the end of our four months' course
we were able, after a fashion, to do every job in the
submarine ourselves.

There were thirteen in our training class and in
accordance with the Blockhouse traditions it contained
some fine rugger players, a category in which I was not
included. Rugger was just starting to lose some of the
glamour is enjoyed in the Royal Navy, though Portsmouth
Services still fielded five teams of a Saturday. But these
were shortly to reduce, for the car was becoming com-
monplace even for impecunious junior officers and week-
end amusement was being sought farther afield.

The wardroom garage contained a motley collection
of vehicles, which did, however, possess some characteris-
tics in common. They were more remarkable for the
performance demanded, and claimed, by their owners,
than their appearance, which had usually long lost its
luster in the hands of previous owners. They ranged, at
this time, from an early Edwardian Mercedes with chain
drive and mighty exhaust pipes, to a 4½-liter Bentley,
which was then only just coming into production. Some of

them should have known their own way home from London in the early morning.

There had been a marked change in wardroom mess life since the war. The formal dinner, with boiled shirt and the Royal toast, with its glass of port or madeira, was then a nightly affair. It is probably economic stringency which has more or less killed that nightly glass of port, so often the forerunner of further decanters of that civilized mode of inspiring conversational fluency. I do not think that the traditional taboo of "Shop" at dinner was strictly observed at Blockhouse, though the various restrictions in conversation, such as that on ladies' name, are lifted after the Royal toast. Shop amongst submariners might be considered by some an occupational disease, and it must be hard for outsiders to understand how submarines and their vicissitudes, vices and virtues, could provide such an endless source of conversation. But to a young sub-lieutenant there was an infinity of knowledge to be picked up and amongst other things I owe my life, and that of my boat's crew, to a chance story of a German U-boat which I heard told in an after-dinner "cag" in the mess.

Another change in mess life has been the virtual disappearance of bridge as an after-dinner game. At this time, after dinner, there would usually be several tables of bridge—auction, of course, as it was to be another five years before contract came in to sound the death-knell of bridge as a social game. Other games of skill and chance were popular in submarine messes at this time—though I do not remember poker, which had been a popular game amongst some of us sub-lieutenants during our courses, being played. The numerous and various games of dice were very popular before lunch or dinner, and at other times; they were usually played for drinks, but sometimes for money. I suppose gambling is not a very laudable amusement and in any case frowned on by the regulations; such games as Slippery Sam, or cutting through the pack for a pound, have little to recommend them. But I am not sure that the cut and thrust of such games as poker are not a good grounding in character study for those who are being trained, as leaders, to live dangerously. Certainly I feel that they provide better schooling for the wits than watching television or filling in pools. Any junior officer at Blockhouse in the 'twenties who embarked upon a game of skill or chance with a certain venerable and skilful submariner was getting education, even if he had to pay for it.

They were happy days, during my training class, and we were not worked too hard. There was method in this, for half the training class were conscripts; they had not volunteered for submarines and in three years would be free to return to general service. In practice, once bitten with the bug, the majority used to volunteer to stay on. We had a good deal of free time and I got to know the road to the New Forest well. At this time my future in-laws, this should be a warning to all parents, had unwittingly ensured that their daughter would marry me by forbidding me the house and their daughter to see me. An impecunious sub-lieutenant compared most unfavorably with other suitors and much ingenuity and connivance with friends went into our meetings. I should add that, once they accepted the inevitable, no one could have had a kinder welcome than I invariably received at their house.

In due course our training class finished and we were faced with the passing-out exam. I remember that our training class got special congratulations for the outstanding results they achieved in the wireless exam. This was scarcely surprising, for in the "resoom" before the exam we had, having I fear somewhat neglected the subject during the course, received inspired guidance. It went somewhat as follows:

"Of course I don't know what sort of questions you gentlemen will be asked, but this is the kind of question you might be asked. I would advise you to take notes. Question One: Describe the Polson's arc"—and so on from question one to eight.

By a curious coincidence, not only did the questions exactly follow the forecast, but they even conformed to the order.

But for the most part our exam was practical and oral, conducted by a number of experienced submarine officers. We had to—and we did—know our stuff.

Having passed out of the training class we were now submarine officers and the occasion was one for celebration. As training class we only entered the wardroom ante-room at dinner-time. At other times we were segregated in what is now the entrance hall; on one wall of this now hangs the portrait of one of our class, a posthumous V.C., Tubby Linton. There have been many changes in the old fort and many splendid new blocks built on since 1927, but I expect that dinner the night the training class passes out is still a matter of moment. One of the hazards of such an occasion was that not only did debagging almost certainly result, if the subject resisted, in irreparable damage to the trousers, but the numerous broken glasses on the floor were exceptionally harsh on the anatomy thereby exposed. On this occasion the very popular C.O. of one of the boats which used to take the training class to sea, was unfortunate enough to get a rib broken in the melee.

Theoretically the appointments available were open to the choice of the training class in the order of passing out. In practice, the rugger players were distributed amongst the Blockhouse flotilla, thereby achieving the derogatory, if enviable, title of Blockhouse Loungers. The remainder were distributed elsewhere and I was appointed to the Second Flotilla, based on Devonport and attached to the Home Fleet.

The Hispano having had an argument with a cow on the way down, I arrived at Devonport rather late and made at the start the acquaintance of Harry, whom I was to meet many times, at all hours of the night, in the months to come. H.M.S. *Lucia,* our depot ship, used to lie at moorings on the Cornish side of the harbor and the last boat out to it left a good deal earlier than junior officers found convenient. Harry was the proprietor of a rowing boat at Mutton Cove and made his living by providing an all night service across the harbor.

I arrived at H.M.S. *Lucia* to find once again a dance in progress. *Lucia* had started her life as a German merchant ship and having been taken in prize early in the 1914 war had been converted into a submarine depot ship. She was then in the process of taking over from the old H.M.S. *Maidstone,* a herring-gutted vessel which had actually been designed as a depot ship. She was extremely "tender," that is to say she had not much stability. The dance was taking place on both ships, secured alongside each other. Since most of her equipment had now been transferred, *Maidstone* was very light and more tender than usual. During the dance the stokers down below were employed shovelling coal from one side to the other to keep her upright. Next day she was towed away to the breakers.

My boat was L.52, one of the six "L.50" class boats composing the Second Flotilla. They had been constructed at the end of the 1914-18 war and, in line with thought at the end of that war, just as—strangely enough—at the end of the 1939-45 war, had had great attention given to their gun armament.

L.52 and L.53 still had the two 4-inch guns with which they had been designed, but the other boats, since in peace-time it would seem that a submarine's surface weapons lose favor with the staff, had had their after gun removed to make room for an asdic set. They also had six torpedo tubes, so their armament was first class, but as submarines they were most indifferent. Owing to a designer's error, their tails were so constructed as to restrict the free flow of water to their propellers; at some speed over about twelve knots the propellers would "cavitate"— or whizz round in a sort of vacuum—and extra revolutions merely produced much noise and vibration, but no extra speed. They also required a good deal of care when surfacing or they would take on alarming lists. Nevertheless, given the gun armament of an L.50 on a good hull, I should have been able to inflict a great deal more damage on the enemy in the 1939-45 war than with any submarine we had during that war.

Because of this chance appointment to L.52 I was able to appreciate the marked advantage of two guns over one in submarine gunnery control and the tremendous potentialities of a submarine armed with a gun—or a rocket, these days. Although our British boats had a bitter struggle to extract even one decent gun out of the staff in World War II, I well remember in the closing stages of the Pacific war the American boats, with which I was serving, having a second 5-inch gun added abaft the conning tower.

Another advantage of a different sort which I gained from being in a double-gun boat was that we carried an extra officer. Complements in the Royal Navy of those days were scaled to some degree on gun armament, and the second gun entitled us to an extra officer. It did not entail the slightest bit more work for the officers, but in fact the extra officer could well be used, and all the boats carried them in war. The officer complement of the "L" class in peace was a Commanding Officer, a First Lieutenant, a Third Hand (a sub-lieutenant or junior lieutenant) and some forty crew. The C.O. was not expected to have anything to do with the routine work of the boat in harbor, except of course for overall responsibility and administration. When alongside the depot ship it was not etiquette for him to come down to the boat in the afternoon, when he was expected to be ashore, or, without due warning, in the forenoon when he could be greeted with proper ceremony. The First Lieutenant organized things in harbor and was responsible for all maintenance outside the engine room—and in that, too, in the small boats without an Engineer Officer. His special responsibility was the electrical installation and the battery; he was also usually the Torpedo Officer. The Third Hand was responsible for gunnery, navigation, correspondence, signals and confidential books—as well as such other of the First Lieutenant's duties as that great man chose to delegate. The Engineer Officer, apart from his direct responsibilities in the engine room, was the technical adviser, mentor and guide to all. At this time he was a warrant officer and nearly all of them had tremendous submarine experience, having worked their way up. It was very difficult, though not impossible, in those days for these warrant engineers to get promoted much farther, thus they remained in similar appointments for many years. They were great characters and of great ability.

To them the submarine service, mechanically, and the junior executive officers in advice, owed a great deal. It was to be many years before their worth was recognized, as with the other officers of the service, by a suitable grant of rank and status. But it was not, even then, impossible for them to go further, and indeed one, now Rear-Admiral Sir Sidney Frew, did go to the top, and his portrait hangs with other illustrious submarines at Blockhouse.

Luckily, during my time as a Third Hand, the era of the typewriter had not dawned, though it was only just below the horizon; everyone got on with his job without writing letters about it. Even so, there was some correspondence which the sub would collect from the Captain (S)'s office, log in and show to his C.O., who would initial it. If that great man felt very strongly on the subject he would write a line or two by his initials; then it would be passed on round the other C.O.s of the flotilla. The Captain's Secretary would draft a reply from the remarks, if any, for the Captain (S) to collate. Actually, since rank was far more sparingly distributed fifty years ago, the Second Submarine Flotilla, with a depot ship and six moderate-sized submarines, was only considered a Commander's command and the flotilla was commanded by a Commander (S), the suffix (S) indicating a submarine flotilla command.

One of the best things about submarine training for a young officer is that responsibility falls on his shoulders early. From the moment he joins he is being schooled to be a submarine C.O. himself and that is a comparatively young man's game. It is the same with the crew, in general more responsibility falls on the individual than would be the case in a bigger ship. Everyone has a definite responsibility, there is no room, at any rate in the smaller boats, for spare numbers. Every depot ship carries one or more spare crews, for if a man in a submarine crew goes sick he has to be replaced by a corresponding man from the spare crew. If a man has it in him, responsibility brings the best out of him and although submariners are basically no different to anyone else in the Service, nevertheless I think that their general standard of morale is higher.

I was fortunate in L.52, because my duties were shared with a Fourth Hand, an R.N.R. sub-lieutenant, the "rocky" navigator traditional to submarines in war. The great advantage of a Fourth Hand was that there were three watch-keeping officers—the C.O. took no standing watch, though he was constantly on the job during exercises and permanently on call when at sea. Otherwise the First Lieutenant and Third Hand took watch and watch about at sea; four hours on, four hours off, day and night, apart from their other duties. Our seafaring forefathers always worked watch and watch, but it is a hard life and one to be avoided.

Although L.52 carried a Fourth Hand, I did not get away with it completely; the First Lieutenant gave me the torpedoes to look after. My job as Torpedo Officer of L.52 came near to putting a premature end to my submarine career. We were being inspected by the Commander (S) and the result of the inspection might have had a considerable bearing upon the promotion of our C.O. Amongst the other evolutions was the firing of a full salvo of torpedoes, fitted with practice heads instead of the explosive warheads used in war. The torpedo would be set to run under the target and from the position of its wake it could be deduced whether it was a hit or a miss. In a submarine there is a tendency to break surface after firing a torpedo, due to the loss of nearly two tons of weight forward, and it takes time until the water can be taken in to replace the weight lost.

Firing several torpedoes in quick succession accentuated this tendency, which in modern boats is largely taken care of automatically. In the earlier boats a good deal of nice judgment in getting the boat going down before firing, and in flooding and blowing tanks, was required to prevent breaking surface and thus giving away your presence. The torpedoes required a lot of careful preparation and any small omission in that preparation tended to make the unreliable brutes misbehave or, worse still, sink and get lost. Upon the performance of her torpedoes the reputation of a submarine largely depended and the loss of one, for they were valuable, meant a Court of Enquiry, which could result in an expression of their Lordships' dissatisfaction.

When the war came, and with a shortage of that highly trained and skilful man—the submarine Torpedo Gunman's Mate—the torpedo just had to rough it; and a lot of trouble they gave—many an enemy owed his survival to their vagaries.

In pre-war days the highlight of an inspection was the salvo. In L.52 the attack was just developing. Our C.O., "Snakey" Leathes, was an artist in attack and he had nearly reached his firing position.

Suddenly there was a roar, as of an aero engine, at the tubes where I was stationed; the fore-ends were filled with vibration, noise and smoke.

It was a "hot run" in the tube.

The first movement of a torpedo when leaving the tube, pushed out by compressed air in a submarine, throws back a lever which starts up the torpedo's engine. The torpedo is driven by its own engine and the air required for the combustion of the fuel is supplied from an air vessel, an immensely strong steel tube which forms the majority of the body. The engine is cooled by the water around it as it travels along. If the engine starts before the torpedo is propelled out of the tube, it lacks this cooling water, whilst the propellers are racing round without the water to effect the propulsion. The result is that it gets so hot that it may even weld itself into the tube.

I knew what must have happened in this case. There was a little stop that had to be unpinned before firing. Due to some mistake in the drill, this stop which kept the torpedo back must have been prematurely withdrawn. The torpedo had crept forward sufficiently to start itself up.

This mistake in the drill would reflect badly on the boat. I hurried down into the tube space, full of exhaust gases—it was a bottom tube—and slipped the side stop back into place. By a freak of chance the torpedo had come back into its original position and the stop went back over the fin. The fore ends had now been cleared and I came back and went up to the bridge to report to the captain, who had now surfaced the boat. I reached the top of the conning tower ladder and fell back into the control room.

Many hours later I woke up, feeling like the morning after, in my bunk in the *Lucia*. It had been carbon monoxide poisoning and a little more would have been the finish.

Two Courts of Enquiry failed to establish how the hot run had occurred. Looking back, this suppression of evidence appears, as it was, most reprehensible; but to a young sub-lieutenant, with his loyalty parochially attached to his boat and his C.O., the defeat of the expert investigators gave much quiet satisfaction.

Snakey Leathes was a man from whom I learned much. He was to lose his life shortly afterwards as C.O. of M.2. He could, and did, sleep at any time, anywhere, at a moment's notice—a most valuable quality in a submariner. He was long and thin, liked his quiet glass of gin, and never apparently took any exercise. I asked him once why and how he lived without exercise. He told me that as a junior officer in submarines in World War I, he noted that those who came in from patrol, during which they got no exercise, and then played violent games, went sick. He had schooled himself to do without exercise, which suited a submarine life in war, and he had seen no cause to alter his habits since. I remembered this and when, ten years later, the clouds of war were rolling up on the horizon, I trained myself to do without exercise too. Throughout my three and a half years of submarine life in war I enjoyed excellent health, which I attribute to this training.

At this stage of one's education one learned much from those who had served in submarines in the 1914 war. At twenty-two the events of a decade before seemed very ancient history, but to those in their thirties the memories were still green. One particular thing stuck in my memory. I had read of a German U-boat which had got home after being heavily hit by the gun of a Q-ship. Our A/S officer in *Lucia* was an old submariner and he told me of trials to sink by gunfire a German U-boat, which had come over with the surrendered German Fleet after the armistice. She had proved extraordinarily resistant to gun fire. This was not unnatural, as the vitals of a submarine are contained in an immensely strong hull, designed to resist sea pressure at depth, and on the surface only a small curved surface of this pressure hull is above water. A popular theory between the wars, and one that was generally accepted by staff officers, was that submarines were very vulnerable on the surface; the result of these old trials was disregarded. Consequently, when it came to World War II, my willingness to fight my boat on the surface was considered by many as foolhardy; actually, it was merely exploiting a great advantage of the submarine. Eventually our boats fought innumerable gun actions, often against more heavily armed adversaries. No submarines were lost in these actions and only one was severely damaged—its tactics in this case being open to criticism.

There was an almost Oriental division of caste in the wardroom of a submarine depot ship, far more marked than the division usually imposed by rank in a disciplined service. The top layer was the submarine C.O.s, then came the First Lieutenants' Union and, finally, the Third and Fourth Hands. The technical and depot-ship's officers provided the leavening.

I suppose it was natural that those with the same responsibilities should clan together and of course the C.O.s were the aristocrats of the flotilla; the C.O., First Lieutenant and Third Hand might all be lieutenants, so there was little division by official rank. It was not unknown for a First Lieutenant to be senior to his C.O., if the former had joined submarines later in his career.

When not away on cruises with the Home Fleet, the Second Flotilla would return to its moorings at Devonport, the submarines leaving the depot ship of a morning for their sea exercises, but usually getting back before evening. The Service inevitably works a seven day week and at this time there was still some truth in the old sailor's saying, *"Six days shalt thou labor and do all that thou hast to do, but the seventh day shalt thou labor a bloody sight harder and do all that thou hast done over again."* This referred to Sunday Divisions, a formal parade and inspection with everyone dressed in their No. 1's, followed by Captain's Rounds, the early part of the morning having been spent furiously polishing brightwork, for his inspection of the ship.

However, in submarines Captain's Rounds were carried out on Saturday forenoon and in many ways a more liberal discipline had grown up. When not at sea exercising, maintenance of machinery, weapons and equipment occupied the crew, and the rule was that the boat must always be kept ready for sea. As things frequently "fell over for a pastime," this latter requirement entailed long hours of work. When all went well the custom was to grant a make and mend, which meant packing up work at

The Old Hispano

midday. On such occasions the old Hispano would rumble eastward the one hundred and forty miles to the New Forest and rumble her way back in the small hours so that Harry could propel me on board before hands fell in at 6 A.M. One of the most enjoyable memories I have of this period was of those night drives back along the narrow hilly road to the west, the wind playing round the body, the great brass headlights blazing ahead, the cut-out wide open except through the sleeping villages, every beat of the long-stroke high-geared pistons seeming directly controlled by the toe on the throttle.

Those frequent runs were eventually to sever my connection with the old red car. I became engaged; finance had to be taken seriously, even though petrol was only a shilling a gallon, and before I left Devonport the Hispano was sold.

I only did a year as a Third Hand, during which time I was promoted lieutenant. In December 1928 I went one step up the submarine ladder to be appointed First Lieutenant of H.M. Submarine R.4, based on Portland.

2

FIRST LIEUTENANT

The "R" class submarine was a brilliant conception, prematurely born. Designed at the end of the 1914 war as an anti-submarine submarine, everything was sacrificed to underwater performance. They were supposed to do fifteen knots submerged. Although some additions to make them less unmanageable had knocked off a couple of knots, it was to be a quarter of a century after they came into service before another submarine, the German Type XXI, equalled their performance submerged. The basic principles of their design are being revived on the dawing boards of today.

They had a hull designed for submerged rather than surface streamlining, the bridge and casings cut to the barest minimum. A single propeller projected from the end of a tapered tail, with the hydroplanes, and originally the rudder, in front of it. For their day and size they had tremendous electric battery power; whilst the engine only developed 240 horsepower, the electric motors developed 1,200 horsepower.

Ten years after the armistice all but one had been scrapped and R.4, the sole survivor, had a reputation for being a boat to which things happened. The trouble was that they were extremely difficult to control submerged at high speed, and not too easy at any speed; the large single propeller sticking out of the tail was extremely vulnerable when going alongside. They were very slow on the surface and it took some twenty hours to fully charge the large battery. They were difficult to detect submerged, owing to their excellent streamlining, and if they got bored with the lesser types of A/S vessels such as trawlers they could show

them a clean pair of heels. R.4 was not therefore popular
with the A/S school for which we worked.

The Sixth Submarine Flotilla at Portland had H.M.S.
Vulcan as a depot ship. Back in the last century she had
been designed to carry six little steam torpedo boats, the
idea being that she would take her charges near to the
enemy battle fleet, hoist them out and send them with
mother's blessing to torpedo the enemy. The conception
was not unlike that of the kamikaze aircraft used by the
Japanese at the end of the Pacific war, though not quite so
ruthless. The torpedo boat idea having lost favor, and no
one having much use for the *Vulcan*, she was secured by
the submarine service as a depot ship, the extra accommodation requirements being met by building various
wooden structures on her upperworks. In the course of time
these had deteriorated and my cabin had quite a bit in common with the one I had enjoyed in H.M.S *Dolphin*. *Vulcan*
was relieved shortly after by H.M.S. *Titania*, a converted
merchant ship, which had a long history with the submarine service.

The Sixth Flotilla was an extremely happy and efficient one. The boats were small, all "H" class except R.4,
affectionately known as the "Slug." They carried two
officers, the C.O. and First Lieutenant, and from time to
time a Third Hand, when one was available, usually a
"rocky" (R.N.R. officer) under training, and a crew of
twenty-odd. They were first commands for the C.O.s and
the first job as First Lieutenant for the second-in-command. A Senior Engine-room Artificer looked after the
engine room and most of the crew were young and new to
their rate and responsibility. Everyone was bound to know
each other extremely well and if we all achieved efficiency
by a process of trial and error, it all helped to weld us into
a team with tremendous enthusiasm.

I had three C.O.s in R.4, the first being a great
character, even in a service of individualists, who rejoiced
in the nickname of "The Night Hawk." However reluctant
he may have been to go to bed, he was equally reluctant to
get up, and one of my worries was to get him up on the
mornings we were going to sea. He gave excellent training
to a young officer and appeared to have a great deal more
faith in my competence on the bridge or at the periscope
than I had myself; he always seemed to delay arriving, when

as officer of the watch, I sent for the captain, until the eleventh hour. Actually, of course, this is the best way to train a young officer, but it needs a great deal of nerve for the man who has the responsibility.

Although my friends had prophesied alarming things from R.4, actually I had a very troublefree run in her. Being the ugly duckling of the flotilla, the "Slug" commanded particular affection and pride from all who served in her, even though her slow surface speed meant that she was nearly always the last home from the daily exercise areas. She had two speeds on the engine—Full Speed and Revolutions for Home. At the latter order the chief would coax more out of her little diesel than her designer had ever dreamed of. Having very little casing she was exceedingly wet at sea and in anything of a seaway one was constantly drenched on the bridge. For sheer misery, the middle watch on the bridge of the "Slug" in heavy winter weather took a great deal of beating.

There are lucky people who have never felt sick, but I believe that few who have served in a small submarine in heavy weather can honestly say that they have not had qualms. Personally I can make no claim to being one of those seadogs with cast-iron stomachs who revel in the discomfort of rough weather at sea. In heavy weather in small submarines some people would lash themselves to the bridge to prevent being washed overboard, but I never found that necessary. You could jam yourself into the corner of the bridge by the voice pipe and duck so as to take the sea on the back when it came over. Down below things were scarely less unplesant. Cooking was impossible, but there was always the slush on the deck where someone had attempted to carry food to their mess, been thrown off balance and dropped it. The all-pervading smell of damp humanity and bilge water, the discomfort of wet clothes you cannot dry, the infuriating experience of being flung out of your bunk—these are common to all ships at sea in heavy weather; generally speaking, the smaller the ship the more unpleasant.

Submarines, being exceptionally strong, are magnificent sea boats, but they are very wet, and R.4 was the wettest I met. If you are in no hurry to get anywhere, you can always dive in a submarine and proceed in comfort below the waves. A certain amount of care is needed in diving a submarine in heavy weather; as the tanks flood she loses the buoyancy to rise to the sea and if she is not handled well will get her bridge smashed up. Similarly, when surfacing in heavy weather, she has little stability as she comes up and is very liable to pooping; again she must be handled carefully. Her submerged performance is limited by the capacity of the battery and that will not take you far.

There are people who are really knocked out by sea sickness and never overcome it, but they are exceptional. Most people, however, have some reaction, if only a feeling of lassitude which they throw off after a few hours. Others are physically sick without apparently much other discomfort. I always remember an incident during my training class whilst I was at sea doing exercises. I had been left on the bridge by myself, by a very confiding C.O., for the first time in my life. We were off the Channel Islands and a nasty sea was running. I had the morning watch—4 A.M. to 8 A.M.—and was feeling pretty miserable when a hoary-headed stoker came on the bridge smoking a revolting-looking little black pipe. He took the pipe out of his mouth, was sick over the side of the bridge, put the pipe back in his mouth and went on smoking. That finished me.

The sanitary arrangements in R.4 were limited and it was customary to make the minor concessions to nature over the side of the bridge. The wireless aerial ran round outside the bridge and, liquid not being too bad a conductor of high voltage electricity, it was possible to receive a paralyzing shock if one was forgetful. Wireless communication was accorded second priority for this purpose and the order to "Stop transmitting" was frequently to be heard being passed to the long-suffering telegraphists.

Ater some eighteen months as No. 1 of R.4, during which Marjorie and I got married, the time came for me to do a year in general service. This was looked upon as a bit of a penance by submarine officers, but was a wise provision of the Admiralty to broaden their training. Accordingly I did a year in H.M.S. *Royal Oak,* a battleship in which I had served as a midshipman, in the Mediterranean.

Although one badly felt the loss of submarine pay, it is of interest that as a junior lieutenant with not much besides my pay I could afford to bring out to Malta an English nannie, engage a Maltese maid, and take a better house than I had in Malta as a senior captain twenty years later. There was no Marriage Allowance nor assistance with passages for wives or families, yet it was common to send your family home for the hot weather.

When my year was up I returned to Blockhouse and was appointed No. 1 of a boat there. Hardly had we taken a house, unpacked our belongings and settled in than I was sent to China at ten days' notice. Wives not being recognized in the Service, no consideration was given to family affairs and one took matters philosophically. A violent pack up, our belongings parked on my in-laws, the baby and nannie on my people and we just raised the money for a Second Class ticket for Marjorie to Hong Kong. I had a First Class Admiralty ticket in the same P. & O. boat, and we compounded with the company by having a First Class cabin and living otherwise Second Class, and a very pleasant five-week trip it was.

We arrived in Hong Kong one winter's morning in January. Whatever may be said of summer in Hong Kong—and for humidity it is hard to beat—the winter is lovely: cloudless blue skies, a sparkle in the air, not too hot and not too cold. We had not been able to make any arrangements for accommodation, but had got some hotel names in Kowloon from fellow passengers. We therefore set out in rickshaws and in due course got in at one of the private hotels. Most of the service families lived in these hotels. For about £20 a month you got a bedroom, bathroom and private sitting-room, with all meals provided in the hotel dining-room. The hotel was built round a central well with a small courtyard at the bottom where the wash amahs sat with their little charcoal fires for heating their irons. Wash amahs charged about a pound a month, for which they did all your laundry, even though in the summer you soaked your clothes with sweat and changed several times a day. Hong Kong was gay, and round about dinnertime the windows looking onto the courtyard would be flung up, a feminine voice would call "Amah!," and an evening dress go floating down. The amahs knew the windows and voices of their "Missies," would field the dress and bring it up shortly afterwards beautifully ironed. A laborer's wage in China itself at this time was about ten cents a day, equivalent to about a penny half-penny, and though the standard of living and wages in the British territory were higher, labor was still very cheap. You could go quite a long way in a rickshaw for ten cents. One never carried more money than was necessary for rickshaws, the ferry across the harbor and *cumshaw* (tips). Everything was done by a chit system. Any hotel, any shop, accepted your chits, though you had to pay cash for the cinema. At the end of the month the chits came in and were settled. It says a lot for the reputation of the colonial British that any tradesman would accept a chit from someone he had never seen before and knew nothing about.

The depot ship of the China Flotilla was H.M.S. *Medway*. She was new, large and magnificently equipped both as regards workshops and accommodation. She had a flotilla of the first post-1914-war-construction submarines —great big boats with air conditioning, which did not work very well, and lots of new ideas; many of these did not work very well either, particularly in the "O" class boats which were extremely complicated electrically.

To my disgust, particularly as I was still paying rent for the house in England, I found that there was no boat for me and I was spare First Lieutenant; I would have to wait till some other First Lieutenant went sick or was relieved.

The China Flotilla was based on Hong Kong during the winter and Wei-Hai-Wei in North China during the summer. The British lease of Wei-Hai-Wei was shortly to expire, much to the regret of the local Chinese, who were extremely loyal, delightful people, and much preferred the benevolent British rule to the depredations of the local war lord.

I was still awaiting a boat when the time came to move north, and I was detailed to take up the target-towing tug. The tug master was a great character, but had no deep-sea ticket, so I had to navigate. It was a bit obscure who was captain for the trip and leaving Hong Kong was an anxious affair. It appeared that the Chinese wives all wanted to come and much altercation went on to make them remain behind. The ordeal had necessitated a good deal of whisky to calm the master's nerves. I had

CHINA

MILES

0   100   200

Peking

Wei-Hai-Wei

YELLOW SEA

Shanghai

CHINA

EAST
CHINA SEA

FORMOSA

Kowloon
Hong-Kong

SOUTH CHINA SEA

never handled the tug and she was in an awkward position in the dockyard basin; it was equally evident that the master did not regard himself in any way incapacitated and intended taking her out.

I need not have worried, it evidently took more than a drop of whisky to affect his skill in ship handling; he took the tug out beautifully and handed over to me outside the harbor for the thousand mile trip. It was my first taste of command. Apart from the master and the mate, the crew were Chinese, and every space in the ship was full of things they were taking north. The spare cabin was full, so I had to sleep in the charthouse. A sister ship had been lost in the Bay of Biscay shortly before and there were most definite instructions to seek shelter if it blew up, but to my relief we had an uneventful trip except for thick fog when we got near the islands off Shanghai. The master was enthusiastic about this; some ship would surely go aground in the fog and we could tow it off and get salvage. Feeling that we were even more likely to go aground in Steep Island Pass ourselves, I lost a great deal of face by insisting on making out to seaward, giving the islands a wide berth. I felt very uncomfortable for the next couple of days and the absence of any distress signals was a tremendous relief. I should never have lived down missing a chance of salvage.

Farther north we ran into a bird migration, the only one I have ever met at sea. Contrary winds had obviously upset their navigation and they swamped onto the ship for rest, fearless of man. The decks were a mass of birds. They perched everywhere—even on the crew. At one time I had three swallows sitting on the peak of my cap. There were numbers of a sort of wader, like a greenshank, and you would see them, exhausted, struggling to keep above the waves; they would touch, struggle on, touch again and finally flop in. We fished some out. The interesting thing was that though the Chinese are catholic in their tastes, I do not think a single bird was put in the pot. I suppose it was a fellow feeling for mariners in distress. They were treated with every consideration until next day, when the wind dropped and they left us.

Approaching Wei-Hai-Wei the ship stopped. Explanations from the engine-room were not convincing, but shortly a small junk came alongside, with much excited shouting. Rapidly it was loaded; apparently the customs were waiting for us. I had unwittingly been commanding a smuggling voyage. I thought it better to see nothing; after all, it was the Chinese customs, not ours, and doubtless I was responsible.

The tug had a very quick, uncomfortable motion, and when we got alongside the pier at Wei-Hai-Wei and I stepped ashore I experienced the phenomenon which gives rise to the nautical roll—the only time I have experienced it. Walking on something flat and firm seemed difficult, one's feet feeling for the deck to come up and meet them.

In due course *Medway* and her submarines and the rest of the fleet arrived. The harbor was little more than a sheltered channel between the island of Wei-Hai-Wei and the mainland; a heavy swell frequently ran in, causing the submarines to bump if lying alongside the depot ship, so they spent much of their time anchored off with a solitary junior officer in the wardroom and a third of the crew. They were, whatever their faults, extremely comfortable boats to live in and the Hard-lying Money you got for sleeping on board was easily earned. Shortly afterwards I became No. 1 of H.M.S *Perseus* and remained in her for some twenty months.

Wei-Hai-Wei was a delightful place. There was a golf course of sorts with sand greens and an unlimited supply of "cheeseyes"—small boys to act as caddies. Never were there such enthusiastic caddies as in China, and some of the opposing caddies frequently wagered their pay on the match, good and bad shots being greeted with cries of "Ting How" or "Boo How," whilst all joined in with the cry of "Out of bow" (out of bounds). Nearly everyone played golf. There were hard tennis courts also and the ships' boats were in great demand for picnic parties. On the mainland there was excellent snipe and duck shooting.

There were a few bungalows on the island, rented by the more senior officers, but most people who had their wives there lived in the one and only hotel, a long bunga-low structure. A long verandah, divided into sections by matting, ran the length of the living quarters. Each family had a section of verandah, behind it a bedroom, and behind that a bathroom and thunder box.* The baths were either large earthenware vessels, which I believe had originally been used for storing tea, or concrete tubs. Plumbing consisted of a coolie with two 4-gallon kerosene tins slung across his shoulders on a pole. The kerosene tins could be used to carry bath water or empty the thunder box, according to the time of day or requirements.

There was also a Club, reserved for the bachelors or unaccompanied husbands, except on Fridays. Skittles, known as bowls, was a great game at the club and, indeed, generally on the China coast. Fridays were known as "Black Fridays" by club habitués, as in the evening women were admitted and there was dancing. Living in each other's pockets, tempers got strained. Women are not as amenable to a community existence as men, and were frequently not on speaking terms with their friends so that the atmosphere was strongly reminiscent of Kipling's *Plain Tales from the Hills*.

Most of our Chinese Boys (Stewards) were Northern Chinese from the Wei-Hai-Wei areas and grand, cheery chaps they were. When we went north they got their only leave of the year and went home to their families. The economics of the families of China depended upon children to provide labor; there was a story of a boy who on arrival in Wei-Hai-Wei requested his C.O. for special leave because his wife was having a baby.

"But I don't understand, Ah Chow," the C.O. said. "We were refitting at Hong Kong last summer and you never came north."

Ah Chow looked puzzled for a bit and then said: "Oh that! My brother, he very good man, he fix."

The following year we refitted at Hong Kong in the summer. The standard uniform rig for officers was white tunic and trousers, a topee and a red and yellow Chinese paper umbrella. It would rain for days on end and the nights were as hot as the days. A submarine lying in a dry dock was like an oven and we were constantly drenched in sweat. Nowadays prickly heat is taken seriously, but in the thirties it was taken as a matter of course. The sailors

*Outhouse.

used to work stripped to the waist, with their backs a mass of scabs, and under their tunics the officers were the same. I can think of few more unsuitable garments for hot weather than the tunic even though it was made of white drill. It hooked up tight round the neck as a sort of choker collar, preventing any ventilation round the body. The open shirt which in these informal days has replaced the tunic except on formal occasions, is far more healthy.

My C.O. went sick and, in my innocence, I had a Brave-New-World idea about diet. Despite the temperature the sailors always ate an enourmous hot midday meal—such as roast beef and Yorkshire pudding, piles of roast potatoes, with a great tot of rum. I felt that a light midday meal, with the main meal and rum after the sun went down, would be beneficial for the prickly heat and health generally. The coxswain protested that the crew would object strongly. I was young and foolish, and insisted. Shortly after my C.O. returned, sensed immediately the rumbling discontent and re-established the traditional dinner, just in time, for tempers are short in such climatic conditions. I learnt a valuable lesson; the British are conservative in their eating and it is sheer stupidity to try and change things quickly.

After a happy couple of years on the China station I was relieved to go home for a C.O.'s course. The next step on the submarine ladder. Marjorie had gone home ahead and I was expecting the usual P.-and-O. passage home, since the submarines remained on the station, whilst their crews changed. But there was one of those periodical economy drives and I was told that I must wait some weeks for a cruiser that was going home. This would have meant no leave, but their Lordships were generous enough to allow me to pay my own passage home and thus get back in time to get some foreign service leave before the C.O.'s course.

Another officer and myself got a Second Class passage in a German ship for the large sum of £42, just £1 a day, for it took six weeks. The German ships were the only ones on the Far East run with all white crews; they were government subsidized and in 1934 all the crew of S.S. *Coblenz* was already being trained for war.

3

COMMANDING OFFICER

The Submarine Commanding Officer's qualifying course, known as the periscope course or "perisher" for short, was training in submarine attack. Since the instruments and equipment were still, and remained so for years, rudimentary, a submarine attack was essentially a matter of judgment by the C.O. He alone could see what was going on and, further, his vision was limited to one sector at a time—rather like looking round with a telescope; he had to be able to piece the picture together in his head as he swept round the horizon. Some people just never got the knack of judging things through a periscope and, however excellent their other qualifications, inevitably failed their perisher.

Most of the instruction was done through a device known as an Attack Teacher. The embryo C.O. was shut in a box containing a periscope. He could train his periscope around and the box, which was like part of a submarine control room, also trained around to simulate the submarine turning, its rate of training varying according to the speed the submarine was supposed to be doing. The periscope looked out at a sort of railway line, along which a small model ship moved; it was all arranged to give a very close simulaton of the real thing. The attacks were controlled by other members of the class, who employed much ingenuity in defeating the harassed student down below. If they succeeded in maneuvering the target so as to "ram" the submarine much joyous jumping overhead informed the "submarine" of his disgrace.

An experienced submarine C.O. was in charge of the perishers, and from him they got their guidance and reproofs. Every attack was analyzed and recorded, and to pass out was by no means an automatic affair. Not that the perishers were subdued or bowed down by anxiety, anything but. The really anxious time was for the C.O. of the boat in which they did their actual sea attacks, for not all training can be done synthetically. The C.O. must let the perisher make his own mistakes, hold himself in whilst he feels that his boat is being run into danger, and only at the last minute take charge and press the hooter. The hooter, a klaxon, was the signal to go deep. It was not difficult to get the submarine into a position where it would get rammed by the target; the way out of this trouble was to break off the attack and go deep underneath it.

As the weeks went by, looking through the periscope and making estimations through it became second nature, and finally the student was pronounced fit to command his own boat. This was the highlight of the submarine officer's career; he got his command young, for it was a young man's game.

I was just 28 when I was given my first command, H.49, which is young for peace time. During the war we had operational C.O.'s of 22. But I think, on an average, probably the best years of a submarine C.O.'s life are 25 to 30—old enough to have experience, self confidence and judgment; young enough not to think too much. At 35 most men are getting too old, over cautious.

In fact I commanded a boat in war till well into my 38th year, but I had been at it non-stop. There were some who after a year or two out of the game and when well into their thirties, tried to stage a comeback—a formidable achievement! I know that I was potentially a much better C.O., despite the later accumulation of wisdom and experience, at 28 than at 37.

H.49 was one of the last of the "H" class, splendid little boats of some 450 tons, constructed in the later years of the 1914 war and basically of American design. Once again I joined the Portland flotilla, though my old love, R.4, had by now been scrapped. The Portland flotilla, besides the old "H" boats, then contained two of the new "S" class, in later editions of which I was to serve during the war. The "S" class was a return to sanity after the flights of fancy which resulted in the clumsy great "O" and

"P" classes; and the long, fast, but weak-hulled "River" class. For long-distance ocean work, a big boat has the tremendous advantage of endurance; the large American boats were splendid for their ocean war against the Japanese and great execution they did. Our own rather smaller "T" class boats were good too. But for tough fighting boats, which could be used either in-shore or in deep sea waters, I think that our "S" class were second only to the German 500-tonner, in my opinion out and away the best submarine of World War II. But that is a personal opinion; like economists, no two submariners think alike.

One's first command is always a milestone. (One of the moments which sticks in my memory is the first time that, in my own boat, I sounded the hooter for diving and pulled shut the conning-tower hatch.) All one's submarine career till then has been watching and learning; now is the chance to really put one's own ideas into effect. It is easy to think how much better one would do oneself and criticize others, but it is a very sobering feeling when it is all yours. I have had a number of much bigger commands since my submarining days, with hundreds of men for each man I had in my submarine, but I know no other job that is so completely yours and yours alone. There is a similarity in the situation to that of the pilot of an aircraft, but the pilot does most of the things himself; a submarine is worked by its crew, each member being an essential unit of the machine, but all directed by the one man, the only one who can see and know what is going on. In attack there is no time to explain or take advice—I speak of the submarine as it was equipped in World War II—and the C.O.'s decision must be instant. And yet there is a long delay before that decision takes effect. Five seconds late in putting the wheel over now and five minutes later you will find yourself that five seconds too late to get your sights on.

It is a strange community in a submarine, the C.O. is an absolute dictator, and yet no man relies more completely upon each and every member of his crew. A good submarine crew is far more than a team; they are as near as possible, during attack, a single composite body using the C.O. as their eye and director. If in my war experiences as a submarine C.O. it seems that it was always I who did this, or I who did that, the "I" refers not just to me but to a number of individuals, all merged for the occasion into one.

So much did the boat depend upon its C.O. that the commanding officer of a flotilla would think of his boats, not by their names, but by the name and personality of the individual submarine C.O. As the war went on and losses mounted, the C.O.s became younger and younger; with this there came an increasing measure of common doctrine, and thus less marked individuality, but fundamentally the C.O.s remained individualists. When, late in the war, I was in charge of operational training and came to inspect a boat, I could sometimes tell by the way the young C.O. did things under which of my contemporaries he had been brought up as a First Lieutenant.

In H.49 I learned to keep a running plot of our position in my head; the First Lieutenant was the only other officer and so the Captain had to be his own navigator. All these things could be done much better by an automatic plotting device, or someone working all the time with parallel rulers and dividers; but, just as a bird knows where it is and where to steer, so we who call ourselves seamen have to develop something of those dormant instincts—if we are not to depend completely on machines, which are too liable to fail. In these mechanized days we make scant use of our natural senses, but it is quite extraordinary what degree remains, even in our over-civilized make-up. A sense of position and direction, which is to be found in men of the open spaces and fishermen, is not really far below the surface in us if we really need it.

I remember once during the war trying to make a landfall after days of thick weather. I suddenly felt there was danger ahead and went full speed astern, not even allowing the few hundred yards to turn round. As the way came off the boat, the fog lifted and close ahead lay great cliffs frowning above us. It may have been just chance; I knew that the time was very close when, if we did not strike soundings we must make to seaward and wait for the weather to clear; but I believe that when you give yourself up to complete and utter concentration, the brain will give you information that does not come from reason.

Whilst I was in H.49 the Abyssinian trouble flared up; nearly all our boats, even the elderly "H" boats, were moved to the Mediterranean in case of war with Italy. To my disgust H.49 had to remain behind and take out the perishers. This meant leaving Portland, which I liked, and going to Blockhouse.

These frequent moves, in the days before allowances, were a source of considerable expense to officers. It must be admitted that we could not have been too badly off really, for as a lieutenant I then had a resident nursemaid and a resident cook at the cottage, but even so the well-known process of upheaval was unwelcome. Open cars were a great help and by time the Lagonda was loaded up for a routine move, some interest had to be taken in low bridges. On this occasion the dog had rather a strenuous passage for, taking overmuch interest in a rabbit, it had lost its hold on the top of the luggage. Equally Marjorie could not get out until some had been removed and so it had perforce to put in some miles of roadwork before help could be found.

I was based on England for two years while I was doing my perisher and then in H.49—the only time in the ten years before the war when I was not on foreign stations. The next move was a wonderful two years serving with the R.A.N. in H.M.A.S. *Australia*, but that is not a submarine story. Then in 1938 I was back in the Mediterranean and in command of H.M.S. *Sealion*.

As it proved this sojourn in the Mediterranean was to be extremely fortunate for me, though at the time I felt that a turn at home would have been more than justified. The First Submarine Flotilla in the Mediterranean was commanded by "Ruckers" (now Vice-Admiral Philip Ruck-Keen), in my opinion the most forward-looking submariner between the wars. As a consequence we got magnificent training and he managed to break down some of the well-meant grandmotherly rules of conduct for submariners in fleet exercises.

These rules were well meant, but it seems incredible these days to recall that between 1927 and 1938 I never dived a submarine at night, nor took part in fleet exercises at night without burning navigation lights. It was obvious to any thinking submariner that night attack on the surface would play a major part in the coming war, but

HMS *Sealion*

we were not allowed to practice it for fear of collision—the kind of risk that had to be taken if our attack or defense were to be efficient. Since Britain had far more to lose by submarine warfare than anyone else, it was the custom to deceive ourselves as to the supremacy of our anti-submarine forces, which were admittedly well ahead of the rest of the world. All exercises were analyzed in the light of this unconscious wishful thinking.

To take an example, submarines operate in the vertical as well as the horizontal plane. Exercises were analyzed in the horizontal plane only and our A/S equipment had no means of estimating the depth of a submarine, and therefore the depth at which to explode a depth charge.

In vain did we protest on fleet exercise when, as usual, we were adjudged sunk, that no allowance had been made for depth. We were merely told that we had been sunk and not to argue. Only a few months later frantic efforts were to be made to devise material and techniques to deal with the deep submarine; many ships were to be lost and the U-boats escape because our own submariners had not been listened to.

In the Combined Fleet Exercises of the spring of 1939, Ruckers had at last got permission for his boats to operate at night without navigation lights. Bickford (*Salmon*) and I (*Sealion*) had spent a considerable period at night, unseen, in the midst of the "enemy" fleet. Bickford had "torpedoed" H.M.S. *Courageous*, with a salvo and she was adjudged to have had her speed reduced by 2 knots. *Courageous* was to sink a few months later from a single German torpedo. The C.O. of the cruiser which *Sealion* torpedoed would admit of no damage. When I asked him why at Gibraltar some days later, he replied that a submarine had no right to be on the surface, darkened, amongst the Fleet at night. A few months later the Battle of the Atlantic was being fought against surfaced U-boats at night.

We also practised "wolf-pack" tactics and, although in the event it was to be the Germans and not us who had reason to use this technique, there was no reason to be surprised by its inevitable development.

I think that even submarine C.O.s in the early days of the war may have been unconsciously influenced by the wishful thinking which was put into the analysis of pre-war exercises. Aircraft were invested, despite their rudimentary equipment, with such magic powers that submariners were recommended to go deep—that is, below periscope depth—where they were virtually impotent as soon as one came along. Stanley—nicknamed "Von Kreishmer" after a particularly stirring patrol—one of the C.O.s in my flotilla in the Pacific in 1945, inaugurated an Aunt Sally technique for dealing with the Japanese "Jake" anti-submarine seaplane—admittedly not a particularly efficient performer. The Jake was small and carried only two depth charges; if he could be persuaded to decant these, he ceased to be a menace and could not interfere with operations any further. The technique on sighting a Jake was to surface.

The Jake would then attack.

At the *moment critique* the submarine dived and got

Stadtlandet

NORWAY

Oslo

SCOTLAND

NORTH

SEA

SKAGERRAK

IRELAND

DENMARK

GREAT
BRITAIN

HOLLAND

London

Berlin

ENGLISH CHANNEL

GERMANY

BELGIUM

Brest

Paris

BAY OF
BISCAY

FRANCE

SWITZERLAND

ITALY

PORTUGAL

SPAIN

CORSICA

Rome

Naples

SARDINIA

TYRRHENIAN
SEA

Algeciras

Gibraltar

Oran

Algiers

SICILY

Tunis

MOROCCO

ALGERIA

TUNISIA

MALTA

Jerba I.

Zuara

Tripoli

EUROPE 1941

MILES

0   100   200   300   400   500

LIBYA

Aichi E 13A "Jake"

clear before the two depth charges were dropped at the position where he had dived. If the submarine dived too soon, the Jake would not drop his charges; if the submarine dived too late—well, it was too late. It called for a nicety of timing.

The war ended before Stanley had popularized the Aunt Sally game and, indeed, I think he only once brought it off himself. But it was a long cry from the staff recommendation of 1939, which amounted to virtually putting your shutters up when an aeroplane came along.

Being of an obstinate nature and no doubt not uninfluenced by some wishful thinking of my own, I used to analyze exercises privately; my conclusions indicated almost as regularly an anti-submarine failure as the staff recorded an anti-submarine success. When I had to admit that for once I might have been "sunk," I was able to see where I had made an error, though of course these analyses disclosed a good many errors on my part which had not affected the issue. Whatever the pros and cons of these analyses, they were to invest me with a confidence in my weapon which was to serve me well. Had I accepted all the Staff conclusions I should have been beaten before I started.

The year before the 1939 war started was one of alarms and excursions; in day and night exercises, the First

Submarine Flotilla worked up their efficiency. So sound was the training that the war order book I wrote up for the conduct of my boat, some months before we even went on patrol, was to remain unaltered through three and a half years of war.

Despite these alarms and excursions, Malta was a gay place that summer of 1939. Most of the fleet and eventually our depot ship moved to Alexandria; the submarines which remained made their headquarters in the old Fort Manoel on Manoel Island, in Marsa Muscetto, the second harbor of Valetta. It had not been inhabited for many years, except by sandflies, but in any case many of us slept ashore when not at sea. The Lazaretto, another ancient building on the little island, was to become the headquarters of the famous Tenth Flotilla during the war.

There were dances at the club, parties night after night, bathing picnics by day and night, scandals and gossip, race meetings and games. The shadow of war caused no depression, Malta between the wars was gay, and gay it remained till the end of that long armistice.

Many war books are written by those who have not chosen the services as their career and to them war must have appeared as an unpleasant upheaval. To me, as a professional sailor, still young enough to take part in the front line, it appeared as the climax of all that for which I had been training for so many years.

Marjorie had gone home, taking the baby with her, and Bill Sladen (now Captain Sladen, D.S.O.), Bickford and myself for a time shared a flat overlooking Lazaretto creek. Handsome, brilliant "Bickie" was to earn fame in H.M.S. *Salmon* some months later. He was to rise from lieutenant to commander, the youngest since Beatty, and lose his life, all within a year. I recall a blustering wet afternoon striding up and down with Bickie above the windswept cliffs on the south side of Malta, whilst we discussed endlessly the tactics we were going to employ. Later in the war, when operating from Malta, we used to make our landfall on these Dingli cliffs; I never sighted them without seeming to see the figure of Bickie, whose gay motto had always been: "Drive on! Drive on! There is an eternity of rest to follow." He found that rest young, in the summer of 1940.

From time to time *Sealion* would go to Alexandria to

take her turn for a few weeks carrying out A/S practices for the fleet. Alex was a delightful place and when in harbor a C.O. had plenty of time to amuse himself. Racing and golf at Smouha and the Sporting Club, surfing at Sidi Bish, shooting on Lake Mazorin, and I used to hire a *felucca* to go fishing. In the evenings there was most stimulating bridge with the Levantine residents, descended from the traders of history; their commercial wits were keen and it was a source of considerable satisfaction if you held your own against them. Round about midnight you would go off to one of the cabarets for which Alexandria was famous.

I have often been asked whether people get claustrophobia in submarines and the only time I have even known a sign of it arose from a visit to an Alexandria night club. The artists of Alexandria, the equivalent to what are sometimes prosaically referred to as taxi dancers, certainly did not deserve the latter name. Many were Hungarians, soignée to a degree, beautifully dressed, exceedingly decorative and inexorably expensive. The dance was only the beginning; bottles of synthetic champagne, bunches of roses, toy monkeys on strings and a host of nonsense purveyed around by itinerant vendors would be requested. Doubtless they were traded back when you had left, your pockets empty, to be resold to other suckers.

Hugo Newton, First Lieutenant of *Sealion,* once hired the tarbush, white robe and tray from a peanut vendor at the Excelsior and did a roaring trade amongst his unsuspecting flotilla mates for an hour or so before he was bowled out.*

I was having a winning run at bridge about this time and would frequently drop in at the Excelsior to dispense of my winnings. As a regular customer with one of the Hungarian lassies, I was privileged to concession rates, or at any rate some easing of the quota of bottles of champagne. In return I invited her to our depot ship, H.M.S. *Maidstone,* for a drink and to see over my submarine.

She was not a girl to pass unnoticed anywhere, let alone in one of H.M. ships, and as we walked across the plank to my boat I was uncomfortably aware of a number of my messmates leaning over the side and taking an

---

*Struck out in the British game of cricket.

unnecessary interest in our progress. All went well through the hatch and down the ladder into the torpedo space; then she clasped her throat, said she felt shut in and suffocated and tried to bolt up the ladder. She went through the motions of starting to scream. I knew nothing about the treatment of claustrophobia; what I did know was that if that girl bolted back up the ladder screaming, the critical audience above would take a great deal of pleasure in jumping to some entirely unjustified conclusions, and I should never live it down. It was a bad moment. There was no time for sweet reasoning.

I seized her round the waist, rushed her aft into the wardroom and forced a double whisky into her hand. It worked, and I give it for what it is worth as a cure for claustrophobia. It was altogether a most unnerving experience.

People might think that being boxed up in a submarine under depth charge attack would affect the crew. The swish, swish of the propellers of the hunter passing overhead, the waiting for the explosion of the charges as they sank slowly down. Had they been dropped at the right moment? Were they set to the right depth? The knowledge that there is no escape, that you must just wait for it. Then the shattering roar, the lights going out, the controls going slack as the power is cut, and the paint raining down.

Then silence and the faint sounds of running water where a gland has started a trickle.

It seems magnified one hundredfold—a serious leak is what you dread. For a few there is something to do, to make good the damage, provide alternative methods of control; others just have to wait for the next attack.

The knowledge that there is no escape—therein lies the secret, I believe, of the magnificent morale of submarine crews of all nations. Normal reaction to fear is to run away; the face goes pale as the blood floods to the legs to give them extra power. The instinct to run away has to be fought, either consciously or unconsciously. The submariner has nowhere to run; he knows he sinks or swims with his boat, he has ceased to be an individual; he is, with his shipmates, part of that boat, and he is spared the normal reaction of the land animal. Of course the crews were first rate men, they had to be for many reasons, but even so I have thought that the almost universal cheerful acceptance of what on the face of it, and my description is inevitably inadequate, might appear a terrifying experience, calls for some explanation. This is mine, though I do not suggest that anyone enjoyed themselves on such occasions.

But all these things were still in the unknown; one might think of them, but not discuss them. The war drew nearer until one day on Manoel Island we gathered to hear the Prime Minister's announcement.

We were at war.

But not with Italy, she had not come in; we had to wait in case she did. For the first time I saw the patrol billets detailed by the staff. They filled me with gloom. Instead of areas in which we could roam, studying the movements of minesweepers and patrols to assess the probabilities of minefields, choosing our moments when to go in or when the conditions recommended discretion, we were given positions. In peace time exercises you have frequently to pinpoint your submarine positions, so as to ensure that the opposing forces meet. In war, on occasions when a concentration is required for a particular operation you may need to pinpoint positions too. But in general, a submarine provides her own reconnaissance; light and wind, sun and moon, sky and sea, depth and shallows, all affect her tactics.

A flag on a chart may look effective, but in some conditions the submarine it represents may be totally ineffective; give her sea room and she will find somewhere where conditions are more favorable. But not unnaturally such things are not appreciated at the beginning of a struggle, we all had a lot to learn.

The anxious weeks passed; we envied our friends in the North Sea flotillas who were seeing action—or might be, though at this period of the phony war there was indeed little chance of it for any of our submarines. I remember feeling more and more worried that the war would be over before we could get into it.

All ship movements were shrouded in secrecy; you had to contact the nursemaid on Sliema front, or the grass widow in the club, to learn the movements of your friends' ships. From time to time we would be warned in secrecy that we were going home; the indigo blue our submarines were painted for the Mediterranean was hurriedly covered over with North Sea grey, the tradesmen noting this from

the road sent in their bills and credit stopped. The alarm
passed; blue replaced grey again, credit was re-opened. But
at last in mid-October, 1939, we got the word to go.
Incredible though it would have seemed later in the war
when submarines made their passages safely and singly,
the Second Division, of which I was senior officer, were to
go home in company on the surface. *Sealion*, *Salmon*
(Bickford), *Shark* (Buckley) and *Snapper* (King). We
had worked up together, we knew each other and what we
should do in any circumstances; as far as peacetime
training made it possible we were completely prepared for
war. And yet *Sealion* was to be the only one of those four
boats to die a natural death; before another autumn came
round *Salmon* and *Shark* had found their final resting
place at the bottom of the North Sea; some months later
Snapper was to disappear off Ushant.

We had no thought of this, however, at last we were
off to the war and if we pressed on would get there before
it was over. Actually it was to be nearly six years before I
was to celebrate V.J. Day in the Pacific, with a feeling
somehow of something lost and over, leaving a strange
emptiness, which I never felt for the peace which ended in
1939. This was the war I had been trained to fight; I was
in command of my chosen weapon in my chosen profes-
sion; no man could ask for more.

We had a very cheerful evening at Gibraltar where
we stopped to fuel and collect intelligence; I remember for
once I won the jackpot on the one-armed bandit at the
Rock Hotel, maybe a good omen; and we were off on the
last leg. As we passed the ports on the Spanish and
Portuguese Atlantic coasts, we studied the particulars of
the potential blockade runners which might be breaking
out to give us our first chance. Two and a half years later,
when on passage south to join in the Mediterranean war,
those selfsame ships were still there.

One calm night leading the other three boats north-
wards up the Portuguese coast we sighted darkened ships
to the westward. I led on, we would go round so as to get
them silhouetted against the young moon to the southward
and having examined their identity and found them enemy
go in to the attack as a division—or, as the Germans
called it, a wolf pack—in the way we had so often
practiced. But the delay was too much for Bickie; thinking

that we had not seen them, he hauled out of the line and went in to attack. Urgently I called him back on the shaded signal light. The moon was starting to silhouette them; the pointed overhanging bow, those funnels could only be a French destroyer. *Salmon* having also spotted they were French had identified herself by flashing light and slunk back like a spaniel that has run in on a hare. Apparently her identification had not been understood; it might have been very awkward. When we got back I was asked by the Admiralty if the U-boats which had been reported as having attacked the French convoy only to be defeated by their gallant escorts, could have seen us.

A U-boat had been reported in the Bay of Biscay, and we spread out on the surface to look for her. It is true that she would probably have been on the surface too, but we relied upon ourselves to see her first. It was foolhardy tactics; if you want to hunt a submarine, do so submerged, or it is more than likely that you will find yourself a hunter hunted.

Snapper had engine trouble, and our progress became slower and slower, but there was no incident till passing Portland on the last night. We encountered some auxiliary A/S craft, recognized as our own, and fired our identification flares. But they were apparently manned by our amateur navy, thirsting for submarine blood, with no interest in recognition signals; they came on menacingly. I signalled Full Speed, watching anxiously to see if *Snapper* could make her getaway. Meanwhile the sky was like a Brock's benefit with our identification pyrotechnics. Miraculously *Snapper* found some speed and we drew away into the night.

After we got in I aked Bill King how he had managed to find the speed, or alternatively why he had been keeping us back with tales of engine trouble. He said that he had got the Chief up on the bridge and pointed out what was going to arrive in the engine room if he could not find some more revolutions. He found them.

For the second occasion on this trip I was to be asked by the Admiralty whether the ravening U-boats so determinedly driven off by Allied action, could have been seen.

A submarine is apt to look upon her own side as far more dangerous than the enemy, and not without supporting experience. It was about this time that one of our boats, returning from a North Sea patrol, made the classic signal to base:

Expect to arrive 09.00 if friendly aircraft will stop bombing me.

The submarine is everyone's enemy, and mistaken identity is not confined to surface and air forces. There was a tragic mistake about this time when one of our submarines, due to an error in recognition procedure, torpedoed and sank another of our boats with the loss of all her crew. The classic case was in World War I, when the Italians were our allies. A boat patrolling in the Mediterranean made a triumphant signal to her base at Malta, reporting the sinking of a U-boat; this was followed shortly after by the amplifying message: *Regret to report that survivors speak Italian.*

4

TECHNICAL INTERLUDE

I have tried to avoid technicalities and I hope that generally there will be sufficient explanation alongside events to clarify our operations.

Nevertheless, some further basic submarine information may assist in the better understanding of our doings.

I. *The Submarine's Operational Role 1939/45*

The submarine is really a seagoing fighting vehicle which has the ability to operate under water, rendering itself invisible. This ability to submerge is only achieved by the sacrifice of other qualities and in general the World War II submarine was a more efficient fighting unit when on the surface than when submerged. Submersion was her defense; and as anti-submarine methods improved, particularly radar, the submarine was driven more and more to operate submerged with the consequent loss of her offensive properties. By the end of the war the Germans were driven back to the practice of the earliest submarines, the fitting of an extensible pipe, the Schnorkel or snort, which could be raised above the surface to admit air without surfacing the whole boat. This device had gone out half a century before with the introduction of the electric battery, which allowed the submarine to proceed submerged, for a limited period, without admitting the air which a combustion engine demands. We could have done with a snort off Norway. But a vehicle can only carry a certain maximum weight and when the Schnorkel goes in something has to go out. This usually meant the sacrifice of some potentially offensive equipment.

46

The atomic submarine has been developed to counter improvements in anti-submarine technique. The conception has changed from a large number of relatively cheap expendable weapons, to a smaller number—all that can be afforded—of vastly more expensive vessels. However powerful it may be, one submarine can only be in one place at a time; there is virtue in numbers.

The World War II submarine was in general a "submersible"—it only submerged when it had to—and it was an expendable weapon. Its success was judged against the amount of enemy losses it inflicted compared with its own inevitable loss; it proved itself a most profitable weapon on both sides. Apart from the actual losses it inflicted upon the enemy, it contained a tremendous anti-submarine force, many times greater in men and material than the submarines themselves. Wanklyn put down in a single forenoon, when he sank two enemy transports, more personnel than the whole of our submarine effort deployed over the whole of the Mediterranean campaign, intercepting about half of Rommel's supplies.

At one time, when I was in Malta during the siege and more amusing occupations were not available, I calculated that we in *Safari* were averaging ten tons of enemy shipping sunk for every 16-pound round we fired from our 3-inch gun. The enemy was expending high explosive, in depth charges, bombs and shells, to absolutely no avail in their efforts to sink us—and at about five times the rate that we were expending high explosive in taking a very satisfactory toll of their shipping. The calculation of the amount of fuel they were using to convey that high explosive to drop on us, compared with the frugal consumption of our diesels, quickly reached such astronomical figures as to quench my temporary enthusiasm as an amateur, and doubtless very inaccurate, statistician.

The submarine, particularly the World War II submersible, is a very versatile weapon. Submarines were used as torpedo boats, gun boats, minelayers, troop carriers, store carriers, tankers, navigational beacons to guide surface vessels, rescue stations for aircraft flying over the sea, reconnaissance units, survey ships, convoy escorts, anti-submarine vessels, power stations to supply electric current to shore installations, and for landing and taking off agents on enemy soil.

But first and foremost their role was to disrupt enemy supplies by sinking their shipping, and since in general the most convenient way of doing this way by torpedo, I think it fair to say that the World War II submarine was primarily a torpedo boat. The Germans and Americans did most of their sinkings on the surface at night in the open sea, preying on large convoys and relying upon their low silhouette to render them invisible in the darkness. The British, having to seek their prey in heavily defended inshore waters around the European and North African coasts, did most of their sinkings submerged by day; or in a brief sojourn on the surface to use the gun.

The great property of a submarine is that it can operate for long periods, entirely unsupported, on the enemy doorstep. A rather embarrassing handicap to such operations was that the submarine could not, like the intruder fighter aircraft which in some ways played a similar very short term role, dash off after making her strike. The submarine had to stay and take the hammering that followed.

II. *The Hunted Submarine*

The technique of escape from a hunt was largely a matter of pitting your wits against the enemy. You could glean a certain amount of information on what he was doing by listening to his propellers on the Asdic set, and when he was using an echo ranging device you could pick up his transmissions, if tuned to the right frequency. When the enemy was getting an echo off your hull you knew he had detected you, and this usually meant that a depth-charge attack would follow fairly soon. But for the most part the Axis relied upon extremely sensitive hydrophones, which would pick up the noise of your propellers, or the slightest noise made by auxiliary machinery. To avoid detection the general rule was to go at the slowest speed, to cut down wake which also gave an echo.

Once detected you would have to speed up, make a wake—which you hoped he would mistake for the submarine itself—and alter course and depth. It was no good doing this till he was committed to the attack, particularly as you usually had more than one hunter and the noise you made would be followed. You wanted to get him to drop his charges. You waited until he seemed to be committed to steaming over you to drop them; then, and then only, you would speed up and alter course to get out of the light. This maneuver called for a nicety of timing, but even if you did not judge it very cleverly, he still had to set his charge to the right depth, so you had an extra chance, except in shallow water. To aid you in your escape, you could make use of density gradients in the sea and variations in the temperature and salinity of the water, which deflected his detecting beam. You could also make use of water noises, such as the sea breaking on rocks and shoals, or the noise and disturbance of ships breaking up and sinking—if you had been fortunate enough to arrange that in advance—but best of all was the noise and disturbance caused by the last pattern of depth charges dropped on you.

For the C.O. it was an absorbing business, you had far too much to think about to have time to be frightened. I always imagined it was very much worse for the crew, though most of them were kept pretty busy in controlling the boat as you twisted and turned, speeding up and slowing down. However, they never seemed to mind though critical interest was taken in the performance of the chaps up top—all of whom, judging by the remarks, had not only been born out of wedlock, but, blessed with amazing stamina, were credited with an almost continuous indulgence in the sexual act.

I do not want to suggest that anyone enjoyed being depth charged, but it was accepted as all in the game. When you could hear the swish, swish of propellers coming in to the attack, and particularly during those anxious seconds just after they had passed close over, waiting for the charges to sink and explode, there was silence.

After the shattering roar of the explosions credit was accorded if they had been close on the target, ironic contempt if they were bad shots. If, however, they had been so near as to cause damage, everyone was much too busy putting things right to indulge in critical analysis of enemy technique.

III. *Trimming*

A submarine cannot submerge or surface, proceed at a steady depth or change depth without a great deal of

care and guidance. All ships are feminine and a submarine
is a very self-willed lady who must be humored.

In order to make her really controllable, you must
have her trimmed exactly right. The essence of a submarine is her pressure hull (see the diagram on pages viii-ix).
This is an immensely strong steel tube, shaped like a cigar
and containing all the essential machinery, the living
quarters and, in both *Sealion* and *Safari*, all the torpedoes.
Some boats had external torpedo tubes, mounted outside
the pressure hull but controlled from within, as well as
internal tubes. *Sealion* and *Safari* had six torpedo tubes, all
in the bow, three on each side, pointing straight ahead;
they carried six re-load torpedoes making twelve in all.
The only parts that really mattered external to the pressure
hull were the conning tower, gun, hydroplanes, rudder,
propellers and periscopes.

Even when the boat is on the surface, very little of
the pressure hull is above water. The part visible above
water is for the most part the casing—a light steel structure, full of holes to ensure that the sea is free to enter and
no air pockets can collect in it. In some ways a submarine
would be far more efficient purely as a submarine, without
a casing at all; the less casing there is the better the boat's
behavior submerged. But for operating on the surface you
had to have some upper works—both to break the sea and
to give you a bridge from which to keep a lookout without
being washed away. The conning tower, which was pressure tight, led on to the bridge. It also had a hatch at the
bottom, level with the top of the pressure hull and known
as the lower lid, so that even if the conning tower were
flooded, as might happen after shell fire, depth-charge
damage or collision, you could still keep the pressure hull
water-tight. The gun tower was a similar, though shorter,
tower to facilitate manning the gun.

Mounted on both sides and also external to the
pressure hull were the main ballast tanks; all, except No.
1, being saddle tanks, blisters of light plating, molded to
the shape of the pressure hull. These were kept open to the
sea at the bottom, but full of air when on the surface. To
dive you opened, hydraulically, valves in the top of the
main ballast tanks. These valves were called vents, they let
out the air allowing the sea to enter. The main ballast
contained enough water to overcome your surface buoy-

ancy—more or less. To surface you "blew" main ballast; the vents were closed, high pressure air loosed into the top of the tanks and this blew the water out of the bottom of the tanks, giving you your surface buoyancy again.

The more buoyancy you had, the longer it took to flood the tanks, and the longer it took to dive. In any case you did not want more buoyancy than was necessary to make you a safe sea boat on the surface and, compared with surface ships, submarines have very little buoyancy. That is why they are so wet in a sea way. An "S" boat in favorable circumstances took about 50 seconds to get under from the time of opening the main vents. With wind and weather from ahead, the sea tended to get under your bow and throw it up, delaying diving. You would try and avoid such a course when in enemy waters with a sea running. If such a course had to be steered you could keep the main ballast tank flooded a bit to keep the bow down. Apart from making you wetter, this made you a difficult sea boat and could result in a dangerous condition. It meant holding a nice balance between the dangers of the sea and the violence of the enemy. Everything in submarining in war is a nice balance of risks; if you balanced them right there was nothing to worry about.

As I have said before, in submersion lay your defense. You frequently had to dive in a hurry. The main ballast counteracted, more or less, your surface buoyancy. Trimming dealt with that "more or less."

Every day, even every hour of the day, the displacement of a submarine was changing; you might be full of torpedoes, stores, fuel and fresh water; you might have expended some of these since the last dive; your bilges might be dry or they might have water in them—it could have seeped in through the glands where the propeller shafts, rudder or hydroplane controls went through the hull.

The expenditure of fuel was roughly compensated for as you steamed on the surface; sea water was admitted to the bottom of the fuel tanks and this forced the fuel out of the top of the tanks to the engines. Being heavier than the fuel, the sea water remained at the bottom of the tank and, strangely enough, very little mixing took place, even in rough weather.

To compete with the adjustments there were auxiliary

ballast tanks distributed inside the boat. The First Lieutenant calculated how much water to put into each to give him a "good trim"—to ensure that when the boat submerged it displaced just its own weight of water. In addition to this he had to have the boat balanced, so that she was not heavy forward and light aft or vice versa. If a man walks from forward to aft in a small submarine you would notice the the shifting of his weight in the trim.

Now if the First Lieutenant had got his sum wrong so as to make the boat very light it would not dive at all—most embarrassing with an enemy destroyer coming at you at thirty knots, or an aircraft diving out of a cloud. If he had got his sum wrong so that you were much too heavy you would dive all right, but you would not be able to stop diving; a boat hurtling down fast takes a lot of stopping, even blowing main ballast would take time to stop her. If there was a bottom to hit and you hit it hard, it would not be a good thing; if it was hard and rocky you would damage the boat, possibly holing it; if it was soft you might stick in it and never get off; even if the bottom was many hundreds of feet below, that might merely increase your danger. For every couple of feet you go down, the pressure increases nearly one pound per square inch. There are lots of square inches on a submarine hull and pressures soon become formidable.

Boats are designed to stand a certain depth, in *Sealion* it was 200 feet, in *Safari* 350 feet. These were conservative estimates. I took *Sealion* down to nearly 300 feet when out of control during a depth-charge attack, but she did not like it much and groaned alarmingly. I used regularly to take *Safari* to about 450 feet when hunted, but that was getting near her comfortable limit. I saw an "S" boat, *Stubborn*, which had lost control in action and been down to over 500 feet. Her plating had started to cave in and, though she lived to tell the tale, her ribs were sticking out like a starving race horse. She required extensive rebuilding. Both *Sealion* and *Safari* were riveted boats and they would creak and groan under pressure to warn you that you were trying them hard. I am told that a welded boat, as all the later boats were, though stronger weight for weight, would not give you that warning. They would collapse suddenly, but needless to say I cannot speak from experience.

It was always a moot point whether, with every rivet straining under pressure, a boat was more vulnerable to depth charges; it could be that the pressure would also reduce the lethal range of the depth charge. But anyhow you used depth to take advantage of density layers, to put more water between you and the enemy hydrophones and to keep him guessing, for he had to set his charges to somewhere near your depth. It was the usual nice calculation of risks. As you went deeper, the boat got "heavier" to the submariner's way of thinking. In reality the boat was being compressed by the pressure, becoming smaller and therefore displacing less water; you had to pump out some water from the auxiliary ballast tanks to compensate.

From all this it follows that the First Lieutenant had a lot of interest in getting his sums right; but he could not, and indeed was not expected to, get them dead right. As long as he was somewhere near—and in war he would take care that he erred on the heavy side, otherwise you got sunk before you started—the boat dived all right and you went down fast so that the hydroplane's fins forward and aft, which could be turned to plane you up or down, could take effect. You could hold quite a large error in trim on the hydroplanes provided the boat was going fast; but if you were being hunted you wanted to slow down as soon as possible. So the First Lieutenant would trim the boat by flooding a little water into a tank here, pumping out a bit there, and gradually reducing the speed until the planes could hold her at her slowest speed. The planes were largely used to put an angle on the boat, bow up or down, so that you used the whole surface of the boat as a plane.

At diving stations the Coxswain worked the after planes, the Second Coxswain the fore planes. When twisting and turning, and particularly in a sea way, it required a lot of skill and anticipation by the planesmen to keep depth. In calm weather you could catch such a fine trim that you could stop the boat altogether. By raising a periscope you would displace a few gallons more water and that would bring you up; lower it again and you would sink. It called for a very fine trimming.

Everything happened very slowly in a submarine— you were dealing with nearly a thousand tons in the "S" class and it took a lot of starting and also a lot of stopping.

Periscope

If you were to keep under perfect control you had to anticipate, start correcting the wayward lady almost before she started to stray.

IV. *Periscopes*

We had two periscopes, the high power (H.P.) periscope, and the attack or small periscope. Both were about 34 feet long.

The H.P. periscope was bi-focal, it could give you 6 magnifications or 1½ magnifications. Owing to the loss of light in the various lenses and prisms, the 1½ magnification gave you about the same picture as you would see with the naked eye. But only "about," judging range and so on through a periscope required a lot of practice.

You changed the power of the periscope by a twist grip; it was as well to remember which power you were using; if you thought you were in high, when in fact you were in low, you would think that you were much farther from the object—four times as far—than you really were. Collisions have been caused that way.

The 6 magnifications gave you a much more detailed picture if visibility was good, but it gave a much narrower arc of vision; you could only take in one thing at a time. In lower power you got a wider picture.

The H.P. periscope also had a skyscrape; by twisting another handle you could search the heavens, and the top window was set at an angle to allow for this. Being sloped, it drained slowly, and with the sea breaking over it, as it did when one was looking into the wind, it fogged badly. Also, being on a slant, it could reflect the sun, producing a flash which could catch a surface lookout's eye.

I never worried about being able to look up to high elevations, I always reckoned that if an aircraft was in that position you had no right to be using the big periscope anyway. I had a special top window in my big periscope in *Safari* which was vertical. It drained better, did not flash in the sun, and enabled the top to be a little smaller. No one else seemed to like the idea of losing some of their sky search; but it suited me, and as I believe I survived more hunting and harassing than anyone else, I had no cause to complain.

For the majority of its length the H.P. periscope was 9½ inches in diameter, the top four feet or so tapered down to about four inches at the window. Everyone had their own ideas as to what color to paint this top taper, but I think any nondescript dirty color served. The rest of the periscope was shining bronze as it had to slide up and down in bearings and was not normally exposed above the surface.

The attack periscope was only 7½ inches in diameter, with a much smaller top window. It tapered down to about two inches, and therefore made little wake travelling through the water. It was much harder for surface look-outs to see, but it was also harder to see out of, as it had a much poorer light transmission. In practice, you used the big periscope as close to the enemy as you dared. Actually I seemed to dare less than anyone else, I was very shy of using the big periscope within 4,000 yards of the enemy on a calm day. There was always a tremendous temptation to have a good look. I used to resist that, even to the extent, when close to the enemy, of not raising the little periscope above the surface sufficiently to get it clear of ripples. In my opinion the art of using a periscope in action was to be able to make your estimations on a very hazy and brief look. When close to A/S craft my rule was that if you could see clearly you were showing too much periscope. It was probably over cautious, but I believed in both caution and survival.

Normally the periscopes were lowered, the eye pieces sliding down into wells close up against the keel. They were raised hydraulically until the top window came clear of the water; you could not do that if you were deeper than the length of the periscope, 34 feet. Deeper than this you were below "periscope depth."

V.   *Periscope Standards and Jumping Wires*

Our periscopes were bronze, which had some advantages, but had not the strength of steel. They needed support when raised to stop them whipping about. British boats, therefore, had heavy supporting standards, as shown in the diagram, reaching up above the bridge to within about 10 feet of the surface at periscope depth. The standards also acted as a support for the jumping wire.

This was a heavy serrated steel wire running from the bow, over the standard, and secured at the stern. The idea was that they would guide A/S nets over the gun, bridge and excrescences, should anyone be foolhardy or unfortunate enough to get mixed up with nets. Apparently the earlier submarines looked upon competing with nets as part of the game; we were not so tough in my time; we reckoned to avoid getting mixed up with nets, but the jumping wire lingered on as a feature for many years.

VI. *Submerged Attack*

Everyone is inclined to invest their own trade with an aura of black magic, and perhaps I too am biased. But I do believe that submerged attack, with the facilities submarines had in 1914–18 was far from easy. Lack of money for development between the wars found our submarines in 1939 with no advance in torpedo control over their 1914–18 forebears. The difference was that they now had to compete with World War II opposition, though this fortunately also had its weaknesses. In support of my contention, it is a fact that in 1914–18 the Germans found that a handful of their C.O.s achieved a preponderance of their sinkings. Others just had not got the knack, the seamen's eye. Accordingly the Germans devised attack computers and accommodating torpedoes which would alter course, so as to take much of the strain off the C.O. The Americans went further and evolved a truly wonderful computer and backed it up with radar ranging. The attack I describe is the World War I attack, as used with considerable success by the British World War II C.O.s.

Nature seems to have equipped the British more generously with seamen's eyes—the ability to calculate velocity triangles in your head, on data judged by eye, and to do them when, if not actually frightened, at least under considerable pressure.

In the days when the exploits of *Sealion* and *Safari* made headlines in the press, I found myself described as "dashing." I can think of few more unsuitable adjectives to use in a trade where the needle business, the closing stages of attack, was carried out at a speed of three knots or less.

I had the honor, after the war, to be head of the

submarine service when Churchill unveiled the submarine memorial in Westminster Abbey. I remember he attributed to us an "ice cold brain in danger." I do not claim this attribute personally; but it certainly describes the kind of intellect I should have liked to have had as a submarine C.O.; the dashing part was best left to those less interested in survival.

During an attack your speed was restricted so as to avoid detection. Then you had to point the whole submarine to aim your torpedoes; it took about four minutes, in reasonable circumstances, to turn your boat ninety degrees; it could take considerably more if the escorting vessels were being difficult.

At reasonable firing ranges, say under 2,000 yards, the target was crossing your sights much faster than you could swing the boat; you had to be lined up in advance. Then you had to attack from ahead. You had not got the speed to catch up.

The ideal firing position was about 600 yards on the beam of the enemy, though anything between 500 and 1,500 yards was fair enough. Outside that range you were starting to rely upon having made very good estimations of enemy course and speed—to calculate the angle to aim ahead—and you were asking more of your torpedoes, though actually our torpedoes had a magnificent range, getting on for 10,000 yards, which was just about double that of the Americans and Germans. At its best a torpedo would only run to within a degree of the course set; and at its worst was more likely to torpedo you than the enemy. The element of luck entered increasingly outside a range of 2,000 yards. Long range shots could, and occasionally did, work; but they were more suitable for a browning shot at a line of ships than at a single target.

Calculation of enemy course was done by eye and was not all that difficult with practice. The line of his masts and funnel and his side would give you this if you were fairly fine ahead. An experienced C.O. would expect to get the enemy course within 5 degrees if within 45 degress of right ahead of the target. From further to one side it became increasingly difficult. Some ships were far more difficult than others; camouflage painting did not help or the light might be difficult.

Judging speed was more difficult. First and foremost

you had the type of ship and what she was engaged upon.
That gave you a clue as to the probable range of speeds
she might be doing.

Bow waves were deceptive, they depended upon the
wind and sea and the shape of the ship's hull. Stern waves,
when you could see them, were more help. A ship going
fast tucks down her stern, a destroyer at speed will have a
stern wave mounting higher than her quarter deck. But
again this is only a rough guide.

Then there were the revolutions of her engines; the
Asdic operator could make a shot at counting the beat of
the propellers. It was difficult, but some were quite good at
it. Then you had to decide what revolutions per knot of
speed that type of ship would be doing; they varied
enormously according to the type of engines, and whether
or not the propellers were geared down. But again it was a
help if the Asdic operator could get a count.

The most valuable method of all was to plot the
enemy's advance, the rate at which he was closing you. To
do that you needed ranges. The periscope had a device
whereby you could make two images of the target and
separate them one above the other. You then balanced the
water-line of one image on the mastheads of the other and
you could then read off on a scale the number of minutes
of arc subtended by the masthead height of the target. If
you knew the masthead height and had balanced the
images right—which was nearly impossible to do without
showing rather a lot of periscope—you could then calculate the range. But you did not actually know the masthead
height, you had to judge it—or some might say guess it.

If the target was hugging the shore you could plot
him along the coastline as he passed various salient features—if there were salient features, that is—and if he
were close enough to them for you to judge when he
passed them.

Finally the rate of change of bearing, either by taking
bearings at set intervals, or just by eye. In the end, after
checking up on the speed in every possible way, you used
your seaman's eye and with experience this was not a bad
range finder. When we were going to surface for a gun
action, I always gave the range to be set on the sights as
judged by eye, after a quick mental sum to allow for the
relative movements between starting to surface and getting

off the first round; it was seldom appreciably out. The professional should know his trade.

If you had got the enemy course and speed right—you had your attack team to help you in computing it from your estimations—you knew what angle to aim ahead; that angle could then be set on the periscope. There was a bearing ring where the periscope passed through the pressure hull and you could read on it the bearing from dead ahead, on which the periscope was pointing. The actual sight was a graticule, or line down the center of the periscope lens (this can be seen in some of the illustrations). There was nothing to stop the enemy altering speed during the attack, though he seldom did; but he could also, and regularly did when zigging, alter course. Zig-zagging is a recognized and quite effective method of confusing submarine attack, and is regularly practiced by shipping in war. You could never be certain of your estimations of course and speed until you fired.

These estimations were only a minor part of the whole business, though they were running through your head all the time. The trouble was to maneuver your boat to be in the right position, at the right range, pointing in the right direction at the right time. You had to do all this without using much power on your propellers, which could give you away to the escorts, if the target was screened; with a minimum use of the periscope to take your observations; and without asking too much of the First Lieutenant and planesmen by turning the boat about too violently, making it difficult to keep depth accurately. In a seaway you might also have to plan to avoid driving the boat on certain courses where the sea would make depth control difficult.

The target was always going a lot faster than you and to a large degree your position was dictated by her movements. If she were sighted in such a position that she was going to pass a long way off, all you could do was to run in as fast as the circumstances—escort vessels and aircraft—permitted, and get off your shot from as near as you could get. Then you just had to trust that you had made a good estimation of enemy course and speed, and that the torpedoes were feeling co-operative. It would probably mean that you would have to fire from outside the screen, the torpedo tracks would probably be seen by

the escorts and the target could be warned to alter course
so as to avoid your torpedoes.

There was no particular skill in this sort of attack; if
you got a hit you were duly grateful and it gave no
satisfaction to your professional pride—there was too
much luck in it. It was also more dangerous, strangely
enough; in the same way big game hunters who take long
chancy shots at dangerous game seldom survive. It needs
some nerve to stalk within a few yards of a vicious quarry;
there was some strain on the nerves in taking your boat
through the screen; but if you did it, you were safer. You
let off your shots on the side of the escorts where they
were not looking out; your noises and those of the torpedoes were mixed up with the noises of the target. Above
all you were fairly certain of making a kill and that is
always upsetting for the opposition.

VII. *Screens*

The air patrol was more or less beyond your control;
you merely had to maneuver your boat so as to make no
wash on the surface—which meant going deep, say fifty
feet below periscope deph, before you speeded up. That
took time and, if you were going to make a worthwhile
distance at speed, it meant running a long time blind. The
enemy might have altered course whilst you were deep and
so changed the whole picture. In some circumstances you
had to accept a longer firing range, rather than go blind
for long.

Apart from that small handicap the air screen did not
trouble you very much; if it did, it was either through
plain bad submarining, or extraordinarily bad luck. There
was just one exception to this. When you were actually
firing the torpedoes, you had to stay up at periscope depth
to get your sights on and you could not avoid the bubbles
and disturbance made by the torpedoes. I was caught by
an aircraft twice whilst firing torpedoes; once in *Sealion*
when we very nearly got sunk in consequence; once in
Safari when we merely got shaken up a trifle. It was just
one of those things you had to accept.

The surface escort screen was different, they could be
a nuisance from start to finish. It is true that if you got
detected before firing it was almost certainly due to bad

submarining, but to avoid detection you could not go where you wanted, when and how you wanted.

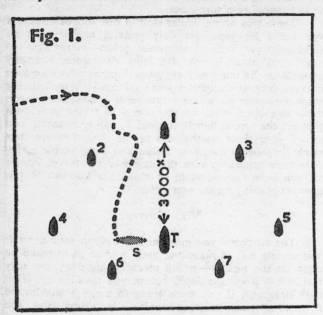

Fig. 1 shows a typical screen of seven escorts and the relative track of submarine would take to penetrate it.

The escorts were usually about 1,500 to 3,000 yards from the target. The 3,000 yard screen was not so bad; you had time—nine minutes for a ten knot target—to turn into your firing course after penetrating it. A 1,500 yard screen was getting a bit needle; it was much closer and you might have to be content with firing from outside the screen; in that case the escorts would not have time to warn the target of the approach of your torpedoes and so let her take avoiding action. At 3,000 yards you had time to go deep under the screen, if they put you in an awkward position, and still come up again for your shot. Provided they all maintained a steady course, escorts 1-5 would not be much trouble. The real brute would be escort No. 6. It would be within a thousand yards of you when you fired, and if it saw the tracks starting it could be on you in a minute or so. It was very unpleasant firing torpedoes with an escort pointing at you like that; you had to clear your firing position very promptly.

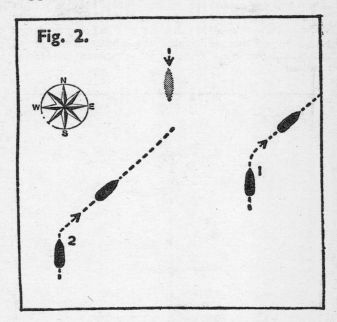

A small point to notice in the diagram is that when actually passing through the screen our submarine does a slow turn so as to present her bow and stern, smaller targets, to the escorts as they pass her.

Unfortunately the escorts would be unlikely to maintain a steady course. Fig. 2 shows the predicament of the submarine if they alter course whilst she is about to pass through the screen.

Whilst they were steering north, the submarine was comfortably placed to pass through the screen between escorts 1 and 2. She would probably turn a bit to point her bow and stern at the escorts as they come past. Suddenly they alter course to the north-east. Escort No. 2 looks as if she will pass over the top of the submarine, as she is going much faster; she is going to pass unpleasantly close in any case, and the submarine will probably have to go deep. She will not have much time as she will not risk increasing speed. If there is an escort placed as No. 4 in Fig. 1, she also is going to menace the submarine and hamper her just when she wants to turn to port and speed up. The target will also have altered to starboard and is going to pass a lot farther off than anticipated; the submarine has got to get cracking at once if she is to get into a good firing position.

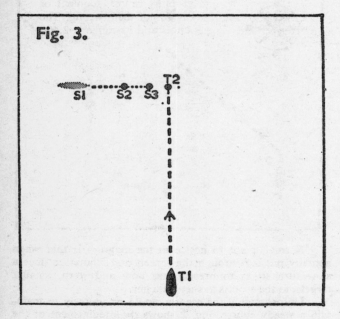

Fig. 3.

S1   S2 S3   T2

T1

VIII. *Getting into the Firing Position*

Even with a slow target steering a steady course it is not as dead easy as you might think to arrive at a satisfactory range, say about 600 yards. At under 400 yards the torpedoes had not time to settle to their depth and might well run under the target. In Fig. 3 the problem is illustrated. We will assume that on the day in question the submarine has to do 3 knots, about 100 yards a minute, to keep depth, which would be the case in a slight sea.

Our submarine reckons that the target at T. 1 is doing 12 knots and is about 2,000 yards off. At 12 knots (400 yards/1 minute) she will take 5 minutes to get to T. 2. Meanwhile the submarine will have done 500 yards and arrived at S. 2 in time for a sitting shot at 600 yards range.

But all these calculations are based on estimations and, perhaps because of bad visibility or misjudgment of the size of the target, she may have got them wrong. The target is perhaps only doing 9 knots and its range is 2,400 yards, therefore it is only doing 300 yards a minute and will take 8 minutes to arrive at T. 2—three minutes longer than estimated. In that three minutes the submarine will have done another 300 yards and will be at S. 3, range 300 yards and too close for the torpedoes.

On top of this, the submarine might have misjudged the enemy's course a trifle; the target may be steering a bit more to port than the submarine reckoned; before the submarine knows what is happening she will find herself in danger of being rammed and will have to break off the attack and go deep.

The submarine should spot that things are not going according to plan and take suitable action to correct matters; but it is not all that easy to do so and she is quite likely to end up by tying herself in knots. If the air throws in some odd escorts as well to confuse the situation, she is going to be really worried. It might seem easier not to attempt such a needle attack, but to shoot in comfort at 2,000 yards range from outside the screen; the enemy might well not notice the torpedo tracks and within 1¼ minutes of their appearance they would have hit anyway. The trouble with this is that a three-knot error in the submarine's estimate of the target's speed would result in the torpedo's being 400 feet off the point of aim at 2,000 yards—even if it ran true. It would only be 120 feet off at 600 yards range and a liberty ship of some 7,000 tons is about 400 feet long.

If the target was zigging, or altering course, the picture changed continually. When the target was doing a regular zig and you had him in sight for a long time, as

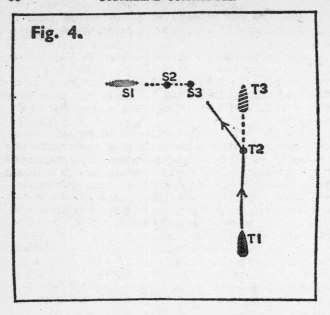

Fig. 4.

you might in good visibility, you could make a forecast of
his next alteration. However, this was a dangerous practice; it is always unwise in war to bank on any future
action by the enemy. The best thing was to attack every
leg of the zig. Sometimes, however, one could and did
anticipate the enemy's action, particularly if he was in the
swept channel of a minefield—the course of which you
could have plotted by watching the mine-sweepers at
work—or when he was rounding navigational hazards.

The permutations of a zig-zag's effect upon the attacking submarine are legion. An example of the worst
sort is shown in Fig. 4; it was what happened to *Sealion* in
the chapter describing her collision. Luckily in this case
she had another target placed more favorably, because an
escort prevented her taking the one way out of the difficulty with her original target. Unluckily she was not
successful on the other target either, but that is not our
present story.

In Fig. 4 our submarine at S. 1 is sitting pretty for the

target at T. 1. When the target gets to T. 3 the submarine will be at S. 3 ready for a nice shot. Unfortunately for our submarine, when the target gets to T. 2 she alters course to port, so that if the submarine holds on both will arrive at S. 3 together.

The submarine has to do something about it. If she could go astern it would all be quite simple. An efficient submarine is in fact capable of diving astern but control is precarious and not good enough to risk it in action; it is certainly not good enough for firing torpedoes.

The best way out of this situation would be for our submarine to go deep, speed up to run across the target's bows and turn round to fire from the target's starboard side. If the target was fairly slow she would probably have time to do this, but might have to fire on the starboard quarter of her target rather than the beam, which presents the best target. This is shown in Fig. 5.

The submarine at S. 1 spots the target at T. 1 changing course to port. The submarine speeds up, runs

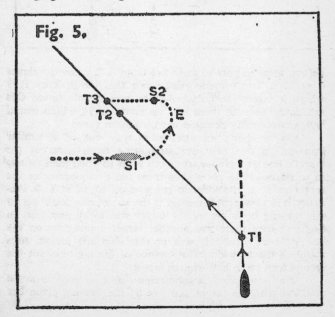

Fig. 5.

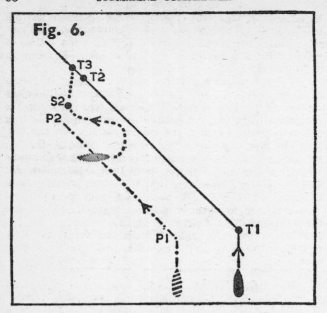

Fig. 6.

T3
T2
S2
P2
P1
T1

across, turns to port so as to fire from S. 2 when the target is at T. 2. The torpedo runs along the line S. 2 to T. 3 where it meets the target. *Sealion* was unable to do this maneuver because there was an escort at E, which would have undoubtedly detected her turning at speed.

Fig. 6 shows an alternative way out of a similar impasse. In this case our submarine turns short of the target's line of advance, runs out a bit to port, then swings in to starboard to get a shot from the port quarter of the target at T. 2, the torpedo running on to hit at T. 3. Actually it is very problematical if the submarine could get all this turning done before the target was away past her. In *Sealion*'s case there was another target coming up on the line P. 1–P. 2 and it was at this ship she aimed, thus avoiding the very doubtful chance of finding time for the second turn on to her original target.

If all else failed, a submarine could go deep to avoid collision with the target and fire by the bearing given her by Asdic listening equipment. Hits have been obtained in this way, but it was a most inaccurate and chancy business —a last forlorn hope.

IX. *The Battery*

There was yet one other thing that the C.O. had to think about during submerged attack: the state of his battery. It was of limited capacity and drove the electric motors when submerged; you had to surface and run the diesels to charge it up.

At full speed submerged it only lasted about an hour, during which you did rather more than eight miles. At slow speed, say two knots, it would last about a day and a half.

A submarine's battery is quite a hefty affair; in the "S" class it was in two sections, each weighting about 50 tons; when discharged it could take the whole power developed by one main engine to start charging it up. If you charged it too fast for too long it got too hot and that finished things.

Without battery power you were helpless. The constant anxiety of the C.O. was to nurse his battery and he only used speed as sparingly as possible. You needed some amps left to make your escape afterwards if you wanted to live to fight another day.

When you wanted to go places at night, the C.O. and the Chief got into a huddle to decide how much of the power the engines could develop should be used to drive the propellers and how much to charge the battery. On a normal diving patrol you needed about six hours a day to charge your battery.

The battery is continually mentioned in the operational tale because the whole submarine routine evolved about its demands; it was the submarine's very life blood on a diving patrol.

X. *Main Engines and Main Motors*

The motive power of a submarine consisted of two diesel engines driving the propeller shafts; the electric main motors were mounted on the same shafts abaft the main diesel engines, with a clutch in between, known as the engine clutch. Abaft each main motor was another clutch, the tail clutch.

With the engine clutch engaged, the main electric motors on that shaft revolved with the diesel engine; if the tail clutch was also engaged so did the propeller. This was the normal way of proceeding on the surface, with the main motors disconnected electrically so that they revolved freely on the shaft as a sort of flywheel.

The main electric motors could equally well be used in reverse as dynamos. In this case electrical connections to the batteries were made and the main diesel engines drove the dynamo to charge the batteries. If you wanted a high charging rate you had to disengage the tail clutch; the engines were not powerful enough to drive the propellers and give a high rate of charge through the dynamos at the same time. However, if a low rate of charge was enough, the engine could drive the propeller as well and this was called a running charge.

To proceed on the main electric motors, as when submerged, the engine clutch was disengaged, leaving the tail clutch engaged, and the propellers were driven using power from the batteries.

Safari could do about 15 knots on the surface, her engines developing about 2,500 h.p. At 12½ knots you could proceed indefinitely with a small running charge to keep the battery topped up; this was our normal operational cruising speed.

5

THE PHONY WAR

We were soon away from Portsmouth, leaving *Snapper* behind for her engine repairs, and groping our way along the darkened south coast and up through the Downs before spreading for patrol off the Dutch coast. In the well-known Naval prayer which Queen Elizabeth the First ordained should be read in her ships daily and which is still read at least at Sunday Service, we ask to be protected from "the dangers of the sea, and the violence of the enemy." The author appreciated which of them required most divine assistance and like most seamen I too always rated the dangers of the sea before the violence of the enemy.

In the early days of the war the coastal passage of the south and east coast of Britain was not one to be taken lightheartedly on a wintry night—with all navigation lights extinguished and a concentration of shipping in both directions. It was not long before the losses from collisions and groundings outweighed any protection afforded by denying the enemy navigational aids, and lighthouses and buoys were provided again. A submarine being more or less invisible at night normally possessed some advantages, as it was fairly certain that you would not be seen and merely had to avoid everyone. In narrow channels this advantage disappeared and a collision inevitably meant loss of life to a submarine with her low buoyancy.

We lost two boats on the east coast in this way. It was October, 1939, a night of low visibility with wind and rain, and I was not enjoying myself, more particularly because I was extremely uncertain of our position and had *Salmon* and *Shark* to keep out of trouble as well as myself. In due course I lost them as we wove our way through the darkened shipping in the Downs. Somehow or other we found our way out into the North Sea through the gap in the minefields and in the grey light of dawn got together again, none of us very certain as to what route we had followed, and moved on to our patrol positions. This patrol was nicknamed the "Thin Red Line" in the submarine service. There was an invasion scare; all available submarines were deployed in a line up and down the North Sea. It was to be an introduction to the realities of war, which had seemed so romantic in anticipation—but which was for many, most of the time, a weary waiting for an enemy who never came.

Submarines were still bound by the rules of war, agreed to by the Hague Convention. It looked as if these rules were designed by the British for the British. With our far-flung Empire, utterly dependent upon sea communication for our daily bread, we had far more to lose than gain by submarine warfare. Unrestricted submarine warfare was taboo. The submarine had to visit and search a merchant ship before, having established her hostile occupation and given the crew time to escape, the ship was sunk. Since it is a legitimate *ruse de guerre* for ships to fly an ensign other than their own, it is easy for a merchant ship to disguise herself under a neutral flag. Only the largest submarine can carry a boat suitable for more than inshore boating, and that would have to be stowed in a casing open to the sea and extremely vulnerable to damage in rough weather. In fact boats for patrol submarines are not practicable, though they may be embarked for special operations, and the submarine had to rely upon the merchant ship sending a boat. She could be forced to do this; but there would be no future for a submarine lolling about on the surface in enemy waters, whilst her boarding party searched the ship. In practice the rules meant that, except on the high seas, far distant from patrols, a submarine could only attack warships. This suited the British and we obeyed the rules, hoping thereby to set the form and above all enlist American goodwill. For America was still sitting on the fence and it was to be over two years before, stimulated by Pearl Harbor, she was to come in on our side.

Needless to say, the Germans, having everything to

gain and little to lose except world sympathy, did not obey
the rules which seemed to them completely illogical. Aircraft could bomb ships or cities; armies could shell towns
regardless of the loss of non-combatant life; but submarines were to fight in kid gloves. War is ruthless; treaties
and agreements become so much waste paper when it suits
a combatant to break them. No logical person could ever
have believed that Germany would obey the rules, but it
was to be another six months before our own submarines
were unmuzzled.

This did not mean that these early patrols of our
submarines were not conducted with the utmost enthusiasm; nor without some success. In a single patrol, *Salmon*
damaged two cruisers and sank one of their escorts and a
U-boat. But for the most part it was a ceaseless barren
watch through the North Sea winter. Night after night
went by without a star to fix the ship and if by day the sun
broke through the grey skies for a few minutes, enabling
you to surface and take a rapid observation, you were
lucky. For the most part we groped our way around by
taking soundings. There are of course definite depressions
and elevations on the sea bottom which, when found, will
give the mariner, in well charted areas, a definite position.
The North Sea is magnificently charted, but the submarine
at war must approach such places with discretion. An
enemy specializing in submarine warfare, knowing the
anxiety of the submarine to fix her position, could be
expected to mine such banks and deeps. However tempted
I always studiously avoided these obvious soundings. The
North Sea is shallow, but even so our echo sounder was
neither accurate nor reliable enough for the purpose when
there were small variations in the soundings. The technique we used was to sink the boat gently on to the
bottom, read the depth gauge, take her off, run on a bit
and repeat the process until you had a line of soundings
which you would endeavor to identify with similar soundings on the chart.

One of our main concerns was to devise clothing
suitable for those North Sea winter nights with short seas
breaking over the bridge. On this first patrol, in common
with many others, I started to grow a beard as a first step
toward weather protection. It was great fun as we compared each other's progress. Beards do not grow to order;

they sprout luxuriantly where you do not particularly want them and show a marked reluctance to grow in other places; some people can never produce more than a patchy coverage. However, given time, most people can produce enough vegetation to give them a wide choice of design. Between patrols, when operating from Harwich, I would go up to London where under the Ritz Hotel lived an artist of a barber, old enough to remember the days when beards were *de rigueur*. After the days of squalor on patrol it was delightful to relax and be trimmed, shampooed and anointed whilst a long-suffering manicurist tried to make something of your dirt-ingrained hands.

No one shaved much on patrol; fresh water was limited and in any case hot water gave off steam which added to the damp condensation in the boat. One wore layer upon layer of clothes; it is cold in a submarine in the Northern winter and submariners get special issues of warm clothing; also at this time kind persons knitted us lots of balaclavas and sea-boot stockings. As C.O., at constant call, I never undressed for weeks on end and, since we all smelt alike, no one noticed. But when one got in from patrol, one and all would strip off their seagoing layers to luxuriate in a bath of indefinite duration. After the last layer of clothing you would find yourself covered with white powder like scurf; this was skin which we slowly change day by day, but which normally gets away.

We did, in *Sealion*, have one who disdained to adjust the niceties of hygiene to the requirements of patrol; and, since he was only one, the limited condensation made his foibles acceptable. Daily he stripped off and washed himself, and was rewarded in due course by developing scabies. There was much to be said for the comfortable theory that by not undressing you kept such things out.

There is no privacy in a submarine and we in *Sealion* had been together with only an occasional change for a year already, but now we were to get to know each other better still. A submarine C.O. was still allowed to hold on to his ship's company, even though his officers would trickle away, Third and Fourth Hands to be First Lieutenants, First Lieutenants to become C.O.s. It did lead to a team of outstanding efficiency, but in a service where losses were to be the highest in the services, it became unacceptable. Each time you lost a boat you lost the whole highly trained team, who could have provided several times over the nucleus for another crew. I served over three years in *Sealion*, peace and war, and a number of us were together throughout. Together we entered the unknown; and although it proved that, thanks to the enlightened training of Ruckers, our theories were justified, they had still to be proved.

I was particularly lucky in *Sealion* because I had been in her for that year and we had adapted her to be suitable for war, whilst the letters we had written stagnated in in-baskets. We knew that the Germans used hydrophones; we knew that some of our machinery was excessively noisy; we devised means to enable us to operate—at some loss of performance—silently. Our solution was not acceptable on technical grounds to the Staff but they produced no alternative until the bitter experience of war stimulated matters.

Meanwhile *Sealion* competed very satisfactorily, however technically unacceptable. We asked for sufficient night binoculars for our lookouts. Despite the fact that upon her lookouts the life of a submarine depended—and the cost was negligible compared with the value of the boat and her crew—the office pundits considered them unnecessary for all the lookouts. It was my ambition to survive and as it seemed a good insurance policy I had bought some out of my own pocket—German ones, ironically. Soon after the war started the country was being combed for binoculars, out submarines having top priority. We also had a homemade night sight; I had got the idea from the German ones of 1914/18, which were at least serviceable, and later developed a similar contraption for night use on the gun.

The gun itself had defeated me; I could find no way to make the breech reliable. As it was originally an army Ack Ack gun, I sought guidance from the gunners at Malta. I found an elderly warrant officer who said he remembered it, and I enlisted his advice. However, when he saw it, he could only suggest that we should throw it away as the army had done years before. Actually, apart from the fact that the breech jammed at the most inopportune moments, that its shell was too light for the job and that it was in no way designed to withstand the exposure of submarine life, it was a very good little gun. Most of its ailments could be cured by a strong man with a lead mallet, though some favored kicking with a heavy sea boot.

Such things, however, were only minor annoyances and the *Sealion* class were splendid boats. They were uncomfortable for the crew, but that is the sort of thing that must be accepted cheerfully in war. I personally suffered by being above average height. The Naval constructors, always hard put to find space, sought refuge in a standard man, who was apparently five feet nine inches tall and fitted a bunk six feet long—a couple of inches less than my height. One very tall submarine C.O. got over the trouble by cutting a hole in a bulkhead and welding a box on the other side into which he could stick his feet. When a couple of years later I went to build *Safari*, I got round Cammell Laird, who were very willing but somewhat doubtful about departing from Admiralty specification, to make my bunk long enough. I then went on leave and, on return, found to my disgust that someone had seized on the extra few inches to locate a particularly knobbly valve. It was too late to alter despite my protests, and in due course my feet got used to taking up the only position in which they would share the bunk harmoniously with the valve. *Safari* was the first of her class and some time afterwards I met another C.O. of a later boat who complained about sharing his bunk with a valve. He said that he had put the matter to Cammell Laird, but been informed that Commander Bryant liked it that way.

But to have a bunk at all was a great luxury and in any case you were never in it long enough to suffer more than passing stiffness from the cramped position. Even working on the hot bunk principle, the man coming off watch taking over the bunk vacated by the man who had relieved him, and using every conceivable space where a hammock could be slung, there were not enough beds for all. Men slept on the deck, on tables, under tables, on top of lockers, anywhere they did not get trodden on—much. In rough weather, the decks were not only damp and covered with slime composed of upset food, bilge water and lub oil, but the deck head would drip condensation, so that the men had to cover themselves with an oilskin.

On the surface, the ventilation was good with the diesels running—too good for those into whose sleeping billet the fans discharged an icy blast. If they failed in their endeavor to shut off the ventilation altogether, an old sock could be used to mellow the supply. The electric battery also used to give off gases. If salt water got into it, it gave off chlorine, but fortunately that could only happen if there was an error in the drill for shutting off ventilation; or a cell cracked under depth charging when there was salt water in the sump. But that was a matter that could be competed with, unless, of course, it happened in a big way. When the battery was being charged great care had to be taken to ventilate it through its own special ventilation system; the battery could give off gases that were liable to explode and smoking was taboo once the battery started gassing; a battery was liable to do this at any time and one near the end of its useful life could be particularly troublesome.

Despite the lack of oxygen, the concentration of carbon dioxide, the lack of exercise, the crowded conditions and all the other discomforts of small ship life, the standard of health was excellent.

Some time later in the war this matter was investigated by the medicos and I actually took a distinguished physiologist on patrol. He laid out little glass saucers containing pink jelly after we had been dived for fourteen hours. He would then, after about half-an-hour, seal up the saucers and with them all the germs which apparently flocked to this jelly. On return to harbor the germs were counted—the whole process was of course far more scientific than my description suggests—and I was informed that there were fewer germs in the boat than you would find in the drawing-room of a country house with the French windows open. We reckoned that the germs could not take the battery gas.

Submariners were a healthy lot on the whole and sickness in submarines was very rare; what there was, was taken to sea with you. Very occasionally there would be a stomach case; then there might be someone who had been unlucky in love, but the introduction of the sulphonamide drugs more or less solved that one; and lastly there was T.B. Before the days of mass radiography there was a danger from T.B. and in the congested living conditions it could spread. Actually in *Sealion,* though we did not know it then, two of our petty officers, invaluable men, were to die later of T.B. I must have picked it up myself and thrown it off, for the scar was revealed by X-ray later on. Nowadays chest X-ray rules out that risk.

Sealion's battery at this time was on its last legs and smelling evil. One of the battery ventilation intakes was in my bunk and I always used to wake up with a red hot feeling at the back of my throat where the nostrils seemed to discharge. I think that this was the cause of the only sickness I ever experienced in submarines.

It was *Sealion*'s third patrol in January, 1940, and soon after going to sea I started to feel very rotten. I could hardly drag myself onto the bridge at night and when I got there sometimes I could hardly stand up. I could not consult anyone and—it being the phony war—nothing happened to put any real strain on me. I was the only person trained to do any attack; either I stuck it out or the boat had to leave patrol. I felt confident that I was so well trained that I could do an attack if half dead, as indeed I felt, and so stayed it out. Our diet was simple in those days, chiefly bully beef in its various disguises and ship's biscuits, known as dog biscuits, with which they were identical in appearance.

We never saw each other in daylight and in the dim artificial light one's face always looked a pretty indifferent color. I did not know the symptoms of jaundice, which of course are unmistakable, and if I had there was nothing I could have done. Strangely enough as the days wore on I started to feel better, despite the diet.

Besides biscuits, we did have bread at the start of a patrol, and it lasted for about ten days. Everything being damp it soon lost its crisp newness. The first step was to put it in the oven and tune it up a bit; that would last another couple of days. Then if you cut off the moldy crust, sprinkled it with condensed milk and heated it up again; that improved it for a time. After that, no amount of baking did any good. The only thing was to cut off the worst bits of mold and eat the rest; actually moldy bread is not too bad, particularly if you work up to it slowly. I have always wondered why my spaniel, which will eat practically anything whether hungry or not, always disdains moldy bread. Perhaps it does not suit dogs, but submariners did very well on it. Later on submarines were to have special wrapped bread which kept much better and in due course got trained cooks who could make bread at sea.

We also used to take a good deal of half-cooked meat to sea with us, small boats could not afford refrigerator space, and this cooking improved its keeping qualities. Some believed that when it was going off a sprinkling of Milton was a good thing. Personally I did not really fancy this twice, thrice or more cooked meat. We did not have trained cooks till later though most sailors were expected to be able to cook; but whatever the standards of the professional sailor as an amateur cook I was always thankful when we gave up the so-called fresh meat and got on to the bully beef. Later on we had excellent tinned food and submarines always had magnificent tinned soup. Various attempts were made to educate us to celery, asparagus and such-like soups, but at this time anything of less specific gravity than oxtail was despised. A substance known as "meat and vegetable ration," which might have been considered by some, including the designer, as a stew, was popular as soup.

Anyhow, nourished on the above diet, I started to feel better and at the end of the patrol, coming down the east coast on the surface in snow storms, I did not feel particularly done up after twenty-four hours on the bridge in a blizzard. Even the sea had frozen at Harwich when we finally got there.

My knowledge of medicine is simple and I have always found whisky and aspirin can compete with most troubles. In this case I felt that all I needed now was whisky and my complaint would be finally defeated. As a matter of principle, we did not drink whilst on patrol except that the ship's company got their tot of rum at a time when the C.O. reckoned that there were unlikely to be alarms and excursions; usually after surfacing for the night, when the charge had been started, the air compresses got going, and all was settled down. The officers, who did not get a rum issue, would then have a bottle of beer, or a small tot of spirits. I never gave an order, and I do not think any C.O. did, about this ration of the one small drink a day. No one could risk being below maximum alertness. The effect of alcohol when diving with a pressure in the boat and a concentration of carbon dioxide was unpredictable so the tot was never taken when submerged. There was usually a pressure in the boat from air leaks and care was required when opening the conning-tower lid on surfacing. At least one man was lost overboard from a submarine by being blown out when he opened the hatch. It was often a good thing to start the diesels as you surfaced to suck the pressure out of the boat before you opened the hatch. But if you had been diving a long time the diesels would not start. They were far more particular about the oxygen and carbon dioxide content than the human body.

As soon as I got back to the old *Cyclops*, our depot ship at Harwich, which we did as darkness was falling, I took strong medicinal action and went up to London to catch the night train to Liverpool. I had four days' leave and Marjorie and I were going over to the Isle of Man to my people who were looking after our little daughter. I felt miserable again that night in the train.

We arrived at Liverpool in the cold gray dawn; Marjorie took one look at me and said: "You've got jaundice."

It was the first time anyone had seen me in daylight for a fortnight except muffled up on the bridge in snow storms and largely covered with beard. I had had jaundice for nearly all that fortnight and the surprising thing is that, until the whisky cure, it had seemed to mend itself, for early on I had been dubious if I could keep going.

Besides a few well-known remedies and some morphia, submarines carried a wallet containing a formidable set of instruments; at least, they seemed formidable to an amateur who had barely grasped the principles of first aid. Amongst these was a tube like a very large hollow needle, which you were supposed to stick into the belly of the patient to relieve a stricture. It was a fairly lethal instrument and I viewed it with some alarm; it was obvious that it had to be stuck into the right place and I sought qualified medical guidance.

I was told: "About where the hair ends."

This did little to relieve my anxiety as in the case of the more hirsute warriors this would have been about the Adam's apple where he started shaving. Fortunately I was never called upon to perform as an amateur surgeon, though others were not so lucky. In the Pacific, where boats travelled vast distances, spent weeks on patrol, and the wide dispersal of the opposition made the breaking of wireless silence permissible, boats would report symptoms and get medical advice back, or else transfer sick men to homeward-bound boats.

I have said that sickness was very rare, but actually on her next patrol *Sealion* was struck down by an epidemic. While I was being nursed in my people's home *Sealion* was taken on patrol by "Shrimp" Simpson, Second-in-Command of the flotilla. With nearly half the crew down with what was described as 'flu he had to bring the boat home early. Personally I believe that battery gas was the cause; the battery was now past its useful service and we installed a new one before the next patrol, for which I was fit again. A submarine battery is a large and expensive thing; each cell weighs about one thousand pounds, and there would be 220 to 330 of them depending on the class of boat.

I think that battery gas might have been the cause, because on Christmas Day, 1939, while we were on patrol, we attempted to put Christmas cheer into the boat. Someone had produced some decorations, people were wearing paper hats and races were being run along the battery boards with clockwork motor cars. For some reason someone in the wardroom produced a clinical thermometer and put it in his mouth, to simulate a cigarette, I think, for we were dived and there was no smoking. Anyhow he ended by taking his temperature and found it to be about 100°. All the wardroom then took their temperatures and though checked on another thermometer we found that we were all running temperatures. It did not worry anyone, but it was peculiar. All I do know is that once we installed the new battery we had no more trouble.

One of our C.O.s (the late Lieutenant-Commander D.S.R. Martin, D.S.O.) did once do an attack from a bed of sickness. He was in the Mediterranean later in the war, lying in his bunk, sick and running a fever. A tanker was sighted, he was called, pulled himself together with determination and sank the ship. It was extremely bad luck; it turned out to be a tanker which had been accorded a safe conduct to fuel an Italian liner being used for transport of refugees. He had all the information about it, but in his fever could not think more than to force his brain to do the attack. The follow up was also unfortunate.

After political apologies we agreed to release a tanker which had been blockaded in the neutral Spanish port of Algeciras, opposite Gibraltar. There were two tankers there. The Italians, unknown to us and, ostensibly at any rate, unknown to the Spanish authorities, had very ingeniously converted one into a depot ship for human torpedoes. The Italians were very good at human torpedoes and sank several ships in Gibraltar Bay; we could not discover how they got there. When we captured one of these frogmen types he got away with the cover story that he had been brought there by a submarine. Their security was excellent and we did not discover about this tanker-depot ship till long afterwards; unfortunately the tanker we released was not this depot ship; it would have been an amusing "concession" to the Italians.

Few of us got any action in those early patrols, though I got a chance at a U-boat during my very first. We were returning from the Thin Red Line to the Firth of Forth. Passing the Dogger Bank a gale was blowing; in the short sea kicked up by the bank, depth keeping was nearly impossible and you could see practically nothing with the seas breaking over the periscope. We sank to the bottom for some breakfast, coming up every few minutes for a look round. On one such occasion we found a small U-boat passing close down our side. Although we had our periscope standards and half the bridge out of water so as to get the periscope clear of the sea, she did not see us and presumably the watch on her bridge must have been blinded by the driving sea.

As was always the case when I sighted a U-boat, we were pointing in the wrong direction and by the time we had turned round at full speed only half submerged but still unseen, the target was a long way past and only presenting little more than her stern. It was asking a lot of the torpedoes to run sufficiently shallow in that sea to hit him, but we fired a salvo and then went deep and waited hopefully for the bang. It came at exactly the right time for the running range and we surfaced triumphantly to see if there was anyone to pick up. To our bitter disappointment there was the U-boat still on the surface; it was far too rough to man the gun and anyhow she dived immediately. The only explanation of this I have ever been able to think of is that the torpedo, which like a submarine has great difficulty in keeping her depth near the surface in a seaway, must have been passing just under as the U-boat, having risen to a wave, was falling back again. Thus the U-boat would come down on top of the torpedo near the tail but abaft the warhead, damaging the controls so that the torpedo would be deflected to explode on the bottom of the sea.

The nearest I got to attacking any other warship in those early North Sea patrols was in March, 1940, our last patrol before the submarine war started properly with the Norway invasion.

We were patrolling inside the "Cabbage Patch," as we called the German declared minefield which protected the Heligoland Bight. The Germans had declared it mined and whether or not it was we had treated it at first with due respect, but by now boats were traversing it regularly. A German anti-submarine trawler started to patrol near us and she seemed a possible torpedo target, although small. To hit a ship of her size necessitated getting in to point-blank range, for one could not afford to miss.

Once you had given away your position by firing, she would become the attacker and the water was uncomfortably shallow. She was fitted with hydrophones to hunt submarines and so the utmost discretion, which meant the slowest speed, had to be used. Every time we were just getting into position she would alter course and start a beat in another direction and so it went on for some hours, Sealion going round in ever decreasing circles. After a bit her movements became so erratic that it became obvious that she had picked up something on her hydrophones and was trying to locate us. The roles changed, we became the hunted and, though she never managed to carry out an attack, we were very pleased when we shook her off. Trying to torpedo small A/S vessels is not a profitable pastime, but when you have been long on patrol without a target one is apt to attempt such things.

We had little knowledge of the German A/S methods or efficiency during these early patrols and we would hear all sorts of noises which could not be diagnosed. The unknown always inspires some respect, and very properly people who live dangerously are very suspicious of any phenomenon they cannot explain. Noise travels much better through water than air and one of the noises all our submarines heard was given the title of "North Sea Grunts." It sounded rather like a large bubble being released under water and was usually heard when a trawler was in sight. The North Sea was still full of fishing boats during this phony war and it was hard to tell whether they were legitimate fishing boats or trawlers converted into A/S vessels. If they had no seagulls round them they were particularly suspect, but all required to be treated with discretion. It was not unnatural that our submarines should suspect that the North Sea Grunt was some sound-ranging detecting device employed by the enemy and scientists were asked to investigate the matter. In the end it was diagnosed as fish noises and if the diagnosis was correct, then flatulent porpoises were the cause of a lot of anxiety.

A good deal more strain on C.O.s was involved during the changeover from peace to war, when you were finding the form, then later on when one had become acclimatized to war. Even so, harmless marine creatures were to cause an alarm much later in the war that the enemy had evolved some infernal new detecting device. A boat patrolling off Taormina, in Sicily, heard a continuous tapping noise and shortly afterwards a destroyer appeared from over the horizon and started to beat her up for no apparent reason. Tappings were heard by other boats and the "Terrible Tappings off Taormina" were treated with the gravest suspicion and gloom. It was some time before the noise was diagnosed as emanating from turtles, numbers of which frequent the Mediterranean at times—the tapping being ascribed to their tactics whilst courting.

Turtles also caused some other unnecessary anxiety. A boat in the Mediterranean found herself surrounded by the low humps of mines which had obviously been set too shallow and were just awash. Wherever the C.O. looked through his periscope he found himself surrounded by mines, and he spent a sweating forenoon avoiding them. It was not till everyone had been reduced to apprehensive exhaustion that one of the mines was noticed to dive; they were all turtles basking on the surface.

By way of relief from the boredom of these early patrols waiting for the enemy fleet, or possibly a blockade runner, to come out, it was decided that we should carry boarding parties. Shipping with neutral markings were still using the North Sea freely and it was decided that we should establish the right of visit and search; if our suspicions were aroused we were to send them over to the British side of the North Sea, with a boarding party on board, for further examination. One of the things we learned from these boarding parties was that the extra men on board not only took up a lot of room but used up a lot of the air we had to breathe. We found ourselves panting, a phenomenon we were to become only too used to later, but which was still something new then.

It was caused by the concentration of carbon dioxide which you breathe out. Not only does it make men pant, but it makes them feel rather clammily cold and it numbs the judgment. In fact, like other mild poisons it has the effect of dulling your higher reasoning power and so to make you rather stupidly brave. Although we did not achieve anything with our boarding parties, they warned us of the carbon dioxide danger, and by the time the Norwegian campaign got going we were being supplied with carbon dioxide absorbent which we needed badly.

I did stop two merchant ships—one claiming to be a Latvian and the other a Finn. Although they sent a boat, the weather was too rough to transfer the boarding party from our casing. It was not rough by any ordinary standards, but the waterlogged hull of a submarine and its narrow casings are singularly unsuitable for taking a boat alongside in anything but calm weather. Visit and search was just not a practical proposition. In any case, if the merchant ship had refused to stop and send a boat, there was nothing you could do about it; to have shelled a merchant ship, especially a neutral, at this stage of the war, would have been most unpopular politically.

Salmon intercepted the large German liner *Breman* running the blockade. *Bremen* refused to stop and Bickford let her go unscathed. The most his little gun could have done was to have caused some superficial damage and *Breman* had over twice his speed; you cannot parley and do a torpedo attack at the same time. All we could do was to make propaganda out of *Salmon's* magnanimity. From the submarine point of view until April, 1940, it was indeed a phony war, but it gave us some useful training.

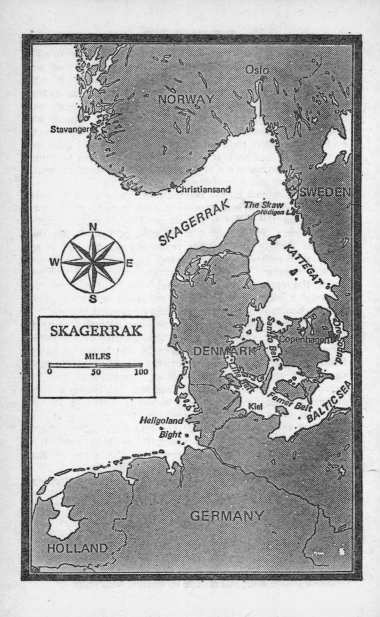

6

FIRST BLOOD

At the end of March, 1940, it was obvious that something was brewing. All our submarines were collected in from patrol and replenished. All was very secret. We did not get our patrol positions until we sailed.

Max K. Horton, the Flag Officer, Submarines, was a man with a flair for the conduct of war and tremendous power to influence others. But even he, at this time, was unable to get government permission to unleash his boats with their muzzles off. There was some relaxation in that we were allowed to sink transports at sight, but other merchant ships were to be given safe conduct except after "visit and search."

Our boats were to be concentrated in the Skagerrak and the entrance to the Kattegat, that shallow stretch of water between Denmark and Sweden, but *Sealion* was placed right down at the south end of the Kattegat by the Sound and Belts which lead into the Baltic. It was not known whether the Germans were going to attack Sweden or Norway, and we were there in case there were such landings in the southwest of Sweden. It was a position of honor, although not likely to inspire one's insurance company with enthusiasm.

One after another on April 1st, 1940, the Third Submarine Flotilla, all "S" boats, slipped from our depot ship, the old *Cyclops,* a veteran as old as the submarine service, and made our way independently up the East Coast channel, which was by now well marked. Boats from the other flotillas on the East Coast were being similarly sailed. As was usual the A/S trawlers out on their lonely patrols, the minesweepers carrying out their dangerous

87

task, and the escorts of the convoys we met, wished us good hunting. We were lucky, carrying the war into enemy waters; they had to wait to defend their convoys if the enemy came to them.

Off Smith's Knoll *Sealion* got her first enemy contact, a darkened ship. It was in our waters, she might have been friend or foe, so we had to challenge her by flashing light. Her response was to show us a clean pair of heels. It was a dark night, she was small and much faster than us, and she soon disappeared. She was obviously a minelayer; we sent a report back and the mines were swept before they could do any harm. And so we pushed on across the North Sea, through the Skagerrak, a slow passage diving by day, and rounded the Skaw, the north tip of Denmark, on the morning of April 7th. I will always remember that Sunday, a lovely spring day, and as we passed through a narrow channel amongst the shoals close to Nidigen lighthouse, I felt that now at last we were really going to war; maybe that channel would not be so easy to get past when the time arrived to come out again.

We crept slowly south on the western edge of the channel, only a few fathoms under our keel, and constant aircraft patrolling overhead. Up the other side of the channel, steering north, came merchant ship after merchant ship, neutral markings of every Baltic and Scandinavian country. Great tempting tankers, heavy-laden ships, the German invasion of Norway going north—simple straight attacks, unescorted except for odd A/S vessels patrolling the channel, no doubt looking upon it as a boring routine. But were they transports? To me a "transport" conveyed a passenger ship, the familiar Bibby liner, soldiers crowding the upper works. Had I but known it, the holds of those cargo boats were crowded with German troops. Passing up the narrow channels from the Baltic they could not afford to give away their intentions to the Danes or Swedes, and so to us. *Sealion* was still bound by the Government adherence to the Hague Convention; whatever I suspected I could not be sure. The German invasion passed on unscathed as far as we were concerned. I was obeying orders and Max K. agreed that we could have doing nothing else.

The German Fleet also passed up the channel to cover the invasion but they did so after we had reached the southern end of the Kattegat, a wider expanse of water. We could only cover one of the exits from the Baltic at a time and we did not cover the exit they used. Looking back now, what I then thought of as frightfully bad luck, may not have been as regards *Sealion* and her crew. We should undoubtedly have done great execution on the invasion; a night or two later Bertie Pizey was to drown 8,000 troops with one salvo in the Skagerrak; but it is very problematical whether we should have lived to tell the tale. The German Fleet was not far south of us, as yet uncommitted to action; the odds against us escaping north through those narrow, shallow channels would have been considerable. As it was, with most of their forces occupied elsewhere, we were to have some trouble in making our escape. But a submarine is an expendable weapon and we would have paid for our loss a hundredfold

But so it was and as we crept south another trouble besides frustration beset us. The melting snows had freshened the water of the Baltic and Kattegat, we pumped out more and more ballast water and still we got "heavier." We were ballasted for salt ocean water; our destination had been too secret to enable us to have some of the lead ballast removed from the boxes in our keel before starting. Presently we had only just sufficient ballast water in our auxiliary tanks to give control. We had to pump out our fresh water, leaving only just enough to drink. The order went round "no washing, not even the hands." And so we arrived off the Sound, our patrol position, at the eastern entrance to the Baltic. The water was shallow, the sea glassy calm, and overhead were air patrols which should have been able to see us—the worst possible conditions for submarining. That night we burnt all our confidential matter, except for a few essential signal books, and waited. If we were sunk it would have been easy for divers to get up those confidential books.

We were not bored, though; it seemed that every fishing boat in Denmark and Sweden had concentrated off the Belts and Sound. By day we were in constant danger of being trawled up; at night, as we charged our batteries on the surface and strained our eyes through binoculars for German warships, the fishing boats harassed us continuously; if they sighted us they might report us. Luckily I had an extra officer, George Salt, a newly qualified C.O.

who had not yet got his own boat, embarked for experience. George was great company to have on patrol, a cheery rotund type—no one would have guessed that he had held the Squash championship of the Navy for several years. His presence was to cause a good deal of umbrage at Northways, submarine headquarters, for he had been embarked before we knew where we were going. The odds were considered against *Sealion*'s return and Max could not afford to lose two C.O.s at once. George was to be lost in his own boat in the Mediterranean not so long after.

Meanwhile we waited. In those calm waters with air patrols constantly overhead and sometimes only a fathom of water under our bottom, which meant that the boat would answer only sluggishly, if at all, to her helm, our operational efficiency was distinctly limited.

To add to the squalor of unwashed decks, the gangways were lined with sanitary buckets. In a submarine the manipulation of the lavatory was quite a complicated affair. If you did things in the right order you blew the discharge overboard against sea pressure. If you did it in the wrong order you blew it back in your face. But if you blew it overboard that caused bubbles, sufficiently obvious to advertise your presence to an aircraft in a calm. Some of the most romantic language I have ever heard was voiced when the bucket chain was passing the buckets up the ladder to the bridge after we had surfaced at night, and a clumsy fellow at the top slipped and decanted the contents on to the upturned faces below.

At last, on the 11th, four days after we entered the Kattegat, we got a welcome signal. We could sink on sight vessels definitely established as German. I believe Max K. had been importuning Churchill constantly and now, at last, our restrictions were somewhat relaxed.

We had been ordered over to the west side to intercept a damaged pocket-battleship, the *Scheer*, which had been torpedoed by *Spearfish* and was now being towed south. It was a particularly uncomfortable position as there was barely water to dive. *Sealion* at periscope depth drew about eight fathoms, less than a fathom under our bottom at periscope depth. But *Scheer* never came our way. By now the invasion was mainly past us and shipping thin, but at last a ship was approaching. She wore no ensign, but I could read her name; feverishly we turned the registry of German ships, the *Otterburg* did not appear. We let her go. Later I discovered that she was German all right, but had been omitted from the list. She was stopped by one of the German A/S vessels on patrol shortly after and we worked ahead of her again, hoping that she might hoist her ensign, and show her nationality, but she maintained her secrecy.

Shortly after another ship was sighted, rather broad, and we had to use high speed to close, the boat behaving badly in the shallow water. She proved to be Danish, but not before our high speed had excited the A/S vessels, and we had a rather anxious time before we shook them off and found some rather deeper water.

Then in the afternoon we sighted the bridge of another ship rising over the horizon and once more we "grouped up" to run in to the attack. Very shortly we had to slow again for an A/S patrol, and could not get in close. She was wearing an ensign which hung down limp in the lifeless air. It was red, but so were Danish and Norwegian ensigns. Slowly she closed our sights; I simply could not establish her identity, it was all getting very depressing.

Just before the sights came on there came a little puff of breeze. The ensign blew clear and there was the Swastika.

It was a longish shot, nearly 3,000 yards, and we fired two torpedoes.

The A/S vessels which had been troubling us earlier had gone off on a wild-goose chase over the horizon; and the air patrol had disappeared to the northward. It was one of those occasions, rare for a submarine, when one could wait and watch the shot. Normally after firing one would go deep, and get away from the firing point as soon as possible. Here one could not go deep, one had to remain at periscope depth and so might as well watch.

The seconds ticked away; at 45 knots the torpedo would take over two minutes to get there. The Torpedo Officer was counting the seconds. Two minutes and still the ship sailed on.

An awful feeling of despair came over me; at last, after all those months of waiting, we had got a chance to attack and I had missed.

Suddenly a great column of water rose high above her masts. Almost immediately she started to settle by the stern. Her fore foot slowly reared out of the water, to fall back as the whole ship sank upright to the bottom leaving her bridge, funnel and masts above water. It was too shallow for her to sink further. In turn *Sealion*'s crew came to the periscope and watched their first victim sink.

Submarining is often painted as a brutal game, but submariners are no more brutal than anyone else. Nobody should criticize the submariner unless he himself has been hunted; for it is when harassed that an animal becomes vicious.

I remember one stoker as he came away from his quick turn on the periscope, saying to me anxiously: "Will the crew be all right, sir?"

I replied that as it was a flat calm day and not far from land, they would get ashore in their boats safely enough; he seemed happy.

A patrol or two later, after we had had a pretty tough time, we torpedoed a ship and I remember, as we went deep to make our getaway, that same stoker said to me: "What's the weather like up top, sir?"

I told him a flat and glassy calm.

"Oh, hell," he said, "I suppose the b——s will get away."

We had got our first ship, but it gave us little satisfaction. We were getting reports now from our boats up north in the Skagerrak, sinking ships right, left and center. And here were we stuck down in this glassy calm, these shallow waters thick with trawlers, and all the invasion past us. The new moon was starting to show at night. In moonlight in those restricted waters with constant patrols, things were going to be strenuous.

When we came up that night we had been dived for 17½ hours; what with the sanitary buckets, three attacks and a hunt, the air was very foul and everyone panting. The crew are in three watches when nothing is happening, so that except when doing routine maintenance, two thirds of the crew are off watch. This condition, with only one third crew closed up, is known as "Watch Diving" and anyone who is not actually engaged in work sits or lies down, you breathe less air that way. We had been closed up at diving stations nearly all day and we had used a lot of air. We were to get used to being short of air in the months to come.

At last I received a signal moving us further north; it was a great relief. I did not fancy staying down there with a moon.

That night the Coxswain came to me and said he had a defaulter to see me. The First Lieutenant would normally see a defaulter before passing him on, if necessary, to the C.O., but No. 1 was on watch. In submarines defaulters were very rare. I scarcely remember having had one in *Sealion* before. In any case a submarine on patrol was no place to carry out extra drills. The normal life was far more strenuous than any official punishment routine.

Well-meaning people who decry the severity of prisons and detention quarters forget that to the small-ship sailor—and, undoubtedly, frontline soldiers as well—detention quarters, although far stricter than civil prisons, were a subject of good-humored contempt. Regular meals, unbroken sleep, safety, warmth and dry quarters, these were things the sailor on patrol never got.

Still, a defaulter we apparently had and the Coxswain brought up our cook; the able sailor was a splendid man, who transformed bully beef into its various incarnations. The charge was disobeying orders by washing and the defaulter denied it hotly.

I was invited to look at his hands and, sure enough, they were soft and clean. I glanced at the Coxswain's and my own filthy, grimy claws. The evidence seemed clear.

I asked him how he explained his hands; he merely stoutly maintained he had not washed and seemed very puzzled himself.

Suddenly, the penny dropped, he brightened: "Oh, I know sir. I have been rolling the meat balls."

After moonset that night, a misguidedly enthusiastic attack on a darkened ship nearly proved our undoing. It is not easy to judge by eye at night; the dark silhouette against the horizon may be a large ship some way off or a small ship much nearer. We were nearly on top of the anti-submarine vessel when I spotted my mistake and slipped by unnoticed under her stern. A lesson learnt. It is just as well for a submarine to make sure what it is at night and close cautiously.

Next day the Kattegat was empty. What made it more

infuriating was that Max Horton had at last got us the "free for all." We could attack anything in enemy waters on sight. For *Sealion* this had come a week too late; everything was north, nothing moved. But at least the fishing boats had disappeared; for the first time since we entered the Kattegat I could get a little rest.

I had learnt another thing; when you need it, the endurance of the human body is astonishing. In face of danger you find your wits sharpened beyond your usual ability and you need very little rest. Twenty minutes bottomless sleep here, another fifteen minutes there, is all you need. You come out of these deep trances with every faculty alert, your brain crystal clear. I am certain that the long seven hours or so sleep, half of it little more than dozing, through the night is unnatural. It is a necessity of civilized existence, transport timetables and working hours. You come out of that long sleep the senses dulled and drowsy.

Most animals sleep immediately after eating. I had always heard that this was a bad practice for human beings, but found it highly satisfactory in the life we led. I believe that it is natural for the human being to sleep thus, for fairly short periods, but sleeping deep. Once you get used to it, and can sleep deep—you have to be pretty short of sleep to learn how—it is surprising how fit you feel. In civilized routine, it is impossible and you have to fight nature during the long drowsy afternoon at the office desk. I think it quite likely that you would do much better work if you put your feet up and slept for twenty minutes, but it would not look well.

At this time there was considerable discussion as to whether submarine C.O.s should use benzedrine or a similar drug, like the German paratroops, to delay fatigue. The idea was attractive. In such a patrol as this with very little let up for the C.O., the only person on board trained to handle the boat in action, there might come a time when he felt that he could compete adequately no longer and a pep drug could make the difference. The difficulty would be that sooner or later there would come a time of reckoning, the pep drug would cease to work and complete exhaustion would follow. It was not a case of hours or days, but of weeks. Max K. Horton decided against it and

he was undoubtedly right. I never heard the idea mooted
again, but then we never had to compete again in such
unfavorable conditions as in the spring and summer of
1940.

Fortunately our frustration was not to last long, nor
were we asked to face a patrol in this area with a waxing
moon. That night we were ordered to return and thankfully we headed north.

As we closed the narrower channels, running on the
surface at night, a main motor bearing chose its moment
to wipe. Chiefy Reavill and his team wrestled with the
defect in the main motor bilges. With one shaft out of
action we made slow progress, the single engine striving to
charge the deflated battery as well as drive us. Our
maneuverability was drastically hampered at a time when
we were likely to need everything we had. It was April
13th.

Suddenly ahead of us we saw the loom of searchlights. Closing farther we saw a line of eight A/S vessels
strung out across the channel. We had to dive as they
swept down towards us and went into silent routine to
defeat their hydrophones. This meant stopping the Sperry
gyro compass, one of whose motors was noisy, and left us
with the magnetic compass which was full of bugs. De-
gaussing was in its infancy and we had been degaussed, as
a protection from magnetic mines, before this patrol; we
had not realized the effect upon the magnetic compass,
which had gone very peculiar.

Men worked on the main motor bearing with muffled
spanners, cramped in the inaccessible space. Slowly we
turned back, listening on the Asdic set to our foes, and
although one passed over the top of us, we remained
undetected.

One of the more anxious moments when being hunted
is when you hear the swish of propellers closing—then
passing overhead. The operator of the Asdic set can hear
this at much longer range and reports the movements of
the hunter. But when they come really close you can hear
them plainly without hydrophones. If they pass overhead it
means that depth charges could have been dropped at a
lethal moment. You have to wait for them to sink, though
they still have to be set to the right depth. In shallow water

like the Kattegat there is no escape in depth, probably the submarine's greatest ally. You cannot burrow into the bottom; your depth is known near enough.

It was hopeless to try and make the passage submerged through the A/S screen with a phony compass and on one propeller. We had to get back into wider waters. The A/S craft started to drop astern, then they would close again and so it went on for an anxious hour. We had to get up somehow. Before long it would be too light to surface and we would have to face a long day with a depleted battery.

At last their noises grew faint and up we came. We could still see the patrol strung out across the channel. There was no hope of getting through them that night; there was no reason to suppose that they would not be there the next night; they knew that we were down to the south of them and must try to break out some time.

But the deep water channel was not the only way out. It was the only way out in water where a submarine could operate submerged, but it was high tide; we could get out on the surface over the shallows by the Kobber Grund on the Danish side.

They would not expect us to do that—or would they? We would not stand much chance if they came into the shallows and caught us on the surface with only one propeller in action, but it seemed the best bet. By the next night the battery would be even lower and there would be more moon.

So *Sealion* set off across the sandbanks on her single propeller and her dubious compass; we still had some time before dawn.

Slowly the A/S craft dropped out of sight except for the glow of their searchlights playing in the channel as we worked round to the west of them. We were not charging the batteries now, we needed all the speed we could get. Then Chiefy Reavill's welcome voice came up on the voice pipe; they managed to fix the top half of the bearing, which was undamaged, at the bottom where it took the weight; the damaged half could compete at the top. The other engine was started up and we could afford to charge batteries as well, giving us the precious amps we should need next day.

And so the dawn of the 13th broke; we were in

deeper water again and we were clear. I had thought when we entered through those narrows at Nidigen that it might not be so easy coming out—it had not been—but we were through.

We still had plenty of A/S vessels to get past, but deep, open water stretched ahead. First came a group of eight, perhaps the same lot we had met in the darkness. We went deep beneath them, but had to use the ballast pump to do so. One obviously heard something and closed on us. We stopped everything and waited whilst he searched around. We were still new to the A/S game; we had our methods of avoiding detection worked out; we knew exactly how we intended to compete; but our theories had not yet been proved in war. We could only guess at the efficiency of the Germans.

Sealion was efficient, highly so by the standards of our training, but we were not yet seasoned, our training still unproved. Things change later, but never again will everything be new. In due course we shook off the hunting group and made our way north.

Another group of three blocked our passage. They were assiduously depth charging an imaginary submarine as we worked round them, leaving them engrossed in their game. They were not the only A/S craft dropping depth charges. Just as our submarines were concentrated in the Skagerrak, so was the German anti-submarine effort. They were dropping a lot of charges and their rumbling roar could be plainly heard. Sound does peculiar things in water. A distant explosion may sound so close that you imagine that it is shaking the boat.

About this time a German U-boat was sunk by our fleet, but not before the crew, or some of them, got out and were picked up. They claimed that they had been depth-charged a day or two before, and even gave the time. The matter was investigated and it was found that at that time there had been a bombing attack on the fleet many miles away. The U-boat, deep and anxious, had heard the bombs exploding all those miles away and cowered deeper thinking that she was being depth-charged.

It seemed part of the Axis A/S technique to drop depth charges frequently, either on suspicion or just to scare. The noise at a distance is not unlike the roar of a mighty lion and is apt to give a turn to the stomach. When a depth charge is really close it has more of a crack in it, but the only real test of range is when the boat shudders, lights break, paint flakes off and so forth. Amongst the wide selection of equipment which later in the war American C.O.s could fit at choice was a device to take the range of depth charges.

Why exactly one wanted to know the range of the last depth charge I never knew; it was where the next one was going to explode that was of absorbing interest. It was a most elaborate bit of equipment, with festoons of wires and lighting like a Christmas tree. I only met one C.O. who had fitted it; he told me that at the first adjacent charge there was a brilliant flash and the whole equipment went up in smoke, far more alarming than the depth charge. Although personally I considered this a useless gadget, there was nevertheless method in such gadgetry. If there is room, after all essentials have been crammed in, then gadgeting is a good thing. Every C.O. has his foibles, most have their *bête noir*—my personal *bête noir*, as it was for many others, was the fear of another submarine, more than anything else, except shortage of air. But as to foibles, if you can satisfy them with a gadget, then that gadget is worth a good deal.

At this time the roaring rumble of depth charges was so frequent in the Skagerrak that it seemed almost continuous. One imagined that it must be from attacks on other boats, and one wondered whom; in some cases this was undoubtedly the case. But for the most part I think they were being dropped on nothing but suspicion.

To *Sealion* the Skagerrak seemed security itself after the Kattegat. At last we had a decent depth of water under our keel and we were thirsting for blood. But nothing came our way as we wended our way home.

Strangely enough we came as near to being sunk closing the British coast as at any time during this patrol. We were proceeding on the surface by day—one could not afford the loss of time to make passages submerged except in enemy waters—and the visibility was very poor. We were in a bombing sanctuary, where none of our aircraft were supposed to bomb a submarine on the surface. There was a good deal of low cloud, behind which an aircraft could approach unseen, but I spotted one in a gap, rather hazily, and took it for an R.A.F. Anson. We flashed the recognition signal to establish our identity, but not being too sure, we dived as well. It was just as well we did, for as we got under, down came a stick of bombs; they were fairly close, but we had made it in time.

Anson

In every ship in which I have served there has always been someone who seemed prone to minor misfortunes, a constant object of mirth. We had such a one in *Sealion* and he was the only casualty. A drip pan, a small tray hung under things which are prone to leak—in this case under a hydraulic vent—and well-filled with oil, was shaken down. It fell on this unfortunate's head, causing a minor cut and soaking him with oil. I wondered what the determined aviator overhead would have thought if he had known that the only result of his attack was to cause general laughter throughout the boat.

When at last we reached Harwich, the only person feeling really satisfied was George Salt, who had got a signal as we cleared the Kattegat that he had become the father of a daughter. Our bag was only one ship, and that of no particular importance; accordingly I was very surprised to receive the most tremendous welcome from Ruckers. He had got Marjorie down to meet us, and she told me that four days earlier she had been rung up by Ruckers who could only say:

"It's all right, Marjorie. It's all right. We've heard from him."

She could not make out what it was all about and of course had no idea where we were—except that we were on patrol. Apparently no one had rated our chances of return from the Kattegat very high.

Others had not been so fortunate. At last our submarines had had a chance and they had taken it with both hands; but they, in their turn, had had to pay for their successes. The Third Flotilla was to lose over half its boats before the summer was out and the other flotillas were to lose their share.

Although later in the war I was to be Captain (S) of other flotillas, it was not till after the tide had turned and our losses small. In these earlier days they were very heavy, it was a difficult time for the captain of a flotilla. They felt the losses of their boats and they were denied the privilege of captains of destroyer flotillas and other senior officers of squadrons, of leading their commands into action and sharing with them the dangers; by the chance of age, they did not have the consolation that they were only asking others to do what they themselves had done. They felt far more anxiety for their boats than ever the boats felt for themselves. It was the same with wives and mothers; women do not get much fun out of war.

Despite considerable success by our submarines, the Norwegian invasion had gone very well for the Germans. Targets in the Skagerrak became fewer and the days were lengthening. The Kattegat was not attempted again except for minelaying submarines, who could slip in and out without giving themselves away—a dangerous game; even the Skagerrak became a doubtful proposition. With the shortening nights our losses seemed to make operations there uneconomical. Accordingly our boats were withdrawn to operate nearer the Atlantic coast of Norway. On their next patrol *Sunfish* (Lieutenant-Commander Jackie Slaughter, D.S.O.) and *Sealion* were sent up to check the form and report back to Max Horton as to whether it was reasonable to operate there still.

Sunfish and *Sealion*, feeling a trifle like a pair of Aunt Sallies checking up on the throwing technique of an American baseball team, duly set off again for the Skagerrak at the end of April. Already night was ceasing to exist in those northern latitudes and the twilight which was all there was in the middle of the night provided little or no cover when we wanted to charge batteries. Air patrols were concentrated and progress was slow; if one was to charge the batteries at all one could not dive for every aircraft. Luckily visibility was good and so were our lookouts, they had to be, and we used to stay up and watch the aircraft who frequently passed by without spotting us. If they were obviously going to pass very closs indeed, or if they turned in to bomb, then down we went. It was a strenuous existence and somehow one seemed to develop eyes in the back of one's head, a sixth sense, for spotting aircraft. Despite this, we were sent down so frequently by aircraft or surface patrols that it took a long time to work up to the top of the Skagerrak and when we got there shipping was hard to find. We only got in one attack and, although the torpedo hit, the sinking has not been confirmed so presumably the ship was only damaged. In fact, operations were so restricted by lack of air to breathe and shortage of battery power, through being kept down so much by the patrols, that the submarine had little chance of paying its way. Whilst we were up there *Seal* attempted a minelaying trip into the Kattegat. With the crew stupefied from lack of air to breathe, she was damaged and captured. Things were a bit too tough.

When I returned I went up to Northways (submarine headquarters) to report; I said things were difficult but not impossible. Max Horton asked me for a day-by-day account of our doings and I gave it to him, missing out one day.

You could not get away with much with the shrewd man and at the end he said, "Yes, that is all right, but what about the Thursday?"

So I had to admit that on that day I had withdrawn from the more infested area, gone deep, settled on a layer, and got some sleep. Even C.O.s needed a bit of sleep sometimes; at least, I did, but I was not so sure that Max, a great C.O. of World War I, suffered from such human failings.

He broke into a broad grin: "Quite right too, I always used to do that."

For our next patrol, however, we got plenty of rest. Our submarines were strung across the North Sea covering the Dunkirk evacuation. We could see the glow of fires ashore; we knew vaguely what was going on; it was reasonable to suppose that the German Fleet would come out to interfere, but they preferred the shelter of their harbors. We viewed their lack of enterprise with mixed feelings. We wanted the evacuation to go through successfully, but a crack at the German Fleet was what every submarine dreamed of.

7

MY WORST PATROL

Sealion had been sent up the Skagerrak in June, 1940, to
test operating conditions. Our submarines had been driven
out and it was important that the enemy should not realize
this; if he had and relaxed his A/S effort, then we wanted
to take immediate advantage of it. Once again *Sealion*
found herself the guinea pig.

No sooner had we threaded our way through the
floating mines, which somehow collected at the entrance to
the Skagerrak, than it became evident that air and surface
patrols were in full force. There was no darkness; on the
second day at 01.00, the darkest hour, we sighted a tanker
with seven escorts hull down but masts and bridges silhouetted against the northern horizon. We were unable to
close to torpedo range as our battery was running low.

Lines of A/S craft swept to and fro; it was seldom
that there was not an aircraft in sight; it was scarcely ever
possible to surface to charge the battery or refresh the air
we breathed. We struggled through a third day, making
only forty miles in twenty-four hours; we were forever
having to take evasive action for the patrols; the battery
just could not compete.

It was no longer a case of whether we could operate,
it was a case of whether we could get out again. We turned
back. There was no question of day or night routine, we
surfaced whenever there was a chance. On the afternoon
of June 30th a very jaded and ineffective submarine
sneaked out of the Skagerrak on the surface.

Once we were out we reported that things were too
tough and were ordered to patrol off Stavanger. It was
better, but not much. Those were the days after Dunkirk;

it was believed that an invasion fleet was collecting at Stavanger. No reconnaissance aircraft could live over Norway; submarines were the only possible reconnaissance and they lived precariously with no darkness to shield them. No one was expected to patrol for more than four days off Stavanger without relief; boats took it in turns and then withdrew to rest and charge.

July 3rd found *Sealion* off Stavanger on a day which alternated between glassy calm and blinding rain storms, which cut periscope visibility to a matter of yards. As one of these storms cleared we sighted a southbound convoy of six ships, with nine escorts and an air screen. They had nearly got past us in the storm, but we ran in as hard as we could, somewhat bothered by a flying-boat, which was patrolling low around us.

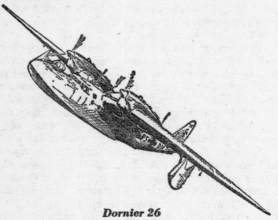

Dornier 26

We were unable to get in close, but we got within range and lined up for a shot from outside the screen. It was right in orbit of a Dornier. As I gave the order to fire I saw a sobering sight; first the nose, then the wings and finally the tail passed a few feet above the periscope.

It could not avoid seeing the gerfuffle made by the torpedoes starting up and, before the periscope dipped as we took the boat deep, I saw the convoy alter away in response to a pyrotechnic fired by the Dornier, whilst the escorts turned towards us.

We went down fast, turning to clear the firing position.

The Dornier had overshot, but it did not take her long to come round again. Her depth charges were set too deep; they exploded below us and seemed to hurl the boat to the surface. Hugo Newton, our No. 1, was flooding everything he could, but still the boat rocketed upwards out of control and we could hear the escorts pounding in.

If we broke surface we had had it—and at first it seemed as if nothing would stop her. Then Hugo caught her with five feet to spare. The next moment we were hurtling down, terribly heavy, and the hunt was overhead. We were going at high speed to try and regain control; our noise must have been nearly deafening to the sensitive German hydrophones.

Down came pattern after pattern of depth charges. The lights went out; the depth-gauge needles went haywire, and then gave up, the Asdic went off the board; the paint rained down as the boat shuddered to the shocks.

We turned on the emergency depth gauge, normally shut off to guard it against the pressure of explosions. In the darkness we went plunging down, past the depth we were designed to stand; Biddiscombe and Denzey, the Coxswain and Second Coxswain, wrestled with their planes, the shafting binding in its bearings as the hull distorted under the pressure. The air hissed as we blew the main ballast tanks; depth charges reverberated; all was noise and blackness except for the wavering pencils of light where the emergency flashlights pierced the dank gloom.

At last her bow started to lift, the descent was checked; we vented the main ballast tanks—no one would notice the bubbles, the sea above must be boiling from the depth charges. We had caught her in time, but it could not have been much above the depth at which the hull would collapse. Actually *Sunfish*, a sister ship, had been a little deeper with no worse effect than a cracked frame. But we were still in darkness, the boat porpoising about like a wounded whale as No. 1 strove to catch a trim and bring her under control. The reverberations died away, and all was strangely silent, except for the creaking of the hull, protesting at the pressure, and then again the shuddering roar of another pattern, but not so close and now we were under control.

I had scarcely noticed the depth charges after those first patterns sent us out of control, but as the immediate danger passed, and the boat responded to her planes, they became of interest again. The next thing was to shake off the hunt. We surveyed the situation. The Asdic set, our normal listening device, had given up. Swift, our senior detector rating, comfortable of figure and imperturbable of habit, changed over to the hydrophone plates. These plates, obsolete and inefficient though they were, had fortunately still been considered worth fitting when *Sealion* had been built six years before. There were four of them, one on each bow, and one on each quarter, but only one remained in action. Hugo caught his trim and the boat settled down.

The hunters had lost us, at least temporarily, in the thunder of their own depth-charge patterns. Rimington, the L.T.O., had already got some lighting into action, we could concentrate on making our getaway. With only one hydrophone it was difficult to locate the hunt, it was largely guesswork, but fortune favored us and the depth charges grew infrequent and more distant. I passed a message through the boat that there were nine A/S vessels up top and I reckoned that they probably carried ten depth charges apiece; we could amuse ourselves counting to see how many they had left. Opinions varied, conversation in the control room changed.

A lively discussion arose as to the effect of the newly announced curfew on the sporting facilities of Brighton beach. I never quite got used to the powers of detachment of the British submarine sailor. The humor and conversation may not always have been drawing-room, but any tension there might have been was always relieved by some wag and the laughter was never high strung.

Our foes must have dashed off on a wild-goose chase; we circled round, but could not pick up a sound, so we returned to periscope depth. The hunt had lasted less than two hours. There was nothing in sight except some smoke on the horizon. Gingerly I raised the big periscope for a better look. A tanker was coming our way, unescorted. Now we would get our own back.

Against time Sarll and his fore-endmen sweated to reload the tubes. We had not been able to risk the noise of doing this when being hunted nor the danger of the heavy torpedo getting out of control when the boat was flung about by depth charges. There was only a minute or two to spare when the fore ends reported ready; the tanker would pass about 1,000 yards off, a nice shot and a fat target.

Then for the second time that day, the fates decreed against us. Down came a blinding rain squall. We could only see a few yards and the target was completely invisible. We turned on to a parallel course and surfaced to give chase. When the rain cleared she had zigged away and was well past clear. That tanker must have led a charmed life.

I was to learn later that an hour or so earlier Bill King in *Snapper,* the next boat down the coast, had experienced exactly the same thing. But Bill had done better with the convoy we had attacked. With its escorts attending to us, he had got in amongst them properly. Doubtless that is why our persecutors had gone off so soon; they felt that they had better go and see what *Snapper* had left of their convoy.

Although the hunt had passed on, the air patrols had been stepped up. We managed to get up and put some life back in the battery, but we were finally put down at about 02.45 the following morning and got no chance to complete the charge. Apart from constant patrols, the next day was uneventful, but it was evident that the heat was properly turned on.

Shark was going to relieve us next day and I decided that I must tell her to keep out; this meant relaying the message home because only Rugby could transmit to a submerged submarine. The skies clouded over, low cloud, but at last there was no aircraft in sight. It might only be because they were behind cloud cover, but we had to charge batteries and we had to get a signal through to *Shark.* It was a risk we had to take.

We surfaced with just enough buoyancy to bring out the conning-tower hatch and I scrambled through as it came clear. I was half out when I saw the aircraft; it came out from behind a cloud straight at us; I pressed the hooter, slammed shut the hatch and down we went; two depth charges straddled us as we went down. Steering, hydroplanes and gyro compass went off the board, some of the lights went and more paint rained down. This time there were no surface craft to follow up, we got things under control and working again, and soon after midnight I decided to have another shot. Somehow we had got to tell *Shark* to keep out. The heavens remained black, one could not see what was behind the clouds. Unless we could charge batteries we were impotent; we could not get away from Stavanger submerged and we would have to run for it on the surface.

Once again our conning tower broke surface. This time I had hardly opened the hatch when there was a roar; a Heinkel came out of a cloud so close that she did not have time to bomb. I pulled the hatch shut and down we went again; we were clear of the position before the depth charges came down and they did no damage.

Now we had to consider things carefully. The air was foul and we were already panting—one always did as the carbon dioxide collected. The conning tower had not been open for more than a few seconds during either of our attempts to surface and no fresh air had reached the boat. The battery was practically flat—another crash-dive would finish it; the enemy knew where we were; we could not get away submerged and equally we could not surface. The only thing was to stick it out submerged and hope that we would be able to last out till they gave up. We found a water layer to sit on; stopped the motors; switched out practically every light and settled down to wait.

From time to time we renewed the trays of soda lime which were laid out throughout the boat. They were meant to absorb the carbon dioxide and so, after a fashion, they did, but without a proper air-conditioning plant to force the foul air through the absorbent it could only be partially effective. We could still receive routine signals from Rugby and from time to time we came off our layer to have a look round, but there was always a hunter in sight. The damage was made good and everybody, except those on watch, lay down to conserve the air. The hours dragged by, everyone had headaches, sleep was impossible, one's body felt cold and clammy. I had always imagined that, if one got stuck in a submarine and ran out of air, one would fall into a stupefying doze and just not wake up. It would seem that this is not so, one cannot sleep. Some cold food was served out with lime juice to drink, but no one seemed interested in the food.

Then we got an enemy report; a ship was coming our way. She would have to come to us. There was still enough life in the battery to turn the boat around, but there was no question of our moving to intercept her. We brought the boat back to periscope depth; the T.I. checked over his tubes and we waited. Panting was getting heavier; it was obvious that we were fairly near our limit, but still the sweeping A/S forces were in sight. They were farther off now, but too near to get away on the surface. I decided to try our small store of oxygen.

When experience of long dives indicated that air was a major problem the medicos were called in; they provided us with the carbon dioxide absorbent, but pronounced that there was no need to provide oxygen since there was enough oxygen available to last us far longer than all the carbon dioxide absorbent we could carry. I knew that the Germans, or at least one German U-boat, had carried oxygen in World War I. Years before during my training class I had heard a story in the mess of how a surrendered U-boat which had no high-pressure air left, had blown her tanks by connecting up the oxygen cylinders she carried. Whilst I believed the experts, I still felt that the German had not carried oxygen for nothing for space and stowage are very precious in a submarine. On the principle of taking no chances, I had secured some cylinders of oxygen, and a reducing valve, just before this patrol.

Everyone was pretty sick by this time and at least it could not do any harm. It was beginning to become doubtful whether, if the reported ship did come past us, we could make much of a show of attacking her. The oxygen was switched on, a gentle hissing in the silent boat; conversation, except for an occasional order, had long since ceased. It is not easy to talk when panting. Some of the men said they felt better; I knew that it must be imagination, but at least it was good to think you felt better.

The long-awaited ship did not come past us; it was probably just as well, but a bit disappointing at the time. We sank back to our layer and waited. The oxygen ran out; the hours dragged past; the headaches nagged. Just before midnight on the second day the sea and sky seemed clear. Men moved to their diving stations and the tanks were blown. I went up through the conning tower; this time all was clear. Then I leaned over the side of the bridge and was sick; not having eaten for some thirty hours, this was not particularly satisfactory, but it helped. The lookouts came up and they too were sick.

Down below they were trying to start the diesels; but it was some time after the fans had been running before they would fire. Diesels are more particular about the quality of air than humans.

Some time later further investigation by the medicos established that oxygen was absolutely essential in such circumstances. My cautious, belt-and-braces philosophy had paid a dividend.

I have said that all was clear, but over towards the landward horizon something was going on. It was twilight, the nearest we ever got to darkness in those latitudes, but one could see tracer bullets and flashes. We tried again to get our signal through to *Shark*. But it was too late; we were watching *Shark* fighting her last action. The hunt had changed their foxes; she was being sunk whilst we lay sick and helpless, unable to go to her assistance.

It took three or four hours for the headaches to wear off; after everything was settled down and we had cleared the coast, I went down below. I was feeling rather despondent; *Salmon* was overdue, *Shark* had gone, two of the four boats which had formed our division before the war. The war was going badly and one felt very alone on patrol; it seemed that the war depended upon you personally and I had missed the convoy and nearly lost the boat; I felt that I had let down the crew.

I wandered for'ard where men off watch were sleeping on the deck, covered with their oilskins to catch the drips, and suddenly the atmosphere of unworried serenity passed from them to me. I realized that they would go into action on the morrow without backward thoughts, that with crews such as I was privileged to command we could not be beaten; the depression left me.

Two days later off Obrestad we went into action again, and we left a wreck to mark the spot.

There was an amusing sequel to our misfortunes. The regulations still prescribed compulsory church on Sundays. Apart from the regulations, I believed that men living as submariners on patrol lived wanted something more than material comfort. I held a little service each Sunday, although it was unpopular with some as it interfered with precious sleep. On the previous Sunday the Coxswain reported hands mustered for church, but the prayer book could not be found. Our solitary prayer book was an

Admiralty issue and I had a shrewd idea why it had been lost. I was tired so I let it go and cancelled church.

The following Sunday the Coxswain, without instructions, reported hands mustered for church. I pointed out that there was no prayer book, but he said that it had been found; and there it was, somewhat the worse for a sojourn in the bilges. We had missed church, we had had a shocking bad week, it was obviously bad joss. Never again would the little Sunday service be missed in either *Sealion* or *Safari*. One could not afford to take chances with joss.

I suppose that most of us were superstitious, particularly in the early days. Most of us had articles of clothing and mascots without which it would have been considered sheer folly to go on patrol; during this one I introduced a new fetish.

The day we got out of the Skagerrak, June 30th, was the date of the announcement of the half-yearly promotions to Commander and Captain. Promotion was a very competitive and selective affair upon which careers depended, and a date of much moment for those in the promotion zone, as I was, for Commander—which meant a brass hat. On that particular June 30th, dates had no significance for me; careers and promotion have no place in your mind when your interest is concentrated minute by minute on survival. That afternoon we were making our getaway on the surface. The date had not apparently escaped others. Clarke, the P.O.Tel., came on the bridge with a signal, followed by Marriott, the C.E.R.A., conveying my sea-going cap, with home-made brass oak-leaves added to the peak; and there was a present of a brass ash tray, made in the shape of a uniform cap. Their Lordships' selection had been anticipated.

The cap was to serve me on every patrol I did and when, three years later, I left *Safari* I was asked to leave it on the boat. That and a little toy dog, given me by Mother, accompanied me on every patrol and also the prayer book she gave me after this patrol.

I personally relied upon quite a battery of fetishes; in particular, I always wore round my neck my wife's confirmation chain from which hung a Church of England St. Christopher, and a Roman Catholic Sacred Heart. One wanted to be certain of backing a winner.

8

COLLISION

Sealion sailed from Rosyth for her eighth patrol on July 27th, 1940. The weather was glorious—for yachting—as it had been throughout that terrible summer for our submarines. As we zig-zagged our way through the gap in our North Sea minefields the Northern Lights laid on for us their most majestic display. The whole sky to the northward appeared to be draped with great curtains of every soft and misty hue, from pink to purple shot with gold, which rolled and flowed across the heavens in a never-ending rippling movement.

Somehow the horror of that grim summer, which claimed half of our flotilla, lies almost forgotten—the translucent seas, with never a ripple to hide us from our foes above; the cloudless skies, that seldom darkened in those northern latitudes to give us the blessed shield of invisibility for which we craved to charge our batteries; the everlasting anxiety as to when we could venture up to change the foul air in the boat; men panting like dogs in the carbon dioxide laden stench we breathed; the plaintively repeated signals from our base asking for one or other of our flotilla mates to report their position—the sign that yet another boat was overdue; all these things are but unreal memories. The sheer beauty of the Norwegian coast that summer remains. Perhaps Nature, who seemed to stack every card in her hand against our submarines, was prepared to relent in this one blessing; or perhaps it was only my personal reaction in a time I never wish to live again.

Looking back, I really enjoyed the submarine war at

sea, as indeed I should have as a professional fighting man;
in the Mediterranean I had far more of the thrills and
excitement of big-game hunting than ever a millionaire
could buy. But, for the C.O. of a submarine, the summer
of 1940 was sheer nagging hell; I think that only two C.O.s
of our front-line boats who saw that summer through,
went on again. I cannot speak for Bill King, but I fancy
that like me, he was never again the C.O. he might have
been. Long after, in the Mediterranean, where conditions
were comparatively easy for submarines, I used to be
criticized for surfacing in broad daylight in dangerous
inshore waters to ventilate the boat. Unnecessary, I know,
but I was never able to eradicate a stupid anxiety that we
would be caught short of air, stemming from those Norwegian days when the main preoccupation of the C.O. was
not mines, nor bombs, nor depth charges, nor navigational
hazards, but air for his crew to breathe.

Once again we were bound for the Skagerrak and,
since we had gained a reputation for survival, what was
becoming the usual rather doubtful honor of patrolling
farther up then was generally considered healthy. Our
losses had caused us generally to withdraw our submarines
from these waters and the idea was to stir up trouble for
the enemy A/S forces and thus keep their effort spread out
rather than concentrated on the Atlantic coast of Norway,
where things were less unfavorable and where our submarine effort had perforce been shifted.

The North Sea passage was uneventful and as usual
done on the surface; the risk of attack by enemy aircraft
and submarines being acceptable, since with our small
effective submarine forces we could not afford the time
spent on a slow submerged passage. The third day out,
however, with the Norwegian coast in sight, we proceeded
submerged, though not yet on the shipping routes. The
increasing A/S air patrols alone indicated we were now in
enemy inshore waters. It was a quiet afternoon, those off
watch lay about sleeping and all but a few essential lights
switched off to spare our precious battery; the dim boat
was silent except for the whirr as the planesman worked
the hydroplanes to keep our depth and the intermittent
rumble of the telemotor pump as "Colonel" Bowker, the
officer of the watch, raised and lowered the periscope.

Suddenly the order "Diving Stations!" rang out and Bowker reported to me: "U-boat surfaced under our stern."

In seconds everyone was at their stations; Sarll the T.I. who lived and slept by his tubes night and day, bringing the torpedoes to the ready; the boat heeling and trembling as the helm was put hard over and the outer screw to Full Ahead to try and turn, bringing our tubes to bear before the U-boat, a green 500-tonner, passed us. She was only about 300 yards away; it was a lucky day for her crew.

Through the periscope I could see the men on her bridge as she slid by, every second rendering her safer; laboriously and maddeningly slowly the degrees clicked past the lubbers line, nearly 180 of these degrees had to go past before the boat would be turned enough to bring her tubes to bear.

If only we had had a stern tube, or any of the modern conveniences fitted to all but the British submarines of that era, it would have been easy; but we still had to turn the whole boat to point the tubes and a submarine submerged, though *Sealion* was a very handy boat as submarines go, is sluggish under helm. The U-boat had surfaced in just about the worst position from our point of view and then gone off on a most unfavorable course. When at last we did get round there was little more than her slim stern, rapidly drawing away, at which to aim. Still a chance at a U-boat, however remote, was worth taking and away went the torpedoes.

As we fired the crew stood by for gun action. Three minutes later, when it was apparent that there was to be no miracle today and the torpedoes had missed, *Sealion* foamed to the surface. A few seconds later the first shell was on its way; but not for along. A splash 400 yards ahead was only a tenth of the way to the enemy. The second round, despite an Up-correction from Tubby Crawford, was little nearer.

There was no question of bad laying. Appleton, the gun-layer, was Dead-eyed Dick himself. This confirmed my suspicions. We had a new sight-setter—these were the days when the men to man our ships had to be produced quickly from somewhere, somehow, and often without adequate training. In the excitement of his first action the lad had forgotten his drill and put 400 yards on the sight instead of the 4,000 ordered; the torrent of imprecation from the bridge failed to stimulate his senses before the U-boat slid under—her lucky and our unlucky day. Our 3-inch shells would not have seriously damaged her, but we might have knocked her bridge and periscopes about, or got her C.O., a man of untold value, in those early days.

That night the familiar black shapes of floating mines reminded us that once again we were entering the Skagerrak. For some reason it seemed that all the innumerable mines that broke adrift from the minefields of both sides collected there. By the Hague Convention, when mines broke adrift a device should come into operation which rendered them safe; but even if the enemy obeyed the rules, the device was very easily rendered useless by marine growths such as barnacles and in any case dodging them gave one something to do. *Triumph* had hit one, which had blown off her bows, but had got home to tell the tale, a chance in a million.

It so happened that night that the sky had clouded and darkened for once and it was difficult to see the faint hump in the water before one was on it. Normally they were swept aside in the bow wave and thankfully one saw them disappear bobbing in the wake.

Bowker, the Navigator, had gone down to work out a sight and I was in his place on the starboard side of the bridge when suddenly I saw one just before our starboard saddle tanks; by some freak of water flow it was sweeping in towards us. There was nothing one could do. I automatically ordered Hard-a-Starboard to swing the stern clear, but the boat had not got time to respond.

As I held my breath, it clanged on the saddle tank just forward of the bridge, and the evil black horned thing went bumping down the side. It did not explode, so perhaps it was not such an unlucky day after all; as it disappeared in the gloom I breathed again, and choked as the sick rose in my throat.

Sealion was past the first flush of youth and by now she was overdue for refit and feeling the strain of the hammerings she had had. The engineers were constantly dealing with a succession of defects. A recurrence of the main electric motor bearing trouble—which had nearly cost us our escape in the Kattegat three months before—

now brought us to a halt and as the weary men straightened after hours of cramped toil to shift it, the port engine clutch threw its hand in. So that the seamen should not be spared, a periscope wire stranded and we had the difficult task of reeving a new wire over the complicated inaccessible series of sheaves around the telemotor ram; the last two days of July were spent as a singularly ineffective submarine. Fortunately no one troubled us, though we saw the usual surface and air patrols through the other periscope; when we dived for an aircraft on the morning of August 1st I thought that now at last we could start operations. This comfortable thought was rudely dispelled when the conning-tower hatch refused to close with the boat going down. I knew John Bromage the No. 1 would shut the lower lid before water got into the boat, but a flooded conning tower, with inevitable damage to electrical equipment, was very undesirable. I sprang up on the bridge again; the aircraft had not spotted us so I sang down the voice pipe to bring her up. No. 1 had already checked the dive and he brought her up. The Chief, as usual, was at the scene of trouble in seconds. The compensating weights, which counterbalanced the heavy upper conning-tower hatch, were hung low in the bridge casing in the *Sealion* class, with long connecting rods to the hinges. This was a weak point in the design and was put right in later boats. In this case a weight had come loose and jammed down in the casing.

I met the eye of Chiefy Reavill as he screwed himself down the little opening which gave access to the lower bridge casing. Both he and I knew that, if an aircraft came at us whilst he was down there, I must dive the boat, using the lower lid, and he would be drowned like a rat in a trap. The weight soon responded to strong blows and cheerful, if muffled, reflections as to the legitimacy of its birth, and before long *Sealion* was ready for action again.

The next couple of days, however, produced nothing and it was evident that the enemy were no longer using the route we were patrolling; even so the lack of darkness and the constant air patrols made it difficult to keep the battery charged. The next day we shifted billet, the A/S trawler patrols intensified and one group of four appeared to get our scent. One of them circled round us for over an hour and, though we were in silent routine, she had obviously heard something and it was an unpleasantly long time before we shook them off. Despite the intensity of the patrols, targets remained painfully absent and I decided next day to run right up to the coast.

In the very early hours of the morning of August 4th *Sealion*, her battery comfortably charged after a series of quiet days, ran in to the coast, still shrouded in mist. Presently we saw a dim shape through the mist—a small coaster—and we speeded up to attack. At this point the fore planes jammed at hard-a-drive and we found ourselves going down much farther than we liked. Strong men with tommybars and imprecations cleared this, but it meant delay, and when we came up again there was nothing in sight.

We went on, inside a little island with a lighthouse, until we were only a few hundred yards from the beach. The mist had lifted with the sun and it was a glorious clear morning. There was a house down by the beach and as I swept round the periscope I paused to look at it. A woman came to an upper window, flung the casements wide open and proceeded to do her daily dozen. She was young and blond, and, which made it a matter of moment, she had nothing on. As I was examining this apparition in high power—six magnification—I suddenly felt an expectant hush. To the control-room crew it must have appeared from my concentration that at least the German High Seas Fleet was in sight.

That evening a sizeable store carrier came crawling down the coast. She was unescorted and gave us a simple attack; in due course she went down with a torpedo in her engine room. I wondered whether the blond was looking and had in her turn taken pleasure in the sight.

We examined Manne Fiord, where a signal had told us there was a concentration of craft with the Germans doing invasion practice, and found it peacefully deserted, and a couple of afternoons later we were patrolling off Christiansand. Smoke to the westward sent us to Diving Stations and shortly afterwards a crop of masts appeared over the horizon.

I have been asked how you felt at "Enemy in sight." For me the first reaction was always the same when you had the difficulties of a screened attack before you; my sensations are vividly described in the Bible. I have the greatest fellow feeling for those ancient warriors whose bowels turned to water; one's stomach descended somewhere through the floorboards; one's limbs felt swollen and paralyzed; and a little prayer went up that you would not let down the side.

I suppose it was fear; fear of responsibility which is said to make cowards of us all. You knew that your crew would do everything you asked, but all their efforts and the efforts of those who had provided you with this potent fighting machine would be set at nought if you made a mess of things. I never had these feelings when being hunted, or other than at the start of an attack, though I have felt something akin to it, though in a minor form, before driving off the first tee in a golf competition.

With the first order came the reaction. It was as if the blood had surged back with twice its vigor after that moment of fear. Everything cleared, the brain worked with a clarity and confidence beyond its normal ability; self, everything, was forgotten in the absorption of the attack.

Sealion was soon at 90 feet at speed to intercept. You had to go deep when speeding up, or the disturbance on the surface would have given you away to screening aircraft. A quarter of an hour later, when we came up to have a look, the pattern was displayed. There was a large ship with ice-breaker bow in the starboard column; a good-sized ship leading a smaller one in the port column; and disposed around them in a rough ellipse were seven escort vessels. Two were weaving about on either quarter of the target line—a difficult screen to operate amongst.

We were still well on the port bow of the target line when they altered course, putting us right ahead. There was lots of time and this was an excellent position; whichever way they turned now they should pass us at a satisfactory range.

At 14.30 *Sealion* was about 3½ miles ahead of the convoy and the next twenty minutes were spent threading our way through the screen which was weaving about as usual.

It was the habit of the German escorts to drop odd depth charges from time to time; I think the theory was to frighten possible submarines. The Italians were also fond of this technique. In practice the submarine could hear those charges at great ranges and they enabled her to intercept convoys which otherwise would have passed unnoticed below the horizon.

Apart from the occasional roaring rumble of such a depth charge, all went quietly and by 14.53 we were nicely through the screen—this always produced a satisfactory feeling of relief—and, though an alteration had again put us ahead of the port column, we were trickling across its bows and sitting pretty for a perfect shot at the large ship in the starboard column.

At this stage I noted in my patrol report: *Decided that only torpedo failure could cause a miss.*

This comforting thought was rudely shattered at 14.55 when the enemy made a large alteration to port, putting us running in very fine on his port bow, too close to get a shot. We could not run across his bow to fire from his starboard side because there was an escort vessel there in a most unfriendly position; the zig had brought us back on his bow again, though previously we had got abaft his beam.

On the other hand the port column, whose bows we had just crossed, had altered course to port and were in a good position for a short-range attack if we could turn round in time; we were now stern on to them.

There was very little time to turn and barely room between the columns. If we speeded up much that unfriendly escort was bound to spot us; on the other hand if we turned right round to get the bow tubes to bear on the port column, it would be from an unfavorable angle on the quarter; they would be nearly past by the time we got round. All the same, at this short range, we had an excellent chance of hitting.

It was a pretty strenuous business at any time, being mixed up in the middle of a convoy making violent alterations of course; but in the Skagerrak at this time of the year it was particularly hazardous.

The melting snows of spring produced a considerable influx of fresh water into the salt water of the Skagerrak which created a layer of low-density water extending to a little below periscope depth. The submarine could sit on the heavy layer below it just as if it were sitting on the bottom. If you wanted to go deeper, you had to take in about six tons of extra ballast water to get through it. This meant that the submarine could not go deep quickly in an emergency—her only escape if a surface vessel turned suddenly and threatened collision. The risk of getting rammed was always present in a screened attack and particularly so if you were taking the boat through the screen at periscope depth.

I had foreseen this difficulty and had prepared for it; I had had *Sealion* fitted with some preventer wires (see pages viii and ix) which would prevent the jumping wire from wrapping round the screws if it were parted; this could otherwise happen only too easily if you lost the periscope standards in a collision.

It was most unpleasant laboriously turning the boat round with all these ships milling about and there did not seem much chance of a favorable shot at the end of it. This time, however, we had one device which could help. Our torpedoes could be set to turn 90°, no more and no less, after leaving the tubes, thus saving the long and laborious business of turning the whole boat that extra 90° to point the submarine. It would have been a tremendous boon if it had worked. The C.O.s viewed it with a jaundiced eye, however; they knew the reluctance of our torpedoes to run straight, let alone turn to order on a given radius—for it they did not do that, you could not calculate the firing angle.

The "Ninety Bender," as it was called, was not popular with the practical man and it was shortly to be discredited by all; but at this time the office pundits, who lived in a world of paper specifications divorced from the facts of life, took a rosier view. The edict had gone forth that the Ninety Bender was to be exploited.

If ever the stage was set for a Ninety Bender, this was it. The war was still young, I was yet to develop the cynicism about our torpedoes which came with experience; I felt that perhaps I had mistrusted our torpedoes unduly and, anyhow, we had been ordered to use the device. It was entirely my own fault that I did so and the responsibility was mine; a submarine C.O. had unrivalled opportunity to exploit the blind-eye technique initiated by the greatest of sailors.* But it was also a very tempting way out of the situation and I decided to have a go.

We were now between the two target columns, point-

---

*Lord Horatio Nelson.

ing at the starboard one but too close to fire at it. The columns were about 3 cables, 600 yards, apart. It sounds a good distance, but at sea it gives you little room to maneuver. A tight turn to port kept us just inside the line of advance of our original target; and as she thrashed by, less than *Sealion*'s length away, we steadied on a parallel course. The sights came on and we fired at the leading ship of the port column, angled 90° left.

As the torpedoes left I suddenly felt a ghastly misgiving; the brutes would never turn to order. Still it was point-blank range; surely it should not be asking too much? Just in case, I decided to swing on, so that I could get another shot off if necessary, straight this time, from her quarter.

The tracks must have given us away by this time; one of the screening aircraft might be along at any minute and we sank below periscope depth for the turn. We could only get down a couple of feet before we hit the heavy-water layer but it all helped.

A minute later when no rending roar of a torpedo hitting had allayed my misgivings, I came up for the second shot. A quick sweep round to take in the picture and all thought of attack disappeared. The small ship, second in the port column, had swung out to starboard and here she was bearing down on us.

She was almost on top of us.

We were very fine on her starboard bow and swinging in to her. We must go deep at once to get under her, but to go deep we had to get through the layer.

At the order to take her down, John Bromage started flooding everything he could, while I put the helm hard-a-starboard and stopped the starboard screw to try and swing us clear to starboard. We nearly succeeded, but through the periscope I saw a reddish sheet of iron coming at us, rusty water seeping out of a loose rivet; then there was a grinding, scraping roar, the periscope went black, the boat heeled over alarmingly to starboard, hung an endless second whilst men hung onto anything to stop slithering into the bilges, and then slowly righted herself as the ship's propeller thrashed by. We seemed to be thrown up tumbling in her wake; but No. 1 had got her going down now. We had swung sufficiently to make it only a glancing blow, and the pressure hull was intact.

In the submarine there was no indication that any-thing out of the ordinary had occurred; everyone went about their business as usual and there was plenty to occupy them. Once through the layer, with tons of extra ballast taken in, the boat was going down like a plummet; the early "S" boats were only designed to stand the pressure some 200 feet deep, though in practice they could and did stand a good bit more. We had to catch her in time or she would be crushed by the pressure of water; the next few minutes were enlivened by much blowing and pumping of tanks.

Then the inevitable depth charges came roaring, crashing down and the boat shuddered to their shocks. We had a considerable interest in those depth charges as we still did not know if the hull had been damaged or weakened by the collison. Surprisingly, the attack was light and not sustained; they must have thought that we had had it.

We slunk away at 230 feet; the layer of heavy water which had embarrassed us earlier providing a welcome shield against the enemy hydrophones.

The hours passed and the noise of hunting propellers died away. The time had come for us to surface and inspect the damage and clear up the mess. Both periscopes had gone, we knew; it probably would not be possible to open the conning-tower hatch, but a somewhat anxious test of the conning-tower drain had shown that this itself was intact. If we could not use the conning-tower hatch, it would mean using the gun-tower hatch, but that was low down and would mean blowing the main ballast right out, leaving us fully surfaced, a sitting target for many danger-ous seconds should an aircraft or lurking escort vessel, lying doggo* and unheard on the surface, be around.

It was now 23.00 and the dusk, which was the nearest to darkness that one could hope for even in August, would have arrived. The A/S operator, who combined the ability to coax surprisingly accurate information out of this un-suitable set with the eye of a hawk as a lookout, gave the All Clear and up we came.

I dropped the clips without the slightest confidence and surprisingly the conning-tower hatch flew open as the

*Hidden.

pressure in the boat was released. There was the sky once again and not a thing in sight, but the bridge was a shambles. A wind had sprung up and there was a moderate sea running. The boat rolled sluggishly. Both periscope standards, heavy bronze castings, had snapped off and both periscopes were bent to ungainly angles. The jumping wire had parted forward of the bridge but remained caught round the wreckage of the after periscope which had been up at the collision. Tough and flexible, the after periscope had not snapped, but it whipped about unsupported, whilst the heavy forward periscope standard, suspended from it by the jumping wire, crashed and battered against the side of the bridge casing like a flail. Only the top of the bridge itself was damaged. The after periscope threatened to crush anyone on the bridge as it flailed about in the seaway; the crashing weight suspended from it threatened to smash up the conning tower.

The first thing was to secure the after periscope; we could not lower it in its distorted condition. Ropes and tackles parted like cotton as it repeatedly broke free and tried to crush the men who strove to tame it. At last we got sufficient wires and hemps around to hold it, listing the boat to curb its backward swing.

Zest was added to this operation by the fact that here we were on the surface close to the enemy coast with a flat battery and, for all we knew, the hunt still on.

The forward periscope standard still battered around like a gigantic pendulum. Its wire was lassoed and lashed to the ship's side; the next thing was to cut it adrift. It is no light task cutting through a heavy steel serrated wire which is jerking about, while sitting amongst the wreckage of wireless insulators and sawing at arm's length with a hacksaw in one hand, holding on to one's precarious position with the other. Men took fifteen-minute shifts throughout the night whilst the engines pumped amps at maximum rate into the deflated battery. Even so we had only got one strand sawn through when we had to dive again.

Meanwhile the Petty Officer Telegraphist had rigged up a jury aerial and got the W/T working. I had to report to Flag Officer Submarines that our usefulness on patrol was ended and we were coming home.

The code book of those days had a number of phrases and words which could be represented by a single group, but any word not in that limited vocabulary had to be spelled laboriously out with a group of each letter; and furthermore the longer the signal the easier for the enemy to D/F us and lay on a hunt, so we wanted to keep it short. There were special groups for being rammed and coming home, but I wanted to convey that we were all right and needed no escorts, air cover or other help laid on; in fact, that we were quite happy. There was no group for happy, but in the geographical section there was one for Blyth, the port. That seemed near enough to blithe, so I ended up *Blind but Blyth*. This caused considerable consternation to the Wren who deciphered it and Max Horton was informed that we were making for Blyth, not our home port, which suggested that we were in urgent need of shelter. Max however immediately spotted the rather weak joke and realized that we wanted to convey that there was no need to worry.

We did, in fact, have one worry and that was a very real one. The next night it had calmed down and we managed to cut away the rest of the wreckage, but I thanked the lucky day I had read of a submarine in World War I which had had its jumping wire carried away by ice and had got it wrapped round its screws; the incident had inspired my preventer wires and they alone were now stopping the loose end of the jumping wire getting round our screws and bringing us to an impotent halt.

I wished I had had them made of heavier wire, they looked terribly thin, and they were exposed to chafing. I watched them anxiously, but they did their job; the last one actually parted three days later as we went alongside the pier at South Queensferry; the jumping wire whipped around the screw and I ignominiously rammed the pier, adding a broken nose to the other ravages to *Sealion*'s beauty.

On return, Ruckers, our Captain (S), met me. I was feeling extremely apprehensive. I had been in collision and hazarded my ship; I had put it out of action at a time when we needed all we had. Court martial, or at least the incurring of their Lordships' severe displeasure, loomed menacingly in my mind. To my amazement Ruckers gave me a tremendous welcome; I found that we were heroes of the press; tremendous credit was given to our bringing the boat home blind, as a feat of master seamanship.

Actually the lack of periscopes made little or no difference; there was plenty of bridge left for The Colonel to wield his "ham bone" and shoot his stars with his usual unerring accuracy—and you had to come to the surface to take a sight whether you had periscopes or not.

Still, heroes we found ourselves, and we got further reflected glory from the fact that Churchill happened at this time to bring up in Parliament the achievements of our submarines despite their grievous losses. C.-in-C. Home Fleet—Admiral Sir Charles Forbes—found time amongst his many responsibilites to hand us a bouquet which ran: "... in carrying out their offensive patrol right up to the enemy's shore and in successfully extricating their damaged submarine from so close to the enemy coast, is worthy of the highest praise. If a tonic is needed at a time when we have so recently suffered the loss of several of our most successful submarines, then *Sealion* has certainly provided it.

All this did much to restore the *amour propre* of *Sealion*'s C.O., but I have never eradicated my disgust and disappointment at missing that ship from point-blank range. It is true that Commander Warner, the kindly historian of World War II submarines, did tell me later that we had actually got the ship. It is possible that by some freak of water acoustics we did not hear the bang or else mistook it for a depth charge; possibly the much maligned Ninety Bender had been unjustly accused. But I do not think that could be so. With imperfect records it is impossible to tie up every sinking correctly with individual attacks and that convoy off Christiansand will always be to me one of the ones that got away.

9

FAREWELL TO *SEALION*

Sealion was refitted at Newcastle after her ramming. The Battle of Britain was being fought whilst we lay in Swan & Hunters' yard, but for us it was a pleasant rest. People were very kind and I got some most enjoyable fishing round about; to provide transport, Fanny the Ford entered the family. I bought her for ten guineas at an auction and she was to serve the family for ten years. Originally she had been a 30-h.p., V8 coupé, but a previous owner had fitted a 15-h.p. 4-cylinder engine which had considerable difficulty in competing with the gear ratio; but she always got there, if not always at the first attempt.

By the time our refit was completed winter had set in and we joined the Sixth Flotilla at Blyth. My old flotilla, the Third, had ceased to exist as an East Coast operational unit; *Maidstone*, our depot ship, had been lent to Destroyer Command and the three remaining submarines distributed elsewhere.

I had served under the dynamic Ruckers for two years and it was strange accustoming oneself to the routine of another flotilla, but we were made welcome, although Blyth is not everyone's idea of a desirable winter resort. The winter off the Norwegian coast with its heavy weather and lack of light was about as troublesome as the summer, in its different way, had been with its calm seas and lack of darkness. Patrols, if dull and uncomfortable, were safe enough apart from the risk of piling up on the rocks as one strove to close the coast in time to take advantage of the brief spell of daylight before darkness forced one to withdraw again from the inhospitable shore. Even during daylight, rough seas and snow storms interfered with

126

periscope vision, so the effective period of the patrol was short and targets and sinkings correspondingly rare.

Thanks to the Gulf Stream it was not as cold as one would expect, though the seas which broke over the bridge felt cold enough. In calmer weather only spray came in and it froze; the gun became a useless frozen mound and the bridge itself was covered with a film of ice. One's beard froze also, though it caused no discomfort.

All the shipping hugged the coast and was extremely hard to see against a background of black rock streaked with snow; in fact, you had to get within two miles of the coast to have any chance of picking up through a periscope; with only about five hours of good light on even fair-weather days, everything depended upon arriving by the coast as soon after dawn as possible. Shore lights would be switched on for brief periods to enable enemy shipping to navigate the headlands, but it was a pure coincidence if this happened at a time when we needed them. Consequently, in the darkness one had to keep well away from the coast; and every morning before dawn, uncertain of your exact position after beating up and down amidst winds and currents the long northern night through, one had to try to get as near the unseen coast as one dared, so as to shorten the slow submerged run in when daylight came. Closing a steep, unlit, rocky coast, of which the sounding machine gave little or no advanced warning, was an anxious business and any ships that one sunk were earned. More often than not these patrols drew a complete blank.

I had one day the same sort of infuriating experience with a tanker as I had experienced farther south off Stavanger in the summer. She suddenly appeared out of a snow squall and then disappeared into another just before the sights came on for a perfect shot. I wasted two valuable torpedoes firing into the squall where I hoped she might be; they were fired more in anger than in expectation.

A ship that we sank off Stadtlandst provided an interesting sequel. She rounded a headland as it was getting dark and then switched on her navigation lights just before we fired. She was a passenger-cum-cargo boat of no great size and I used one of our least valuable torpedoes. The production of torpedoes did not yet keep pace with the demand and we had fallen back on old ones, previously relegated to peacetime practice. For some reason the elderly warhead did not go off properly, there was a very sub-caliber bang, and though the ship stopped she looked a very long way from sinking; we came up to finish her off with the gun and thus save using another torpedo.

Before opening fire I flashed the international signal for Abandon Ship and was surprised to get a reply in English from the very sporting Norwegian captain— "Thank you."

While we waited for the boats to get clear, the gun's crew were getting very cold indeed and had to work the mechanism constantly to stop it freezing up. Many Scandinavian ships have their name in big letters along the ship's side amidships, opposite the engine room, and I told Appleton, the gun layer, to aim at the "writing."

He thought that I had said lighting and with deadly aim he picked off the starboard bow light with the first round. We left her well on fire and settling, whilst the boats, which I believe contained a number of German soldiers, made for the shore.

That night, I remember, it blew up with the heaviest seas I ever saw. High above us, out of the darkness, great towering mountains advanced as if with the inexorable intention of overwhelming us. Always it seemed that the boat would never shake herself clear from her plunge down the previous monster in time to rise to the next. The blowers were kept running continuously to stop the main ballast flooding back; we needed all the buoyancy we could muster. But a submarine, wet though she is, is a magnificent sea boat and as soon as we had got the battery charged we dived. There is always a danger, when diving in heavy weather, of the bridge getting smashed up, as the water-logged hull gets thrown about before it can be driven under; it is a question of choosing your moment right. All went well, but I remember that even one hundred feet down the boat still rolled quite heavily; normally you do not feel the motion of the sea much below fifty feet.

It was some years later that I was dining with a Norwegian submarine officer at Fort Blockhouse; he had come over in a passenger boat and had been talking with her captain. The captain had told him about how he had been sunk by a British submarine off Stadtlandst during the war. It was seldom that one could risk the extra time to let the crew get away—on this occasion I had been fairly certain that conditions were unfavorable for aircraft—and apparently Captain Gausdal had meant his little signal: "Thank you."

Not many men, faced with an unpleasant and somewhat perilous boat journey in wintry Northern seas, and about to have their ship sunk as well, would find time for the courtesies of life and think about others accepting risks on their behalf.

Whilst I was at Blyth I had the amusing experience of being arrested and taken to Morpeth jail as a German spy. Marjorie and I had digs in Blyth and when I was in harbor we would dig Fanny out of the snow, drive clear of the coal-grimed slush and take a walk in the country. On this particular day the snow was quite heavy and after parking the car we walked towards Morpeth along the railway embankment, which provided the only good going. As we got towards Morpeth we passed the jail, which looks like an ancient fortress, and Marjorie remarked that she would like to see inside it. We bought a dry battery for a wireless set and were looking for somewhere to have tea, when a police car drew up alongside and two policemen descended and started to question me.

A crowd collected and the young policeman, doubtless thinking that he was bravely arresting a dangerous agent and apparently wishing to impress the onlookers with the importance of the situation, seemed to me to be getting unnecessarily excited. I suggested that we go somewhere less public for the interrogation and they seemed delighted at the idea. I was put between two policemen in the back of the police car and Marjorie followed in another. Within half an hour of expressing her wish to enter the fortress, she was inside it.

If I were a spy, the last thing I should do would be to wear a beard, but apparently in Morpeth that was the accepted hallmark. It so happened that my photograph was in that morning's edition of a popular picture newspaper and I thought that this could be used to establish my innocence, despite the beard. The police, however, had no opinion of the photographer's conception of a likeness; it was not until I had managed to get through to George Phillips, our Captain (S) at Blyth, that I was able to convince our guardians that a man with a beard, who displayed himself against the skyline on a railway embankment, bought wireless batteries and spun the unlikely story that he walked in the snow-clad countryside for pleasure, was not a secret saboteur. We ended the best of friends.

When March came round the *Scharnhorst* and *Gneisenau* took shelter in Brest after their successful shipping raid in the Atlantic; *Sealion,* and a muster of all available boats, were sailed to surround Brest on a patrol which was nicknamed the "Iron Ring." Even the few old "H" boats available were mustered to increase the strength of the ring.

The weather was pretty foul and even in an "S" boat it was not easy to keep periscope depth; vision through the periscope was often limited to the next wave. In these conditions the ring would not have been very effective had *Scharnhorst* and *Gneisenau* ventured out, but they were not to do so for many months.

Submarines are susceptible to pooping, that is a following sea coming up over the stern and smothering you, and the little "H" boats particularly so. One of them disappeared on this patrol and there is little doubt that she was a casualty of the weather. *Snapper,* who had survived the Norwegian campaign, though Bill King had by now left her, had disappeared somewhere off Ushant in February, and no reason for this could be found; it was thought that she must have been another casualty of the weather. This left *Sealion* the sole survivor of the four "S" boats of the Second Division who set sail from Malta some sixteen months before.

A submarine has little buoyancy compared with a surface vessel and it used to be common practice to reduce that buoyancy still further—in the expectation of having to dive in a hurry—by partially flooding the main ballast tanks. In this condition her stability was reduced and altogether she was not a very safe sea boat. After the Iron Ring, *Sealion* was based on Portsmouth and did a series of patrols off Brest waiting for *S.* and *G.* We would go down the Channel on the surface to save time. There was usually a good deal of low cloud and there was always the danger of being jumped by a German aircraft; diving in a hurry became a matter of great interest.

A submarine is apt to be sluggish when trying to get down into a head sea; the sea gets under her bows and tends to throw them up. South-west winds were prevalent in the Channel, which meant that it was not always easy to submerge quickly when steering down the Channel; to assist matters I would "trim down"—that is, partially flood the main ballast—and it was through that I nearly lost *Sealion* one day.

The wind had freshened from the south-west to half a gale and I was considering blowing main ballast right out; but there was a lot of low cloud, so that aircraft could come at you with very little warning, and I decided to hold on a bit. I did take the precaution of standing by the upper conning-tower hatch with one foot on it; in this way you could slam it shut if a wave came inboard—an old "H" boat practice.

Suddenly there was a wave and *Sealion* just did not lift to it; she tucked her nose down and before we knew what was happening we were under water.

I trod the hatch shut and hung on to the after-periscope standard; the lookouts managed to do the same; but it caught Vasco* without a handhold; he was washed right out of his place on the for'd starboard side of the bridge but luckily caught the jumping wire abaft the after-periscope standard as he was swept aft. When we came up from our involuntary dive, gasping a bit, there was Vasco precariously perched on the wireless insulator at the extreme back of the bridge. That taught me not to trim down in the future. It had been a close thing.

The dangers of the sea should always take precedence over the violence of the enemy. Had the hatch been left open, *Sealion* would never have surfaced again.

The patrols off Brest were a boring business, waiting about for the battle-cruisers that did not come out; the only other hope of a target was a U-boat or blockade runner. In a way I think it was a fortunate thing for me, though I would not have admitted it at the time; the

---

*Lieutenant Stroud, R.N.R.—submarine navigators were often called Vasco after the great Portuguese navigator, Vasco da Gama.

Norwegian summer of 1940 had knocked some of the stuffing out of me and the enforced, frustrating boredom was an excellent nerve tonic.

Reggie Darke, a submarine D.S.O. of World War I, made life very pleasant for his boats at Blockhouse and Marjorie was sharing a house near Fareham with a very charming friend. In between patrols, during that summer of 1941, Shelly Rolls gave me some wonderful fishing on the Itchen and it was a pleasant interlude between more serious participation in the war.

I was fortunate in *Sealion* about this time in having in succession as Third Hand the first R.N.V.R. officers to enter submarines; hitherto submarining had been considered a closed shop for professional R.N. officers, with professional seamen in the shape of the R.N.R. "rockies" as Navigators. First came "Canada" (Lieutenant-Commander Freddie Sherwood, D.S.C. and Bar, R.C.N.V.R.), who was later to be my First Lieutenant in *Safari*, and he was relieved by Teddy Young (Commander E. Young, D.S.O., D.S.C., R.N.V.R.) who has written much about *Sealion* in his book. They were the forerunners of the V.R. tradition in the submarine service.

By way of some relief from the boredom of hanging round Brest we were co-opted into the cloak-and-dagger brigade.

We sailed one day from Blockhouse with a suitcase full of franc notes, a number of tins of petrol and sealed orders. I was allowed to open these when I got to sea and was instructed on a certain evening, at a certain time, in a certain position off, I think, Concarneau, to contact a certain fishing boat.

The reports of these operations were considered so secret that they were not filed with my patrol reports, so I have been unable to refresh my memory with details; the fishing boat was to be white and, I think, blue; a man would climb the mast as a signal. We duly arrived at the time and place, but although the area was as usual infested with fishing boats, none were blue and white.

In due course I did notice, a little way off, a man clambering up the mast of a fishing boat which in no way resembled ours and we closed it submerged. Surfacing hereabouts was not without interest, though it was now growing dark, as the Germans were known to have agents in a few of the boats to control activities of the fishing fleet and some of the trawlers were reputed to be anti-submarine vessels in disguise.

However, I decided to have a shot and up we came. I hailed the boat with the password phrase in my schoolboy French and was relieved to get the correct reply.

One of the advantages I found in dealing with the Bretons was that French was to them but a second language; their rendering of it was easily comprehensible to me, and mine to them. The slurring words of the Parisian always defeat me, and he in turn does not seem to realize that I am talking French.

We were soon alongside and transferred over to them the franc notes and petrol for the secret wireless stations, which were keeping Britain informed of the activities of S. and G. We also gave them coffee and rum in exchange for fresh fish and took aboard a little party of men, fugitives from the Gestapo, men who could tell some of the most thrilling stories of the war and who were amongst the most gallant of its heroes.

It was in this way that I first met Daniel, who was to be my liaison officer on future missions. At this time he was only allowed to use a Christian name; his family were well-known Breton people, in the tunny-canning business, and it did not seem wise to give the Gestapo an excuse for taking it out on the relations of those who helped us. His surname actually was Lomanecq and later on—after he had left us for a series of adventures of which I have heard accounts, but which it is not for me to relate—he became too well known for cloak-and-dagger operations. Like a number of Bretons, they are a singularly independent race, he did not join up with the Free French, but was given a commission in the R.N.V.R. I met him again, some three years later, as a sub-lieutenant in a flotilla which I commanded.

Daniel I had expected, he was in operation orders, but his companions were rather a surprise. They included a Polish aviator, who had been travelling through Europe for about eighteen months to get back to the war. He had escaped from the Russians in Poland and, by way of central Europe, had finally ended up in a Spanish jail. He had somehow got out of this, joined up with the French Resistance Movement, and now he was to arrive in England via *Sealion*. The Poles were undoubtedly the most magnificent fighters, probably on average the best on either side, for the Germans had some Polish battalions as well. There was also a French aviator, with similar determination, on his way to join the Free French; a chemist, whose special line appeared to be extracting iodine from seaweed; and, a less erudite occupation, the late Inspector of Brothels in Brest, the Germans now having assumed this function.

In a way, the last-named was rather a disappointment to us. When you have a number of men living cheek by jowl, all of varying age, background and interest, there is only one subject which is of interest to all. Everyone was most friendly in submarine messes—there was no time for petty jealousies and quarrels, and submarine life was so different from normal life that the two had little in common; everyone was fighting together for survival. The only news one got was from a routine news service, which may have been absorbing for those with financial and political enthusiasms, but catered for no one else. The mainstay of conversation was that common interest shared by all men and one might have hoped that a man who had been an inspector of brothels would be able to shed some intriguing new light on the eternal subject. He, however, was so utterly bored with what he thought of as mere shop, that he was no longer capable of realizing that others might still be interested.

From time to time, when the subject of women came up, he would produce a photograph of his wife. She was a very beautiful lady but obviously of the most unimpeachable virtue—a fact which somehow reduced our interest in her to near zero.

But we were not really so cynically disinterested in our passengers; they had left their families, with the ever-present nagging fear that the Gestapo would get on to them with their foul and brutal methods; they had given up anything that remained to them of their home and possessions; and they had risked all to take part in a war that their countries had already given up. Such men and their families stand out above the normal run of self-seeking humanity. They had nothing to gain, it was sacrifice for an ideal.

Having carried our our mission we proceeded, com-

plete with passengers, to continue our eternal watch for *S.*
and *G.*, the only variation in the day-by-day routine being
the weather and the standard of the nightly fireworks over
Brest, where the R.A.F. were delivering their loads nightly.
One had plenty of time for reading on these patrols, and I
conscientiously studied the issues of *Admiralty Fleet Or-*
ders which had collected over the last patrol and the
period in between. These little books of orders emanated
weekly from the bureaucratic machine and, despite their
title, were usually of more interest to their originators than
the Fleet. However, there had been one fairly recently
which exhorted all, despite their natural distaste for beating up fishermen, to sink fishing vessels operating from the
enemy coast. We were at great pains to blockade German-
held Europe and it was obviously illogical to allow them to
reap the harvest of the thousands of miles of coast they
controlled. Most of the catch of the tunny fleets operating
from the Biscay ports was being canned and sent to
Germany. Daniel and company left us in little doubt of the
loyalty of the Bretons to the Allies and the fact that they
were fishing for the Germans was no fault of their own;
they had no option as a subject people. There seemed a
chance that if we started sinking a few tunny boats we
might force the Germans to step up their protection of the
fleets to such a degree as to make it uneconomical, or at
least give the Bretons some excuse for desisting.

   After five days of the usual uneventful patrol, therefore, and having bethought myself of the A.F.O.s, I decided to relieve the monotony by a little fishing-boat straffing.

   The tunny boats were the most beautiful sailing
yawls; they would sail far out into the Atlantic, hundreds
of miles from shore, with exceedingly limited navigational
facilities. But for the most part they were concentrated
within a hundred miles of the coast, and on these patrols it
was rare for a number not to be in sight. They carried no
navigational lights and avoiding them kept the officer of
the watch well occupied.

   It was a calm, moonlight night in July 1941, when we
closed a tunny boat, ordered them to abandon ship, and
picked up the crew—after first enquiring whether they
would like to be picked up. They were extremely friendly
and philosophical; if it was going to help the war for them
to be sunk, then they were very pleased to be sunk.

With the next boat we sank, we made a mistake. Daniel knew many of these boats by sight and we had wanted to avoid sinking a one-man business; it would not hurt a large owner so much. The crew of this one was not so enthusiastic about helping the war effort; it appeared that they had an interest in the boat's ownership. Having got two crews (ten men) on board, we transferred them to another tunny boat, with instructions to spread the word that all tunny boats were to remain in harbor; we did not want to sink them, but would be forced to do so if they persisted in fishing.

Having, we hoped, given a lesson to the tunny boats we next turned our attention to the steam trawlers, of which there were a few; some were reported to be disguised A/S vessels. We picked out a largish one the next afternoon, waited for the crew to abandon ship, and then sank it. Despite the distaste for doing this sort of thing to fishing boats, the actual sinking of the vessels was great fun. Much money is made at fairs by coconut shies and throwing things to break things; shooting up ships gives one all the fun of the fair, combined with that spark of danger which makes any sport really worthwhile.

This trawler had a crew of sixteen, plus a cabin boy, and it strained our hospitality to accommodate them. They were most enthusiastic and everyone shook me warmly by the hand before they went below. It seemed to the Bretons that at last the British were doing things; it gave them renewed hope. The captain gave me much useful information about minefields and patrols. He also thought it a great joke because the trawler was really British-owned and had been caught up somehow or other by the Germans. The crew smelt strongly of fish, a fact which was somewhat noticeable in the confined quarters of a submarine. What made their single-minded enthusiasm for the British in general, and for being sunk in particular, the more extraordinary was that this was the last day of their trip, their holds had been full of fish and all of them would have got a share in the astronomical number of francs the fish would realize. The only thing they really seemed to feel badly about was the loss of twenty-five liters of wine. Apparently the Germans pinched all the best wine and it really hurt them that this little store had gone to the bottom.

They were absolutely amazed that we had white bread, moldy though it was by then; and the quantities of sugar they saw dumbfounded them. All they heard was propaganda; it was a long time since they had seen white bread, or sugar and coffee in any quantity, and they had been led to believe that we were even worse off. They were pathetically grateful for the presents of bully beef, rum, sugar and coffee we gave them. As usual, we asked for volunteers to join the Free French; as usual, there were none—apparently the Free French needed a first-class public relations officer amongst the Bretons. Actually one of our passengers was, I believe, an agent for de Gaulle. Daniel had been working for the British direct.

The next problem was how to get rid of our charming guests, they had no wish to go to England with us, whilst the smell of fish was one of which the unaccustomed soon grew tired. The weather was blowing up and, just when we wanted one, all the trawlers had disappered; we were due to leave patrol next day. However, soon after midnight we found a small trawler, Daniel pronounced it innocuous, and we closed it and told them to send a boat. In view of the weather they showed a quite understandable reluctance to do so, particularly as their boat was very small.

It was obvious that the situation required a greater command of the French language than I possessed.

I sent for the captain of the trawler we had sunk and explained the situation; unless this trawler took off him and his crew he was bound for England. It was fear for their families which governed their choice; they themselves had expressed their readiness to fight against the Germans and assured us that we could count on them when the invasion came. It was to be another three years before that; I wonder if they retained their faith in the British till D-Day.

The captain, having expressed himself satisfied that the weather was not too bad for the boat, sprang up and delivered himself in the most commanding tones. I remember he started off: *"Je suis un batiment Anglais..."* and went on to explain just how quickly he would open fire if the boat did not come at once.

It came.

It had to do three trips and several times it was nearly swamped, but the last boat made it to the accompaniment of loud cries of *"Vive l'Angleterre."* And so *Sealion* said goodbye to some very gallant men.

While the Breton fishermen were expressing enthusiasm about being sunk—if it would help the war—their governor was anything but enthusiastic. Old Marshal Pétain had long passed the age when action appealed. I was told that personal protests passed from Pétain to Churchill. Whether or not that was so, I don't know, but there was certainly much alarm in high places. Max Horton was asked what the blazes one of his submarines was doing endangering relations with the French and a great deal more besides.

Max sent for his Staff Officer, Intelligence, an officer of brilliance and encyclopedic knowledge; he even knew what was written in A.F.O.s and he produced the one in question, which no one seemed to know anything about. My character was cleared. Max, however, did say to me that what surprised him was not that I had been sinking fishing boats, but that I had not only read, but actually carried out, written instructions. I was not to do it again, he said; not to sink fishing boats, that is.

A number of Breton fishermen, put to a great deal of risk, discomfort and loss of personal property, had cheered and cried out: *"Vive l'Angleterre!"* as the sea threatened to swamp their little boat. They had seen some action carried out, however slight, by those in whom they put their trust for deliverance from the Boche. But, back in London, those who sat in offices and directed affairs in a rarefied atmosphere entirely divorced from the flesh and blood of human nature, had looked on it as a blow to the *entente cordiale*.

It seemed to me a pity that in modern times there should be an unbridgeable gulf between those who govern and those who are governed. In the days when leaders of policy were also directly leaders of men, when even kings went into action, they knew what their men were thinking.

For our next patrol Daniel came down to Blockhouse to join us; D.N.I. took charge of him in harbor, and he used to disappear and reappear in Admiralty transport. We were rather horrified to find him dressed in a magnificent new suit, which showed up to great disadvantage the ragged clothes we affected on patrol. We had to put in to Dartmouth on our way down Channel to collect tommy-guns and things for the resistance movement; they were

Tommy-Gun

late in arriving. I was invited up to the college for dinner and I took Daniel with me. He examined the pictures of old sailing-ship battles, with which the walls of the college are adorned, with great interest, but finally came to anchor opposite one, which he regarded with rapt attention.

After a bit I went over and asked him what interested him so greatly in the picture.

He replied that the French ship was winning.

It then occurred to me that in practically every picture a British ship was blasting some ship wearing a tricolor; so many of our old wars had been against the French. But in this picture, for once, the French ship was apparently giving as good, or better, than she received.

This patrol and the one that followed, which was to prove my last in *Sealion*, were uneventful. The ferry service to the partisans in Brest was the only relief from the monotony of waiting for *S*. and *G*. It is true that on one patrol off Brest I got a chance at a U-boat—it was not my last—but I was never to have any luck with U-boats. On a future occasion, when in *Safari*, I even got as far as hitting a U-boat with two torpedoes, but both had warhead failures and did not explode; we were to learn later that they did no more than dent the plating.

On this occasion *Bismarck* had just been sunk by the Fleet and *Prinz Eugen*, her consort, was running for the French coast; we hoped to intercept. We did not see the cruiser, but a U-boat turned up; as usual, she was only sighted fairly close—except in calm weather, a U-boat is hard to pick up through the periscope—but in a favorable position giving us just enough time to turn round for a nice shot at short range. The trim was upset by going from Watch Diving to Diving Stations and flooding the tubes in a hurry. No. 1 had not had time to correct it as we turned fast onto the firing course and he was unhappy about his trim; there was a moderate sea, but we had to keep the boat up so that I could see through the periscope; he was just managing by using a lot of rise on the planes.

We steadied on the firing course and I passed the number of divisions on the periscope graticule from which the attack team could calculate the range on a slide rule. The slide rule did not compete direct with such a small target as a U-boat and you had to multiply or divide the answer according to the technique employed. The slide-rule operator made a mistake, which was easy to do, and multiplied by two instead of dividing, announcing the range as about 3,200 yards. I spotted the mistake but did not trouble to remark upon it; as the sights were just coming on, I just mentally noted that the range was 800 yards.

No. 1, however, not being able to see through the periscope, assumed that the range was given correctly, breathed a sigh of relief that he had a few minutes to correct his trim, and allowed the boat to sink below periscope depth. My explosion of wrath brought the boat up again, but too late. The U-boat had crossed the sights whilst we were below the depth at which I could see.

Although we turned at top speed it was only at a slim retreating stern that we got round to fire our torpedoes and the chance had been missed.

On the whole *Sealion* was not a lucky boat, except in so far as she survived. After I had been relieved by George Colvin, *S.* and *G.* finally did come out from Brest and *Sealion* was on patrol. There were two routes out that they could have taken; *Sealion* was at the wrong hole. George then took her up the Murmansk coast, where he got a ship or two, and then, nearly worn out, she was retired to training and in her declining years ran for the commanding officers' qualifying course until relieved by *Safari* at the end of her useful operating life. I was captain of the training flotilla which included *Sealion* when her end came in 1944. I was instructed to sink her off the Island of Arran, in the approaches to the Clyde. There she served as a target for the A/S vessels under training, to practice dealing with a bottomed submarine.

I think *Sturgeon*, who had been transferred to the Dutch, was the only other boat of the old "S" class to meet a peaceful end. They were splendid little boats, and were in the forefront of the battle in the early days of the war, including the almost impossible conditions the front-line boats had to face off Norway.

Although I had loved *Sealion* dearly and had commanded her for three years, peace and war, I felt far more regret at parting with those who had served in her with me, than at leaving the old boat herself.

I was to build the first of the new "Repeat S" class. Two years before Ruckers had collected from all his "S" boat C.O.s ideas on the improvements required and he had edited the requirements of the men who knew and fought the boats. In my innocence I imagined that the new boats were going to have all those improvements of which we had dreamed; I was thrilled to have a chance of sailing in the first of them. I had reconned without a charbourne pondit, the new design, once again, was not to be what the fighting man wanted, but what the office brigade thought he ought to have.

10

P. 211

As soon as I had turned *Sealion* over to George Colvin in the autumn of 1941, Marjorie and I piled all our baggage into Fanny and set off for Birkenhead. Leaving Marjorie to find a hotel, I dropped off at Cammell Laird's and was met by Bill Harris, our Engineer Officer; we went straight down to the boat. Names for submarines had been dropped for the time being, and, strictly utility, submarines had reverted to the old practice of numbers; the new "S" boats were to be the P. 200 series, the first of which, P. 211, was to be mine. Chiefy Harris had been standing by the boat for some time; it had new Admiralty diesels and Bill had had the prototypes in *Sunfish* and knew far more about them than anyone else. He gave me a great welcome and said that he was having a lot of trouble in imparting sense to the Admiralty and needed my backing. The boat had been delayed a bit, a bomb during one of the Liverpool blitzes had gone right through her and exploded in the dock underneath. She was but an empty shell at the time, and the damage had been surprisingly light. A good omen; she was going to be a lucky boat.

We talked as we walked down to the dry dock where she lay. I was almost running by the time I got there, seething with excitement. First and foremost I wanted to see what gun we had got; that had been the worst feature of the *Sealion* class. I looked over the side of the dock and suddenly black depression replaced bubbling excitement. On the casing was perched that deplorable relic of World War I, the 3-inch 20 cwt. Mark I—this one had actually been made in 1915. I looked aft; the next most important thing was a stern torpedo tube; there wasn't one. However,

it might be better inside. One of the greatest handicaps in
Sealion had been lack of space in the control room to get
round the periscope and, above all, a decent chart table on
which to keep a plot. The boat was bigger, there should be
room for a sensible grouping of the attack instruments. We
had specially asked for this, which is nowadays called an
action-information center. I went straight to the control
room. It was worse than *Sealion*; there was not even
provision for a chart table; if anything, more room than
ever was taken up by wireless—the Admiralty at that time
were incapable of designing a wireless set suitable for
submarines. It was scarcely possible to squeeze round
between the after-periscope and the things which cluttered
up the bulkhead of the W/T cabinet, let alone use the
periscope in attack. There were, however, two major
improvements on *Sealion*. A much better hull and engines,
both of great importance.

We spent the rest of the day going round the boat. I
had been sent up, of course, to use my experience in the
fitting out of the boat and we made a list of things to alter.
That evening the wires buzzed and a couple of days later I
attended a conference at the Admiralty, Bath.

It was, for me, a singularly unsatisfactory trip, though
various things were approved—"subject to no delay." To
one who had spent the last two years at sea, the peaceful
unhurried atmosphere at Bath, a world of circulating
dockets and delayed decisions, seemed unreal. "Subject to
no delay" proved little different to the administrative
side-step "Approved in principle." When in my declining
years as a sailor I was washed up on the Admiralty shore, I
was never able to get a firm definition; but what it seemed
to mean was that no objection could be found to it but
nothing would be done to implement the matter. At the
time I was cheered by this anxiety to avoid delay and when
the meeting closed I assumed that those concerned would
now get down to it. But the passion to avoid delay had
simmered down. I had forgotten that people still had
definite working hours and the day was not twenty-four
hours long at Bath. I departed fuming.

Max Horton refused to see me; but sent a message
that in his early days he had had a captain who tore out
his beard in handfuls when enraged, and it amused him to
picture me doing the same.

However, Cammell Laird were most co-operative, and we got some things done, though the later boats got the major improvements. In a service of individualists it is said that no two submariners agree and it must have been difficult for those responsible for design to suit all tastes. But I had thought it would have been easy to follow the requests from sea.

While at Cammell Laird's I drove up to Barrow to see a newly-captured German U-boat, a 500-tonner. I could have wept; she had everything I had ever dreamt of and some things which even I could never have dreamt of. It was a boat into which a brilliant designer had compressed every requirement of the practical submariner, a wonderful combination of the ideal fighting submersible and economical production. Obviously the Germans had a very much better liaison between those who went down to the sea in ships and those who used their brains in the design office.

Nevertheless, except for the German U-boat, which was in another plane, I never saw any other submarine I would have preferred as a fighting vehicle in the Mediterranean to our own "Repeat S" class, though the marvels of the American torpedo control system gave cause to hesitate in choice. Experience was to prove that into P. 211, later to be called *Safari*, went all that was best in British workmanship, and a very tough and devoted little boat she proved.

As time went on the officers and crew collected; some of the key engine-room staff were there when I arrived. Freddie Sherwood with his comfortable Canadian drawl was No. 1, representing the R.C.N.V.R.; Devlin, Sub-Lieutenant R.N.R., who had done his training in New Zealand, as Navigator. The key ratings, heads of departments, chief and petty officers, were men who had seen action in our submarines in the Mediterranean. Their experience in building a new boat was invaluable, but most had been in China before the war, then in the Mediterranean, and they were very naturally looking forward to a spell of home service. It was awkard, but their feelings were legitimate, and before we sailed for the Mediterranean everyone with that feeling was changed.

It was absorbing watching the boat complete and a very pleasant interlude in the more strenuous pursuit of war. Accommodation was nearly impossible to get in Birkenhead, but the Yeowards very kindly gave us a share of their house at their farm at Hooton. Several submarines, and warships of all descriptions, were being built at the yard, and farewell party followed farewell party as in turn they left for the war.

When our turn came we had our party and thereafter I banned all women entering the boat. We settled down to the serious business of working up. In those days the time allotted was barely more than was necessary for trials and all new-construction boats joined the Third Flotilla in the Clyde for this brief and intense working-up period. Ionides and Ronnie Mills, Captain and Commander (S) respectively, laid on everything possible in that inadequate time. Things were critical in North Africa and every boat was sent off as soon as she was safe to dive, trusting that the practice on passage and a brief rub-up at Gibraltar would enable her to get her final polish up in action.

The policy was dictated by necessity and those who survived learnt the hard way. Eighteen months later I was destined to relieve Ronnie Mills, in charge of submarine working-up training. Our losses of boats in their early patrols had been so heavy that Claude Barry, who had relieved Max Horton as Flag Officer, Submarines, gave us as much time as we wanted to get the boats efficient before they sailed. By then the tide of war had turned and it is hard to make a comparison, but despite the fact that most of the boats were first commands, only one of those— *Stonehenge*—who went through the long and strenuous training program, was lost. I am certain that only the gravest necessity should ever be allowed to influence the sending of inadequately trained submarines, or for that matter other forces, into action. Flags may look pretty on the maps or charts on the walls of staff offices, but if those flags represent inadequately trained units their value is hard to judge.

We were able to get in a little more working up than most, for as "First of class," the first boat of a new class of submarine, we had to do a number of trials, but it was not a very efficient submarine which left the Clyde in the spring of 1942 to sail for Gibraltar. Most of the new key ratings, the chief and petty officers other than the artificers in the engine room, only joined us just before we sailed.

They may in some cases have been a bit young and inexperienced in their rates, but they were keen. One of them, Duncombe, the electrical artificer, reminded me at a recent old comrades reunion of my reception of him; it had stuck in his mind. I had told him that I realized he knew little or nothing, that I could not care less and that all I wanted were chaps who were prepared to learn and work like blazes twenty-four hours a day.

I had been a little concerned at that time that such an important section of the crew had missed what little working-up practice we had had; but I need not have worried. It was not unusual for submarine C.O.s to believe that they were fortunate in having the best crew in the Royal Navy, meaning the whole world; I think the crews reciprocated this confidence. I know that we in *Safari,* as in *Sealion,* were a very happy little community, though doubtless the crew had a good deal to put up with from me

I remember after the war someone saying to me: "Of course we always knew when things were getting a bit exciting."

This rather touched my *amour propre*; I always hoped that I displayed outwardly a cool, calm and confident appearance whatever I may have been feeling inside; so I asked for further explanantion.

"Oh yes," he said. "You always used, suddenly, to become so polite."

It is possible for some people to fool some of their seniors all the time, but you cannot get away with much with those you have the honor to command. At least I may be forgiven for not realizing that the crew knew when I was finding "things a bit exciting," because I never remember, in either *Sealion* or *Safari,* anyone showing that he looked upon what was happening as being other than all in the day's work.

There came a morning in April when we said goodbye to our womenfolk, goodbye to those in the Third Submarine Flotilla who had tended to our teething troubles, and set forth for the Mediterranean. We were to join the Eighth Flotilla, based on Gibraltar; at that time our submarines had been driven out of Malta by the German bombing and the Eighth Flotilla had to make the long passage from Gibraltar to operate on the west and south coasts of Italy and Sicily. The First and Tenth Flotillas operated from the eastern end of the Mediterranean. Until we had been driven out of Malta, the Eighth Flotilla had been mainly concerned with giving the submarines fresh out from home a general polish up, mechanically and in training, before despatching them further east; now it was to build up into a sizeable operational flotilla itself. At this time the Straits of Gibraltar were not far off being a non-return valve for British submarines, all too few survived a commission—about eighteen months—to return again to the United Kingdom; but we had no thought of this.

My greatest difficulty at this time was to persuade the crew that every minute we could find after routine duties, and at the expense of sleep, must be spent in practicing evolutions. They were keen to get at the enemy, the everlasting repetition of training was irksome. From my point of view, if not theirs, the passage out from the Clyde to Gibraltar was invaluable and we arrived a somewhat more effective submarine, except in gunnery, for which at that time there were totally inadequate training facilities. We would have to learn that in action.

There was always the hope that one might meet a German blockade runner on passage—*Urge* had had the good fortune to sink one on her way out the year before—but our trip was uneventful. Blockade runners were very few and far between and I noted the familiar names of German ships, in the Portuguese ports, supplied by intelligence reports. They had been there when *Sealion, Salmon, Shark* and *Snapper* had sailed north to join in the war some two and a half years before. We had been worried then that the war would be over before we got to it; *Sealion* alone remained of that little party, but still the war showed no signs of ending. The 8th Army was on the defensive, with Rommel threatening Egypt; Malta was besieged and desperately short of supplies; and our submarines alone could operate in the Central Mediterranean. When they were driven out of Malta in the spring of 1942, Mussolini was rash enough to boast that our submarines also had been driven out of the Central Mediterranean; he was to learn his mistake.

Gibraltar was in some ways a land of plenty, the shops were full of those little luxuries which it was hard to get at home. But from the point of view of the thousands of

service men there was one serious deficiency, the female
sex was remarkable for its absence. The few Wrens and
nursing sisters did overtime, with dates booked far ahead,
and they must have longed for an evening off when they
were not bespoke for some party. The arrival of an Ensa
team caused far more excitement than would have that of
the enemy; I remember that one of the periodical alarms
of an air raid did coincide with the presence of a newly
arrived Ensa team and it proved singularly hard to get
people to take the former seriously.

It was possible on occasions to get a run over to
Spain; the currency question could be solved by devious
means. The Italian consul in Algeciras, across Gibraltar
Bay, had a room at the Reina Christina Hotel, the windows of which looked out across the Straits of Gibraltar
and enabled him to report all shipping movements by day
into Gibraltar or beyond. I remember a run over to
Algeciras with two other C.O.s one Sunday between patrols. We did ourselves really well with food and drink,
and later amused ourselves by staring up at the lookout
window of the Italian consul, though doubtless he was too
used to such demonstrations to be embarrassed.

On the whole neutral Spain was very fair; if the Axis
enjoyed certain neutral facilities, so did we. It must be
remembered that at this time Spain, Portugal, Switzerland,
Turkey and part of Russia were the only places on the
European continent which were not more or less under
Axis domination. I say more or less, for in Scandinavia
only Norway was occupied, but our friends in North-West
Europe were not in a position to give us overt backing.

I shall always remember that particular little jaunt
into Spain, a very happy day, but which was to prove the
last "run ashore" for my companions. We all sailed for
patrol the following week. Mackenzie was to disappear in
P. 222 in the Naples area, whilst Sam Ford was to go
down with *Traveller* in the Gulf of Taranto.

Our depot ship at Gibraltar was once again my old
friend the *Maidstone* and happily I found myself again
with a cabin in her C.O.s' flat. During her sojourning away
from the Submarine Service where she belonged, but
which had become too depleted of boats to use her, the
C.O.s' flat had had other occupants. They had gone when
our new construction program started delivering the goods

and our operational flotillas reformed, but they had left behind a legacy. There was a lot of wood panelling in the
C.O.s' flat in which bed bugs had found a secure refuge,
despite the energetic efforts of the commander and his ship-
wrights to eradicate them. Being by now far more senior in
years and rank than the other C.O.s I was privileged to
have the best cabin in the flat and, while others suffered up-
heavals and discomforts as their cabins were stripped and
fumigated, I enjoyed immunity. I had no hesitation in sug-
gesting that the occupants, and not the cabins, were at
fault. When I did eventually vacate that cabin it was seized
upon by an exultant successor. He was quickly disillusioned. I am told he did not last out the first night; the bed
bugs came out in force to rend him. Apparently even bed
bugs have their epicurean standards, which I failed somehow to satisfy.

The Commander of *Maidstone* had a lot to compete
with, as had the wardroom, besides bed bugs. The Eighth
Flotilla was still largely a transit camp for submarines; P.
211 was the first of the R.N. boats which really belonged
to her, though the Dutch boats had already established an
operational nucleus. For the most part a steady stream of
boats joined her en route for further east and occasionally
some war-scarred veteran, the crew covered in gongs and
glory, would slide alongside on her way home. I can
remember only two such whilst I was in harbor during the
four months we were based on *Maidstone* at Gibraltar.
One was *Torbay*, commanded by Tony Miers with his
wonderful record and V.C. to boot; and the other *Sokol*, a
British-built boat, commanded by Boris Karnicski with a
Polish crew who had all escaped from the Baltic in 1939.
Sokol had been severely damaged in Malta during the
bombing and Boris had somehow got her out, patched up
so as to be barely seaworthy. Boris was an old friend of
mine and a raconteur with a pretty turn of wit; but the
deep admiration we all felt for *Sokol* and her gallant
Polish crew did not rely upon his version of her adventures.

But whether coming from or going to the war on
Rommel's supply routes, it was an occasion for a party;
poor *Maidstone* was more than a little tired of those
parties which broke up the wardroom and interfered with
the less glamorous, but infinitely important, duties of those

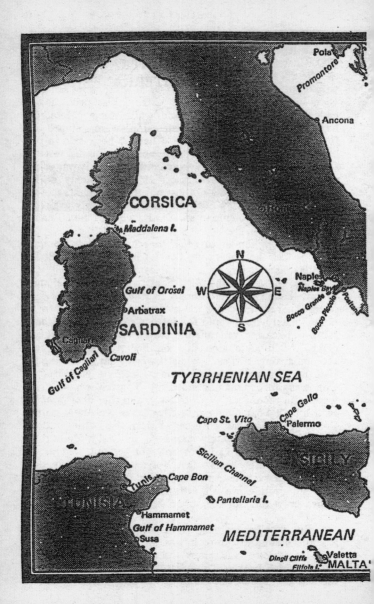

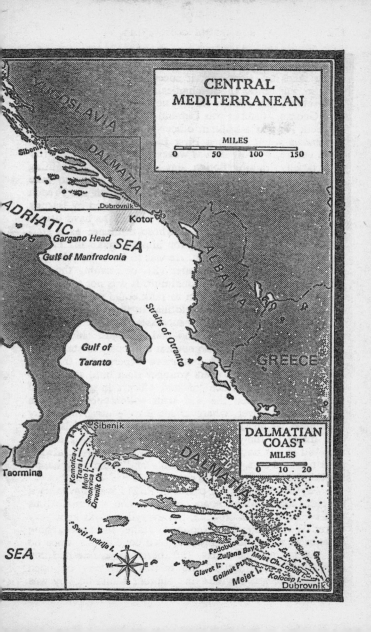

who strove to see that everything possible was done for the
boats temporarily in her care. It is true that the racing
driver takes the risks and, if successful, gets the popular
acclaim, but unless the mechanics and planners in the pits
have served him well the car will never finish.

George Voelcker was Captain (S) of the flotilla when
I joined. He was a brilliant officer who had been my C.O.
in *Perseus* when I was a First Lieutenant in China nine
years before. By now he was weary of being a Captain (S)
of a largely training flotilla and longed to get a fighting
command of his own. He left shortly afterward to take
command of a cruiser, and was lost in her off the French
coast the following year. He was to be relieved by Barney
Fawkes, himself a submariner just too old to have driven
his own boat in the war, and whose brilliance as a staff
officer had made it difficult for him to make his escape
from the headquarters office. He was to have the job, with
Bertie Pizey as his Commander (S), of forming the new
Eighth Flotilla as an operational unit. It was not to be long
before his flotilla could claim to rank equal with the older
established First and Tenth Flotillas in the Mediterranean,
with their long record of successes against Rommel's
supplies. I think Barney, who had only just shipped his
fourth stripe, viewed me somewhat dubiously to start with.
I was very much older and more experienced than his
other C.O.s, only two years younger than him, and apt to
be cantankerously critical of staff officers in general, and
those who confused the war with voluminous orders in
particular. However, whatever his private misgivings may
have been, we were to become the greatest of friends and I
owe much to the consideration and generosity I always
received in his hospitable cabin. Very shrewdly he always
gave me as free a hand as possible and some very happy
hunting I enjoyed under his command.

My first operational patrol in P. 211 was inevitably a
set-piece affair. More boats collected, and it was obvious
that something was brewing, but everything was kept very
secret. We looked at the moon, or rather the approaching
absence of moon, and drew our own conclusions; since no
one was let into the secret, and therefore no one had any
confidential information, the matter was one of open
discussion. It was obvious that another Malta convoy was

being organized and the secret became an open one. It is always very difficult to keep operations secret, particularly in a place like Gibraltar with a ready means of communication across the Spanish border, but I personally believe that it is always better to tell all those intimately concerned so that they will not talk about it. Otherwise there is bound to be conjecture and the conjecture may prove correct; in this case it could not avoid being so and the cat was out of the bag.

In due course the boats sailed and P. 211, which in future I will call *Safari*, although she did not receive the name until later, and a billet on a submarine patrol line between Sicily and Sardinia, so as to guard the northern flank of the convoy from attack by the Italian Fleet.

Although we still only had a number, instead of a name, we had designed ourselves a crest which H.M. ships normally have, but which had been omitted in our utility conception. We preferred to design our own crest, anyhow, though anything with heraldic affinity to P. 211 was not easy to conceive. The number was, however, one degree below boiling point—212°F—and we decided that a "watched pot" was a suitable emblem. There was a very charming Wren, who in less stirring times had studied heraldry, and she produced a very fine witch's cauldron, hanging from a tripod over a camp fire, and above it, keeping watch, a heraldic eye. There were many suggestions for the motto; the ribald were in favor of "Always on heat," but we finally decided on "Hot on the trail," which, since no one could remember his Latin, remained in English. The crest was cast by the foundry in *Maidstone*, painted in gules and azure and, by a coincidence, proved singularly suitable for our name when it arrived.

This patrol was uneventful as far as *Safari* was concerned, though it proved to be the only time I ever saw a major enemy warship through my periscope. We patrolled up and down on a north-south line, turning round every half hour. We were just reaching the northern end of our beat when we sighted to the southward two cruisers and four destroyers steaming east from Cagliari in southeast Sardinia. We had to turn round, and though we ran in at full speed we were unable to get in range; they passed five or six miles south of us doing 20 knots. Had they come half an hour earlier or later, when we were at the south end of our beat, we should have got a favorable attack; such is war.

The epic of the Malta convoys has been told elsewhere and the only excitement we got out of it was when returning to Gibraltar. We sighted a U-boat hull-down steering east, and for two expectant hours, the engine room coaxing all they could out of the diesels and eyes straining, we strove to work ahead of it on the surface, but keeping as far as possible below the horizon. Finally her lookouts woke up, there was no more reason that we should see her than she us, and she dived shortly before we reached a position from which we could approach submerged. Still, it had all been very good practice and we returned, a more efficient submarine, ready to get our final training in action.

Our next patrol was very much to my liking; we were given an area of sea and left to sink what we could find in it, being supplied with intelligence reports of enemy shipping; no endeavor was made at remote control from base. The latter could only occasionally work; submarines in the Mediterranean normally did patrols of two or three weeks, or less if they ran out of torpedoes, of which we carried twelve. They would be given an area of sea, but no one knew their whereabouts in the area unless S O S calls from the enemy were intercepted. Nothing was more infuriating for a C.O. than to be moved just when he had gathered the information to make a strike.

11

SAFARI—OPENING THE INNINGS

It was July, 1942, before Safari got her first chance of action. Our patrol area was the east coast of Sardinia; it was not a very strongly defended area except for Maddalena in the north and Cagliari in the south. As we were still unseasoned, I had no intention of trying to run before we could walk and so I chose the Gulf of Orosei, about halfway between the two, for our scene of operations. The water was, for the most part, deep close inshore, which was where we expected to find any shipping. The Italians did not venture into the open sea much and relied enormously upon coasting vessels for their communications. In particular petrol and ammunition were carried in small coasters which could keep close along the shore, cut across the open to the North African coast by Cape Bon, Tunisia, and then run along the desert shore to the eastward, where they were delivered as near Rommel's army as possible.

It was Sunday afternoon and we were at church when our first victim was sighted. Divine Service came to an unceremonious halt and we were soon grouped up, and running in to attack. She was an old-fashioned steamer and unescorted except for a seaplane ranging ahead of her. For many of the crew this was their first action, except for the abortive attempts to get in attacks on the two cruisers and a U-boat whilst covering the last Malta convoy.

It was very little different, in the way everyone went about their job, from a normal practice dive. Most of the crew were occupied, when diving, in controlling the boat; the job is the same whether in action or not. Only the internal excitement and the cost of a mistake are different. That is why we never used to use the term Action Stations

155

in submarines, but the term Diving Stations, which meant that everything was manned to deal with any emergency whether in action or not. When everything is already under control and you are not doing any violent maneuvering, you can dive the boat on about one third of the crew; this is called Watch Diving. For gun action some of the crew are taken away from their diving stations to make up the guns' crew; the torpedo tubes, for instance, would be manned by a reduced crew. Engine-room ratings as well as seamen manned the gun, and everyone was very busy during gun action.

We were unable to get into a satisfactorily close range for a torpedo shot and I got an early opportunity to exploit my theory that the gun remained a potent weapon in the Mediterranean despite the pretty strong air patrols which were maintained on the shipping routes. The air patrols did restrict your movements by keeping you submerged by day, though in clear weather an efficient lookout—and without one continuously on the job by day and night a submarine's days were numbered—could always see an aircraft and dive the submarine before she was sighted. One always had the night in which to charge and go places, for the enemy still had little or no radar; aircraft never troubled me much in the Mediterranean. Compared with the summer of 1940 off Norway things were pretty favorable. The reason why our losses of submarines were so heavy was that the shipping was never far from the shore, and surface and air support could be concentrated. And always there were the undersea menaces, the opposition submarines, to which I accorded considerable respect, and mines, which were an ever present danger. However, at this time the air was accorded a lot more respect in the general opinion than I felt it deserved and it was to be a long time before the gun became generally popular; in fact, I was considered a bit of a crank. The "U" class, in which Wanklyn and Co. made history operating from Malta, had been equipped with an ancient 12-pounder, with open sights, which was as near a useless weapon as could have been thought of, and they had not got the surface speed to exploit gun action; they also had had plenty of large torpedo targets.

The patrolling seaplane had gone on ahead by now out of sight to the southward, so up we came and were

soon closing at full speed on the surface. Our quarry took
no evasive action and at 3,000 yards we opened fire. She
was a large target and despite our lack of training we had
no difficulty in hitting her; in fact nineteen out of the
twenty rounds we fired before the gun jammed were hits.
This was sufficient to stop her and, having by now gained a
favorable position, a torpedo was fired to finish her off.

Our torpedo left a clear track, a path of lighter
colored water in its wake, and you could follow it all the
way till finally the great column of water rising above the
masts of the target announced its arrival. A fascinating
sight and one which you could seldom wait to see. She was
not far from the shore and I wondered what the local
inhabitants were thinking about it, for there was a village
close by.

All this had taken about seven minutes and we were
keeping a very close watch for the returning aircraft.
However, I could see in my binoculars some men in the
water who had failed to get away in their boats. The ship
went down remarkably quickly. Sometimes quite small
ships took a deal of sinking, others went down in a minute
or two. In any case this one was old, she had been built
the year I was born, and doubtless her bulkheads were not
too sound.

We closed, still with our weather eye lifting for the
aircraft, and fished four men out of the water. I was a bit
dubious about cluttering up the boat with passengers, but
one had grey hair around a balding crown; once the fire of
action has died down the opposition became fellow mariners in distress.

We had been up long enough by then and as soon as
the four were inside we dived. They were sent to the
torpedo room where the reload torpedoes are kept. Seeing
the fore-endmen hauling on a tackle to reload the tube
which had sunk them, they immediately lent a hand. From
then onwards for the rest of the patrol they were accepted
into our little community, always willing to lend a hand,
and became very popular on board. One was detailed to
each mess and they proved magnificent workers; the Coxswain complained that if he gave them anything to polish
he had to remember to tell them to stop, or they polished it
right away. They were pathetically grateful for having
been rescued, despite the fact that we were the author of

their troubles, and the youngest was particularly philo-
sophic. Apparently he was being called up to serve in the
army after this trip and he viewed the prospect with the
greatest gloom, though apparently happy enough to serve
in *Safari*.

The first sinking on any patrol is always a matter of
note. It is rather like breaking your duck at cricket, or the
first fish in a day's fishing; you were spared the mortifica-
tion of a blank patrol. Actually we were fortunate in
Safari, after covering the first Malta convoy we never had
another blank patrol, though targets were not all that easy
to find. By this time, so many of the nice big targets had
been sunk, for our submarines took a heavy toll on the
Axis supplies to North Africa, that any ship over 1,500
tons was satisfactory and frequently you had to be content
with less. Big ships are not only more valuable but easier
to hit with a torpedo; a submarine would pick them out of
a convoy and so they became scarce.

It was three days later before we got another chance.
A steamer of useful size was sighted creeping down the
coast from the northward, again unescorted except for the
usual air patrols which ranged up and down the coast. It
was just after sunset and the light was starting to fail; if we
waited for her to come to us it would be too dark to see
her against the cliffs through the periscope; and if we
waited till it was dark enough to be able to attack unseen
on the surface she might have gone into the little port of
Arbatrax, a short way to the southward. It was another
opportunity for the tactics which had been successful on
the previous Sunday.

Safari streamed to the surface and was soon closing at
full speed on the engines. The ship held on her southerly
course, possibly they were keeping a bad lookout, for a
submarine is not easy to see, or more probably they
thought it was one of their own; after all, Mussolini had
said that our boats had been driven from the central
Mediterranean.

Anyhow, they soon got disillusioned as we opened fire
at 4,000 yards, closing fast. The hits glowed red in the
twilight and though we were hitting all right they were
distributed about her hull and upper works, not in vital
places. After 18 hits had been registered she stopped and I
saw boats being lowered to abandon ship. I therefore

ceased fire. I had felt that I might have given the previous ship's crew a bit more time to get clear; on this occasion I reckoned it was getting a bit dark for the returning aircraft to see us and that we could afford to give them a bit more chance of getting away. I had made the mistake of underestimating our enemy; there were some brave men on board. They had a gun which I could not see and, encouraged by the respite, they seized the opportunity to man it and fire at us; at the same time they got under way again and turned in under the cliffs. Almost immediately a shore battery woke up and started shooting, we were only about 4,000 yards off the beach.

I had taken the precaution of keeping at a fair distance, so we were not hit, and I gave the order to open fire again; unfortunately the conditions proved too difficult for our standard of gunnery. The light was failing fast, the ship was not easy to see against the cliffs and our shots went wide. Before we could maneuver for a torpedo shot she disappeared in the gloom under the cliff.

Meanwhile we must have been clearly silhouetted against the lighter sea horizon and it was only a matter of time before we got hit. The excitement ashore was tremendous, all sorts of flares being fired to make a very creditable firework display. We had been seen off and there was nothing for it but to retire to deeper water where we could dive in safety. It was a dark night and, although we came up shortly after, I never found the ship again, despite a fruitless night beating up and down an unlighted coast with enemy patrols in their turn looking for us.

I had learnt two lessons. Firstly that you wanted to be dead sure of getting your ship before you indulged in the niceties of humanity and not to underrate the courage and fire-power of the opposition; secondly that the old telescopes on the sights had a very bad light transmission.

When we got in after this patrol, *Maidstone* made us adaptors so that we could ship modern binoculars in the sights; they were to serve us well. As usual we had had to pay for our lessons and in this case a ship I could have sunk with ease had I behaved with the proper ruthlessness of war had got away with only superficial damage; also we might have been hit ourselves.

Submarines, both friend and foe, are often painted by propaganda as heartless beasts wantonly murdering defenseless merchant seamen. The ships we attacked were carrying the sinews of war, all directed at destroying the forces of the opposition. By the same token it was entirely fair, all is fair in war though I am not so sure in love, for the Italian ship to take advantage of the respite I gave her to try and destroy *Safari* and escape.

Q-ships, first exploited by the British in World War I, were designed to profit from any let-up by the submarine in its role of ruthless destruction. They were merchant ships, but equipped with a heavy gun armament disguised behind collapsible screens. When attacked by gun on the surface the crew (a decoy crew) would abandon ship in their boats, leaving the crews of the guns hidden behind the screens. If the submarine let up and ventured close, down would go the screens and the submarine would be shot down in a welter of gunfire. Fair enough, but not calculated to inspire undue magnanimity in the breast of the submariner.

On this occasion, just in case of games of this sort, I had kept my distance whilst letting the crew get clear. It had been an error of judgment, our standard of gunnery was not up to requirements when needed.

After we had dived, the senior prisoner, he of the grey hair and balding pate, approached me and enquired politely if all had gone well. I told him that I was afraid not. He seemed genuinely disappointed.

Apparently the prisoners had been infected with the excitement of the occasion and joined in with the ammunition supply. I suppose it must be difficult when surrounded with enthusiasm not to get carried away.

We found no more targets that patrol; it took so long making the passage from Gibraltar, diving by day and having to charge the batteries again by night, that you did not get much time on the job.

As we were approaching Gibraltar the Coxswain came to me and said that Nicola, the leading-hand of the prisoners, had requested to speak to me. He said that all of them were very happy, they liked the food, they liked the company and could they please continue to serve in the boat.

I had to tell them that I was afraid that this could not be.

When we got alongside they left us, their pockets

bulging with little presents given them by the sailors. A guard of soldiers had arrived to take them away. *Maidstone* was alongside the South Mole and I went over the side shortly after to report at the dockyard offices. There was our little party suitably guarded by heavily-armed soldiers, who equally properly were searching them and removing their little possessions from their pockets.

I caught the reproachful eye of Nicola, it said: "Won't you help us?" I felt the dregs of the earth as I turned away unseeing and went on my way.

Gibralter was displaying the unmistakable symptoms of another Malta convoy brewing and we sailed early in August to cover it. The second day out we were diving by day, we surfaced for a minute or so to take a sight of the sun to fix our position. This was quite an evolution; you did not want to be on the surface longer than necessary.

Up you came—not too much buoyancy so that you could get down again in a hurry if necessary. As soon as the lookouts were up and confirmed that no aircraft were in sight, Devlin came up with his sextant, pre-set to the approximate altitude of the sun, "shot" it and down we went again.

You could pick up aircraft through the periscopes easily enough if they were low-flying and in a dangerous position, but if you swept the whole heavens it took so long, since you only had a narrow beam of vision, that an aircraft could very well have arrived on the bearing where you started the sweep before you had completed the survey. When you surfaced by day there was always the chance of an aircraft being in sight, but not in a dangerous position unless it had been hidden by low cloud.

On this occasion there was no aircraft but we spotted the conning tower of a U-boat about five miles off.

Off we set to get into an attacking position ahead of him, for he was steering west and we were already past his beam. Possibly he had also surfaced for a sight and doubtless he too was waiting for the Malta convoy. We should not have been able to get into an attacking position with our slow submerged speed and it was asking a lot to hope that we could keep him in sight, without being seen ourselves, for long enough to work ahead.

It was not very long before he also sighted us and

dived; we followed suit. Then followed a round of that
game known in submarine circles as "Doggy doggy." You
could hear each other on your listening equipment, and
each would maneuver so as to try to fire the torpedoes by
sound.

The opposition had the advantage over us in this
game, for with an up-to-date torpedo control system they
did not have to point the whole boat to aim their torpedoes. The usual pattern followed; you went round and
round each trying to get on the beam of the other to fire
the torpedoes; it usually ended up by both boats going
round in ever decreasing circles, following each other's
tails, hence the name Doggy doggy; it was a most exhausting and nerve-racking process, with only sound to guide
you.

One of our submarines, having encountered a U-boat
at close range at night, to their mutual surprise, and both
having dived immediately, brought their game to its con-
summation by ramming each other, both claiming to have
sunk the other and both getting away, in fact, without any
serious damage.

On this occasion the game went on for some time
until it became evident that there was no future in it for
either of us, and we proceeded on our ways. Normally we
should have waited about hoping to get a shot later on, but
we had a very tight schedule to get to our appointed billet
in time and I could do no more than report the U-boat and
hope that our surface forces would get on to him.

Our patrol position was off Cape Gallo near Palermo,
again with the object of intercepting the Italian Fleet
should it venture out to attack our convoy. In order not to
disclose our position our orders were not to attack anything less than a cruiser. Submarine C.O.s loathed this
restriction, beloved of the staff. For one thing we knew
that our chances of getting a shot at the Fleet were slight.
For another, with such a concentration of submarines as
was out on an occasion like this, the enemy would have to
pass someone if they were going places: they were just as
likely to be deflected into your position by reports of
another submarine as reports of your presence were to
deflect them away. Thirdly, and most maddening, it always
happened that magnificent targets, normally conspicuous
by their absence, would drift past your sights while you

were debarred from torpedoing them. Sure enough on this occasion an armed liner, I could even read her name *Filippa Grimani,* crossed our sights at point-blank range, whilst my blood pressure reached an all-time high.

It was glassy calm, and patrols and mine sweepers kept us from being bored; in due course we received numerous reports of an enemy cruiser force. It appeared that they would pass us early in the middle watch of August 13th. It was one of those beastly nights with a glassy calm reflecting the stars, yet with a mist low down so that you could not see where the sky ended and sea began. There was nothing much to silhouette a target against.

About 01.30 we ran into two destroyers of the screen, steaming at high speed, but the cruisers passed well to seaward of us. Fortunately Mars in *Unbroken,* the next boat down the line, had been driven off shore from his billet by the patrols and the cruisers came close past him. He severely damaged two with his torpedoes.

By the 14th August, Operation Pedestal, the August Malta Convoy, had reached its heroic conclusion and we were released from the patrol line. *Safari* was given the Sardinian coast to reduce my blood pressure by a few days' freelance submarining.

As we closed the coast we sighted an auxiliary schooner under the cliffs steering south. It was an excellent opportunity for some gunnery practice and to make the shoot better practice I kept closing her at full speed during the firing. This meant constant corrections to the sights as the range was coming down rapidly.

I rather overdid it and actually had to go astern to avoid hitting the cliffs as our target went down in a welter of spray.

That evening we sighted a small convoy consisting of a small steamer, a smaller tanker and four A/S escorts approaching from the southward. We ran in to the attack. Things were going promisingly when suddenly they altered course away into the little port of Arbatrax. We followed them down the swept channel and tried to open up the entrance to the breakwater but the water was too shallow and we had to withdraw to wait outside.

It was misty that night and we were much harassed by patrols. It seemed that all four of them were patrolling off the port and it was a strenuous night. In the mist we lost most of our advantage of being able to see the bigger silhouette of the surface vessel first and on occasion had to dive in a hurry as they loomed out of the mist almost on top of us. They served their purpose for at dawn next day the little convoy had gone; they must have slipped out under the cliffs in the mist, possibly on one of the occasions when we had been driven under. You could not see through the periscopes at night, except in clear moonlight, and there is always a large loss of light in the periscope, so that periscope visibility is restricted in anything but clear daylight.

But fortune had not entirely deserted us and just before noon we sighted a small ship to the northward, steering south with a seaplane quartering the sea ahead of her. We maneuvered to attack and as the aircraft passed on ahead we surfaced 1,000 yards away on the port quarter of our quarry.

After our first shot the crew abandoned ship.

She had two sea boats, one on each quarter. They were away in record time, I have never seen better seamanship. In peacetime Fleet evolutions—"Away both sea boats"—such a performance would have brought a "chocolate" signal from the flagship. Their alacrity was soon explained; it was an ammunition ship and the fourth hit touched off the cargo which went up in a truly magnificent explosion.

Such an occasion is not without danger to the attacking submarine; everything which goes up has to come down. A U-boat in World War I was sunk by a lorry, flung high off her victim by the explosion, crashing down on her. One of our own boats came back from patrol with an Italian bedstead wrapped round her gun; another had her pressure hull holed by a beam from a cargo hatch, though luckily the damage was above the water-line and she was close to Malta and got in safely. All these incidents had occurred during night attacks on the surface. I ordered Down Below; it only took a few seconds to clear the gun and the bridge and we were going under as the debris started raining down. Devlin pressed his camera as he went through the hatch and got what was, in pre-atomic days, an excellent snap of an exceptional explosion.

When it died down there was nothing left but a stain

on the water, the poor devils in the boats had just been vaporized. But it was amusing three minutes later to see the poor old Cant seaplane come flapping around like a worried old hen searching for her chicken.

CRDA Cant. Z.501

However, her persistence, and that of an E-boat which joined in the hunt, combined to preserve a north-bound auxiliary schooner which passed inshore of the hunt later in the day.

I now felt, particularly after our night dodging the patrol in the mist, that we were sufficiently worked up for a more ambitious billet. It was also time to start the homeward voyage, and we worked south.

Dawn next day found us in the approaches to Cagliari, where activity of A/S air and surface patrols suggested something might be moving.

At 08.43 the officer of the watch sighted a large tanker approaching from the south-west. We were soon deep and running at high speed to intercept her. Thirteen minutes later we slowed down and returned to periscope depth to see how things were going.

The tanker was coming along nicely, but passing under our stern at rather long range was a U-boat. If we had not sighted the tanker and gone in to intercept her, that U-boat would have passed close to our position, an easy attack. As it was she was a good way off; we had no stern tube and so would have to turn right round to bring our bow tubes to bear. Meanwhile the U-boat would have got a long way past and would present a very poor target fine on her quarter. The chances of hitting were remote, whereas the tanker should give a nice shot. She was unescorted, except for a routine A/S patrol in the vicinity; presumably the Italians reckoned the Gulf of Cagliari safe. I decided to take the bird in the hand. This was typical of submarining; you went for days with no sign of a target and then two first-class ones came along at the same time and you could not get them both.

Still, you did not get a tanker every day and at 09.14 we fired three torpedoes from 750 yards. One hit forward of amidships and one in the engine room. A tanker takes a great deal of sinking; you may only cause the oil to run out and unless she sinks low enough for the heavier sea-water to replace it she is not much worse off. It all depends on which bulkheads you carry away. The most serious damage you can do to a ship is to break its back and the best way to do this is to arrange your explosion underneath the keel.

Both sides had expended a considerable amount of effort to design a "non-contact pistol"—which would produce the desirable under-the-keel explosion—but with equal lack of success. Normally the pistol which touches off the main charge of a torpedo is fired by collision with the target; if you could get one to fire magnetically as it ran under the ship you could set your torpedoes to run deeper, where they would be less affected by any seaway, which upsets depth-keeping in submarine and torpedo alike, and also ensure devastating damage by breaking the back of the target. From the point of view of the submarine, it would also give you the great advantage of being able to deal with the shallow-draft torpedo boats which continually harrassed us, but were generally immune from our torpedoes which did not like running at depths shallow enough to hit them. A further advantage of setting torpedoes to run deep was that they left far less track, which could give warning of their approach, and less guidance to the hunters as to where they had come from. Our first effort at a non-contact pistol had been a failure and a new one had just been designed.

Safari was carrying six of these new torpedoes for trial purposes and the first three ever to be fired had gone in this attack. Being somewhat dubious of this new pistol, called the C.C.R., I had not set all three to run under, but only one of them; the other two were set about the draft of the ship. I believe actually the for'd hit was a non-contact —in a photograph of her taken through the periscope it seemed that there was a hump under her bridge; but the one in the engine room was a contact, but had not carried away the engine-room bulkhead, and the ship, though stopped, refused to sink. The crew abandoned ship and were picked up by the A/S patrol which closed and then patrolled round the wreck. She was joined by a motor A/S boat and a seaplane; we spent the next two and a half hours waiting for the tanker to sink and trying to torpedo the A/S patrol craft. She in turn was trying to pick us up on her hydrophones; she was pursuing such an erratic course that I could never get the tubes to bear; we were also incommoded by the motor A/S boat and the seaplane.

There had been a useful ripple on the water, but about 11.45 the breeze dropped away and it became glassy calm, I had to reassess my chances of torpedoing the patrol vessel; in such conditions the odds were more on her getting us. By this time a salvage party had been sent back to the tanker.

Everyone in the boat, a submarine gets very warm indeed in the Mediterranean summer, was very hot and exhausted, particularly myself, although I was water-cooled. Another experimental fitting in *Safari* was a new type of gland for the periscope. The periscope slides up and down through a hole in the pressure hull and it is difficult to produce a gland which can stand up to high-water pressure and at the same time allow the periscope to be turned freely.

This latest gadget to deal with an awkward problem was the worst I ever met. You pumped up the gland full of grease and for a while it leaked very little but made the periscope terribly hard to train; as the grease oozed out it started to leak and one got bathed in a mixture of seawater and grease. In this condition it was easier to train, but in due course the leak got so bad that the mixture got in your eyes and, worse still, on the eyepiece of the periscope, until

finally, and worst of all, it sometimes seeped inside, so that
anything you saw was as through a glass, darkly. The
engineer then pumped it up with grease again, you started
the muscle drill over again to train the periscope, and so
on for another cycle.

In the cold Northern winter a leaking periscope gland
was most uncomfortable and we used to wear a sou'wester;
in the Mediterranean in summer one could not claim that
it caused physical discomfort, but it was tiring and infuriating.

In addition to the water treatment, manning the
periscope when in close proximity to the enemy was quite
a gymnastic exercise. When the periscope was down, the
eyepiece end was down in a well below the floorboards,
whilst the top was withdrawn into the periscope standards
several feet below the surface. When one wanted to look
around, the periscope was raised hydraulically and, as the
eyepiece came clear of the floorboards, the C.O. was
already grovelling there to seize the handles by which one
trained it; he had to glue his eyes to the sights and follow
the periscope up. He could then see immediately when the
upper lens broke the surface, and order Stop—or, more
probably, give a sign with his little finger. The periscope
operator, who required a lot of skill and practice to work
his hydraulic control valve with nicety, would then stop
raising it.

Thenceforward the periscope was ordered up and
down whilst the C.O. was looking through it so as to have
just sufficient, but no more, of the periscope exposed above
the surface. Even in calm weather it is not easy to keep the
depth of a submarine steady to within an inch or two, in
rough weather, or when twisting and turning, it is often
difficult to do better than to within a foot or two. In a
seaway it is very hard to keep any sort of steady depth and
there is always a danger of being thrown up by the sea so
that the boat breaks surface. When keeping an ordinary
lookout with nothing close you can afford to expose two or
three feet of periscope and work it in comfort; but in calm
weather at close range of the enemy, if it is your ambition
to die later in your own bed, it is inadvisable to expose
more than an inch or two.

The periscope would be moved up and down as the
boat changed depth, even if it was only an inch or two, all

the time you were looking through it. Usually the operation was controlled by motions of the C.O.'s finger and the First Lieutenant would keep his C.O. informed of the depth so as to assist him in only exposing the bare minimum of periscope above water.

The moment the C.O. had seen enough for his immediate purpose, the periscope would be lowered, only to be raised again when next the C.O. wanted a look; at the culmination of an attack, or when dodging escorts, this might be only a matter of seconds later. At such times the C.O. would be alternating between grovelling on the floorboards and stretching out to his full height. If you add to this gymnastic procedure the effort of training the periscope—you could only see in one direction at a time and so you had to walk round it, sometimes on your knees, pulling the eyepiece with you so as to be able to sweep the horizon—it all mounted up to quite a strenuous occupation physically.

Mentally it was, if anything, more strenuous. R.N. submarines in World War II still only had the most rudimentary of attack instruments and you had to keep a running plot of all vessels in the vicinity in your head, memorizing ranges, speeds, rates of change of bearing and courses of both yourself and the enemy. It is quite extraordinary how difficult it is to do quite simple sums in mental arithmetic during the stress of action. Sometimes, when things were not turning out too well, you had a good deal to worry about, and at such times it required considerable mental effort to convert, for example, knots into feet a second. Of course you could always ask one of the attack team for the answer and he had the tables and slide rule to produce it. But when things were needle I used to find this too slow for me and I still carry in my head a mental conversion table of knots into feet a second. I used, at the time, to carry a good deal of information in my head—such as the firing angles to aim ahead of targets at varying speeds and courses.

With modern attack systems, the sums are done mechanically and even in my day the answer could be obtained, given a bit of time, from the attack team; and indeed I used them constantly. But at times, as I have said, I personally found this way of gaining information too slow. I may have been wrong, but I personally thought it

worthwhile to save spilt seconds by doing the sums in my
head, although I was but an indifferent mathematician. It
is certainly a fact that some of the most successful C.O.s I
knew in World War II happened to have very good
mathematical brains—Wanklyn and Linton, who both
gained V.C.s, Tomkinson, Dewhurst, Launders, and many
others. I think it was the same in World War I; Naismith,
who also gained a V.C. but who, unlike the other two I
have mentioned, survived the war, invented what I believe
was the first practical attack instrument. One of Linton's
hobbies was breaking ciphers, which gives an idea of his
mathematical abilities.

To return to the Gulf of Cagliari on the forenoon of
August 18th, 1942, by 11.45 I had been working at the
periscope, except for some fourteen minutes during our
initial run in, for three hours, chasing round an elusive
patrol vessel; furthermore I had done it with a periscope
gland which was better suited as the final punishment for
erring C.O.s in purgatory. It was not till after we had given
the tanker the *coup de grace* and had gone deep and made
our getaway that I suddenly found that, dripping with
sweat, seawater and grease, I was completely exhausted.
One just did not notice these things during the absorption
of attack.

After I had decided that aggression was no longer
going to be profitable, I chose a moment when all the
hunters, surface and air, were the other side of the derelict
and fired another torpedo, this time definitely set to run
under. We could not risk staying up to see, but the
explosion of the torpedo was followed immediately by
breaking-up noises—the structure of the ship cracking
up—and nine minutes later when we ventured up for a
look the tanker had gone. I believe this was the only
occasion when one of our non-contact torpedoes definitely
achieved a sinking. In certain conditions at short range—
and I had heard the torpedo which hit the tanker that
morning do it—one could hear a torpedo hit, with a sharp
noise like a click, a split second before the charge touched
off. Sound travels well in water, extremely well in some
conditions.

I say I believe it was the only occasion for this C.C.R.
pistol had a serious defect which could prove a menace to
the firer. If a torpedo was a rogue, through gyro failure,

and circled back at you instead of running straight you would normally go deep below it; with a non-contact pistol it might still go off and destroy you. In the future, as a result, they were always set to fire by contact only. But even contact pistols had failures too; Haggard had one particularly infuriating experience of this when he delivered a needle attack on a cruiser; he heard his torpedoes click as they hit the enemy's side; there was no satisfying roar to follow; the pistols had failed to touch off the warheads and the cruiser steamed on unscathed.

That evening we turned for home and as dusk was falling we were passing the southern entrance to the Gulf. The officer of the watch informed me that he could see what looked like a gunnery target adrift; Cagliari was a naval port. I knew what that was—the conning tower of a U-boat.

I sang out: "Diving Stations!"

She was homeward-bound, probably scenting the fleshpots, and—as was so easy when in sight of home—she was being a bit incautious. She had surfaced before it was really dark and was making speed on the surface for home. It was longish range and not a very favorable position from which to attack, but the tail rattled as we turned at full speed under full helm to a firing course whilst the T.I. and his fore-endmen brought the tubes to the ready at the rush.

We had six tubes and I decided to fire all six, spread across the target to give the maximum chance of success. I could not see very well in that light and it was impossible to judge enemy course and speed with any accuracy. Two of our tubes had torpedoes with the new experimental C.C.R. pistols, the other four the earlier attempt at a non-contact pistol now modified for contact only and, like most things adapted for another use, not particularly efficient as such. The old contact pistols were out of production, though occasionally odd ones would be found in forgotten stores, and I for one would go to any extreme to get hold of them.

The sights came on and we started firing the torpedoes with several seconds between each one to give a good spread and cover some error in estimation of the firing angle. Before we had fired the sixth there was a shattering explosion just ahead of us and the boat rattled and shook.

The compensating gear on the tubes also chose this moment to fail and we broke surface. A lot of the crew thought this must be a torpedo hitting at point-blank range and there was a wave of jubilation, but I knew that the target was about 2,500 yards off. It could not have been a depth charge as there was no aircraft or patrol vessel near; it could only be that a torpedo had exploded prematurely just outside the tube and much too close to be pleasant.

I wrote in my patrol report that it was *impossible, even for an Italian, not to notice one or both of these disasters*—the premature explosion of the torpedo and the submarine breaking surface—*and for the second time this war I saw the target turn away*. In fact, the credit I gave to the Italian lookouts, a tiring occupation uncongenial to Latin blood, was not justified. During the Sicilian landings the following year, this particular U-boat, the *Bronzo*, was captured by our surface forces and with her all her papers. I had heard by the grapevine earlier that the Italians had claimed to have sunk us on this occasion as, indeed, both they and the Germans claimed on others. However, the story of the *Bronzo's* C.O. ran as follows:

While proceeding in the southern approach to Cagliari he heard a torpedo exploding at the end of its run. Actually, of course, our brute exploded almost before it had started. At the end of their run torpedoes sink and may explode if the nose hits the bottom with a bump.

With a quick appreciation of the situation he turned towards the attacking submarine. Actually of course he turned away, but, if the explosion had indeed been a torpedo at the end of its run, he would have been turning towards; anyhow, he obviously never saw us break surface. He was almost immediately in collision with the "submarine," there was much disturbance in the water and large quantities of bubbles. He claimed to have sunk the enemy submarine. The report went on that, after docking, great dents had been found in the hull, one under the gun and one by the engine room. It was taken as sufficient proof of his claim and he was duly decorated. In fairness to our old foes, it must be admitted that other C.O.s on both sides received decorations for sinking submarines that were in no way incommoded. Of course, the bubbles, fuss and disturbance, to which he refers, were two of our torpedoes hitting; a weight of nearly two tons at 45 knots strikes a pretty hearty blow even without an explosion. In this case both pistols had failed.

On this patrol I had been in contact with three U-boats; it was surprising how often we met each other and it kept you on your toes; to ensure survival you had to see the other chap first. Many U-boats were sunk by our submarines but, as I have said before, fate had ordained that neither of my boats was to be successful at this game. Although three of my torpedoes made contact with enemy submarines, none exploded on their hull or caused more than superficial damage. I never got in another attack at a U-boat to see if I could break the hoodoo. The next time it was to be a U-boat having a crack at us, not the first to do so, and he missed; perhaps the hoodoo worked both ways.

It was after this patrol, being even more submarine-conscious than usual, that I got told off for coming home through our patrols off Gibraltar submerged. The proper drill was to come up about 50 miles off and run in on the surface suitably protected by bombing restrictions and with our time and route known to all patrols. Submerged we would be assumed to be U-boats and, if detected, attacked. I preferred to take this risk, in common with others, rather than expose myself as a target to U-boats.

I may have on occasion made rude references to the staff, but in reality they served us tirelessly; we all owed them a great debt in managing to ensure that our boats were hardly ever attacked by our own forces, in whom any submarine was liable to excite such martial enthusiasm as somewhat to obscure the small matter as to which side it was on.

Although we were yet far from being a really efficient submarine, the period of getting our eye in was over and *Safari* now settled down to some steady batting.*

---

*Continuous play as in cricket.

12

MALTA AND THE ADRIATIC

Our submarines had been forced to withdraw from Malta under the bombing of the spring of 1942. We had lost too many boats in harbor. The Tenth (Malta) Submarine Flotilla had joined the First Flotilla at Beirut; whilst the Eighth, my flotilla, operated from Gibraltar. This meant that from east or west our boats had to steam some 900 miles to get on to Rommel's main supply routes; and since it was not healthy to be on the surface by day, what with aircraft and enemy submarines, the passage took about five days—an awful waste of submarine effort. From Malta one could be on the job within a day, and in the late summer of 1942 the Tenth Flotilla started collecting at Malta again. *Safari*, *Sahib* and *Saracen* were seconded from Gibraltar to back up the Tenth Flotilla, depleted by grievous losses.

We were delighted to be going to Malta, where our submarines had achieved a tremendous reputation, though the glamour at close quarters was not so bright. Malta was hungry, tired and battered. The Tenth Flotilla was somewhat depressed at the recent loss of *Upholder* (Lieutenant Commander Wanklyn, V.C., the greatest of our submarine C.O.s) and others of comparable achievement. There were no amusements; food or drink was unobtainable outside our mess, and food was strictly rationed there. Actually the submariners and fighter pilots got extra rations and did not do so badly; we were able to run in—as the R.A.F. flew in—some of the bottled amenities of life.

In my opinion the real heroes of Malta, forgotten men, were the soldiers. I had gone out in a trooper with the Devons in 1938 and they were still there. I scarcely recognized in the gaunt figure with the flapping tunic and sagging Sam Browne the major who had been so singularly robust a man in 1938. No extra rations, under or over the sea, came their way; they had no relations with a farm in Gozo to supplement their diet by unofficial channels. Unheard of and unsung they unloaded the occasional ship which got through amidst the furious bombing; when others were in their shelters they filled in the holes in the runways to let our fighters down; and they kept unceasing weary watch upon the beaches and annihilated the only seaborne attack the Axis ever made on Malta.

Shrimp Simpson (now Rear-Admiral C. W. G. Simpson, C.B., C.B.E.) commanded the submarine base at the Lazaretto, an ancient building, one-time hospital, lately the sanitary store for the civil engineers of Malta. The glazed products of Mr. Shanks had suffered severely in the bombing, but the sandflies, which shared the building, had thrived exceedingly. They resented our intrusion and we lacked the chemicals to defeat them. They were at their most ferocious in the air raid shelters and many of us preferred the bombs to their attacks.

Films we had in plenty—a priority under-seas cargo —with two different programs daily; some people solemnly saw out two programs each day they were in harbor. In the mess, with boats coming and going daily, the conversation was confined to food and shop. In these endless discussions the infernal machines devised by the enemy for the destruction of submarines assumed a fabulous ingenuity, and the atmosphere might not have been thought particularly conducive to enthusiasm. Actually, under the leadership of Shrimp, morale was good and many a cheery evening we spent in the Lazaretto. With Teutonic lack of imagination, the raids came with clockwork regularity; you could decide whether to have breakfast before or after the morning raid. As lunch drew near, and if a consignment of gin had arrived, you could decide whether to have lunch quickly, or have another gin and take it to the shelters, repelling the sandflies with your breath, until the midday was past. But more probably and stupidly you would go up and watch the orderly flights of bombing aircraft, pinpointed by occasional shell bursts—there was insufficient ammunition to do much more than indicate the target—as they sailed across the cloudless skies.

Then from away up out of sight, hurtling through the shell bursts and enemy fighters, would come a handful of little shining specks—our fighters—to spread disorder and confusion. Odd aircraft would peel off trailing clouds of smoke—at that height it was hard to tell which side they were—and, as the bombs crashed down and raised great clouds of sand, the enemy passed on, the skies cleared again except, perhaps, for a few little white bubbles where parachutes drifted down.

At this time the bombing was concentrated on our airfields, and as our fighters—this was the heyday of Skewbald Beurling and Co.—took increasing toll of the bombers, the enemy fell back on fighter bombers and gradually the odds eased; more Spitfires flew in and impending starvation became the only real, but very present, menace.

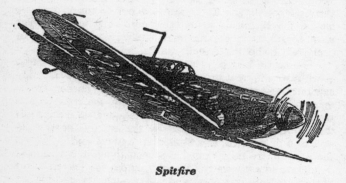

Spitfire

No longer did our submarines have to sit through long sweltering days at the bottom of the harbor, to come up for the all too short nights to carry out essential repairs and maintenance. An occasional bomb would, however, fall in the harbor, and as the spray died down, from cove and cranny would come out the brightly painted—though very faded now—*dghaisas,* the gondolas of Malta, to collect the fish stunned by the explosion.

All coinage had disappeared, reputedly buried in the gardens of Malta and at this time a two-shilling note was the smallest token; if you took a *dghaisa* across the harbor you could give one of these notes or a couple of cigarettes;

probably the latter was more acceptable. A reel of cotton was worth fifteen shillings and sixpence; an immature potato a shilling; the worth of such things as lipstick could not be measured in sordid coin.

Submarines coming from east or west would bring in little things like scented soap, plentiful at Gib, but a fabulous luxury in Malta. Soon after arrival I went up to see the Tenches, one of the only English couples left in Malta. I took up, unthinkingly, some bath salts and when Greta opened the parcel, she took one look and broke into a hollow laugh. Of course it had been many months since Malta had had the fuel for a hot bath. Actually at the Lazaretto, Sam MacGregor, the flotilla chief, had rigged up an ingenious Heath Robinson affair, wherein an old oil drum was heated by a fire of dirty diesel lub oil. This allowed submariners—when supplies of dirty lub oil were available—to have one hot bath when returning from patrol. Of course we had the sea to bathe in, and very pleasant it was even though the harbor was polluted. The lovely bathing beaches of Malta were inaccessible, heavily protected by barbed-wire defenses.

Scabies was rife and it seemed that nearly every other woman of Malta had a bandage round some sore on her stockingless legs. It was said to be due to lack of fats. When my turn came to contract scabies, I duly treated it conscientiously but unavailingly with the only salve we had— sulpher ointment. Months later, when Malta had been relieved, and we had departed to Algiers, I showed the P.M.O. the mess and asked for advice. He simply recommended knocking off sulphur ointment; whether I had been treating what had long ago become only sulpher ointment rash with that indifferent medicament, or whether it was the good living in Algiers, it rapidly cleared up.

In the Lazaretto I shared a cabin with Lynch Maydon (Lieutenant-Commander Maydon, D.S.O., D.S.C., and now an M.P.). It was a singularly well ventilated room containing two beds and a wardrobe. If you opened the wardrobe you looked straight out on to the rubble outside —a bomb had blown out that bit of the wall. There was also a step missing in the stone staircase which led to it. The extraordinary thing was that no one ever fell down this in the dark, even on those nights after a consignment of gin had been run in. Lynch had an unrivalled aptitude

for sleep and when he came in from patrol he would go
into a sort of a deep trance round the clock and round
again. Of course he had quite a bit of sleep to make up, as
there wasn't much time for a submarine C.O. to sleep on
patrol.

The Lazaretto was situated on Manoel Island, which
lay between Sliema Creek and Lazaretto Creek in Marsa
Muscetto. Submarines could go alongside the Lazaretto for
servicing, but for the most part when in harbor they lay
dispersed in trots connected to the beach by floating
gangways. We had some underground workshops and the
aforementioned air-raid shelters lined with bunks. Behind
the Lazaretto was Fort Manoel, the last fort built by the
Knights and in its era the last word in fortifications. It had,
like all the old fortifications, stood up remarkably well to
the bombing, but we left it mainly to the sandflies. Close to
us was a graveyard, presumably dating from the hospital
days, and between the graveyard and the Lazaretto was
our farm.

A farm is rather a grandiose title, but it did contain
several sorts of fowl and a number of pigs. By this time,
late in the siege, it was a far from flourishing concern.
Theoretically, the pigs fed on the "gash"—waste food—
from the Lazaretto. Anyone who has been in the Services
will know the tremendous amount of pig food that is
normally produced when catering for hundreds of men
and originally the pigs had thrived, despite the hazards of
razor blades and tea leaves and other indigestible things
which it is practically impossible to persuade sailors to
keep out of the pig buckets.

But as Malta grew hungrier, so waste disappeared,
and the poor pigs grew hungrier too. The pigs ceased to be
productive, interest in them waned and by this time only a
few razor-backed sows were precariously supported.
Someone had a brainwave. Earlier in the war an Italian
schooner had been taken in prize and it had a cargo, said
to be a product of the oak tree, which was impounded in
the bowels of Lazaretto. No one knew what this strange
brown substance might be and some wag named it camel
fodder. The idea spread, the step from camel fodder to pig
fodder was short and it was fed in with the dwindling gash
to the ravening pigs. That nearly ended the pig farm; the
product of the oak was for use in tanning and it had the

most adverse effect upon the digestive processes of the pigs; it was touch and go before their digestive paths were cleared again. They were being saved for Christmas, and although actually Malta was relieved in November, they did form our Christmas dinner, thin and wiry as they were; they were much appreciated on patrol.

About the only item of food in fair supply in the Lazaretto was a product known as veal pie, which it closely resembled in appearance. I used to make this the mainstay of my diet, but noticing that the more experienced inhabitants seemed to prefer to go hungry, I inquired the reason. They told me that it was made from goats. The goat of Malta, excellent though its qualities may be as an economical method of converting garbage into milk, is—or, rather, was, for like many other things its more romantic associations have now succumbed to modern hygiene—a singularly repulsive animal in look and smell. Its irregular pendulous udders nearly sweep the ground and, interfering with the movement of its hind legs, make even its gait ungainly. It was the general belief that only after advancing disease and years and lack of nourishment had caused those gnarled udders to dry, did the goat qualify for elevation to veal pie. The squeamishness of some was understandable.

Nevertheless the Lazaretto did occasionally provide some luxuries; an occasional piece of toast was one—a luxury because both bread and the fuel to toast it were in short supply. Devlin, our Navigator, told the story of one day coming in from patrol and sitting down for tea. The Maltese steward brought him a large piece of toast.

The officer next to him protested that the steward had just told him that there was no toast.

He was withered by the reply: "Yes, Senor, but this officer has sunk a ship."

Very loyal and long suffering were our Maltese staff and much we owed them.

But though food was carefully rationed, drink never was, except for beer. Two bottles of beer a fortnight was the ration and those two bottles went down in one. Any other consignments which were run in were dealt with while they lasted; the morrow, if there was one, could take care of itself.

One of the greatest advantages of Malta, from a

submarine C.O.'s point of view, was that there was no one on your side for hundreds of miles. Later on in the war in the Pacific I found that the American submarines, like ours, regarded their own Air Force with far greater respect than the enemy. At least you knew what to expect from the latter. In the Central Mediterranean anything that flew or floated, except a submarine, was bound to be enemy and so you had no trouble about recognition. Everything was delightfully simple and since Shrimp and his S.O.O. comprised the whole operational staff of the Tenth Flotilla and they were much too busy to write voluminous orders, everyone knew exactly what to do. It seems that the main *raison d'être* of staffs in war is to try and arrange so that people on the same side do not fight each other; at Malta you were spared such complications.

As I was starting off for this patrol from Malta Bob Tanner, our S.O.O., issued me with his latest economical form of operation order—one of those little purple tickets you tear off a roll, in this case a return ticket across the harbor to the Manoel canteen, dating from the days when there was a canteen; on it had been written: *Adriatic, valid till October 11th*. All was crystal clear; I had to beat up the Adriatic and be clear of it by October 11th.

Actually, of course, I had been told we were to have the Adriatic and had briefed myself thoroughly. In the bowels of Lazaretto was a small room wherein were kept all patrol reports, arranged by areas. All you had to do was to pick out the Adriatic file and see where every boat which returned from there had been, all their remarks about shipping, minefields, navigational aids and hazards, patrol beats and so forth. Then you would study the charts, noting where the soundings suggested favorable operating conditions and memorizing the sailing directions, those wonderful directions in innumerable volumes comprising the experience of mariners throughout the world over the years. One probably would not have much time to consult them on patrol.

Shrimp came down to see us off with some last-minute information and instructions, the last wire was thrown ashore—you carried no wires on patrol because if your casing were damaged they might get round a propeller —and the little flotilla staff waved us off. Theirs was a twenty-four-hour day month in and month out, yet they

were never too tired to see off or welcome back the boats
whose maintenance they tended.

There were four minesweepers at Malta now, commanded by Jake Jerome, himself an old submariner, and
two swept us out round the channel to the deep water
south of the island. They could only just manage to skim
the minefields the enemy laid, so the submarines could not
dive till they reached the very deep water past the little
island of Filfola, close to the south of Malta. Accordingly
the minesweepers escorted us, their Ack Ack armament
acting in our defense, since we were denied our usual
escape by diving. On this occasion we were not attacked,
the sweepers wished us good hunting and turned back for
Valetta and we were out on our own again.

We were lucky to have been given the Adriatic.
Though every ship sunk helped in the long-term policy,
these were the days shortly before El Alamein and it was
vital to get those ships actually taking stores to Rommel.
Sinkings in the Adriatic were of secondary importance,
except in so far as, by causing the enemy to extend his A/S
forces, you eased the concentration on the North African
routes. No submarine had been spared for the Adriatic for
some time and our job was to stir up trouble there and
draw off the A/S effort from our hard-pressed boats
elsewhere. It was a fruitful hunting ground, usually reserved for boats which needed blooding, and we could not
claim that excuse.

We had an uneventful passage and only met one
destroyer as we passed through the Straits of Otranto on
the surface during the night of September 30th.

My first intention was to attack Gruz Harbor. This is
up a short fiord with a narrow promontory on the seaward
side, from the tip of which runs to the northward a chain
of islands that continues far up the Yugoslav coast. The
approach is a very narrow one, too narrow to turn round
submerged, and accordingly on passage we practiced diving astern. We should have to back out about a mile after
attacking. I hoped that the enemy would reckon this
tucked away little harbor naturally secure, since there were
no intelligence reports of booms or nets.

It was a lovely afternoon on October 1st as we closed
the coast north of Dubrovnik. At 13.35 a steamer, coast-
crawling northward and out of range, turned in between

the first and second islands, Kolocep and Lopud from the end of the Gruz peninsula, Grebini, and disappeared in the inside channels. Slowly we crept in towards the coast, our mine detecting unit running despite the risk that enemy hydrophones might pick it up.

The mine detector unit was an application of the Asdic which enabled you to get echoes off mines—and of course many other things, including fish, eddies and rocks. A mine is a small thing to get an echo off, but the M.D.U. was a good gadget and though far from completely efficient, gave some security. Luckily I had not got the charts of the enemy minefields, if I had seen them, I should never have attempted this patrol as we carried it out. Much of the time was spent in minefields, as I realized after Italy had collapsed and we took over her charts. However, the water was deep and a mine cannot have heavy moorings in deep water as their weight would sink it. Light moorings readily part, and since these minefields had been laid some time, many mines must have broken adrift and the fields become thin. I should have a noted a possible reason for the steamer we had seen earlier going between Kolocep and Lopud and followed her track. However at this time I assumed that she was northbound and drew no inference from the fact that she had not gone through the first gap in the island chain, into which I was steering from the westward, before altering south down the Gruz approach. To have taken the next gap northward would have meant another six miles—another two hours.

The M.D.U. recorded a clear channel and at 15.30 we started through the narrow passage between Kolocep and Grebini. There was a lighthouse on the shore and through the periscope one could see a man gardening by it. Slipping along through the lovely Dalmatian scenery on this sparkling afternoon, it seemed absurd that we were bent on destruction and all around destruction was designed for us. Slowly we moved up the fiord, the slim periscope only breaking the surface occasionally to show an inch or two. Any casual watcher on either side could have seen it had we shown more. Even that woman on the beach could have given the alarm.

Closer came the last turn which would open up Gruz harbor; visions of cruisers, submarines, fat merchant ships lying there, sitting shots, rose vividly before me. This had been in my mind for weeks; and now, we had negotiated the channel undetected and around this corner we should know the answer. At 17.00, an hour and a half after commencing the run in, we rounded the corner. There was Gruz Harbor, peaceful and, a bitter disappointment, nearly deserted. There was the steamer we had seen turn into the islands some three and a half hours before and one small torpedo boat, but nothing else. Still at least they were something.

As we crept on to get into a firing position, a worse disappointment awaited us. A regular row of buoys indicated a boom and though we approached it close we could find no gap to let through a torpedo. The Italians had not been as careless as we had thought or intelligence reports had indicated.

There was nothing for it but to retire; the Coxswain and Second Coxswain changed places; the after-planes normally controlled by the Coxswain would now be acting as foreplanes and vice versa. The motors were put astern and we started the long run out faster than we had come in, mostly below periscope depth. The slightest error of judgment by the planesmen and we would break surface and the balloon would go up, or we would hit the bottom and damage our screws. All went well and we faithfully followed our track in, for that we knew was clear of mines. As we passed Grebini our friend was still gardening away his peaceful afternoon.

Now my suspicions—aroused by finding that the first steamer had doubled south after entering the islands—were confirmed. A second steamer was approaching and, as we ran in to attack, she also dodged in to safety between Kolocep and Lopud. Evidently the channel we had used was mined, though our M.D.U. had found us a safe channel. Submarining is like that; it was the second steamer in a day that we had just failed to intercept. Had we managed to save an hour in five days since leaving Malta—our passage had been delayed by being sent off on a wild-goose chase—we could have attacked the first ship before she got inside the islands. Had we come out past Grebini half an hour earlier we could have got in on this second steamer.

But we knew where the first one was now, and I was determined to get her.

I reckoned that she would leave Gruz at dawn and run north inside the islands. We would get inside the islands farther to the northward and intercept her next morning.

In the meantime we withdrew from the coast to charge the batteries. The moon had not yet risen; it was one of those fathomless, black nights. We zigged slowly on one engine and charged on the other, a gentle inshore breeze playing pleasingly over the body, everything dead quiet except for the muffled exhaust of the diesels and the gentle lapping of the ripples against the hull, outlined by the faintest tinge of phosphorescence. The lookouts, however, were not lulled by the peaceful beauty of the night; with a flat calm in that velvet darkness it was hard to pick out the horizon, against which other ships must be silhouetted, if you are to see them first.

Submarines live by always seeing the other chap first. On the surface, in those pre-radar days, everything depended upon the lookouts; it is a most exhausting business concentrating endlessly on glaring into darkness through binoculars. The officers of the watch, as well as generally supervising, would take the sector from ahead to the starboard quarter and the two helmsmen would alternate between the after lookout and steering down below. A selected chief or petty officer took the port sector. Generally an hour at a time was all a man could do as a lookout, before straining eyes in the binoculars grew tired and unreliable. Some C.O.'s spent all night on the bridge when on inshore patrol, but I did not. I always reckoned that it was better to be comparatively fresh when there was something to do. I would be up there until all was settled down for the nightly routine and then again before dawn. One always slept in one's clothes—one could be up on the bridge in a fraction of a minute if required—and the officer of the watch well knew what to do. Usually I could reckon on two or three hours' sleep when things were quiet; the rest of my sleep was made up in odd snatches throughout the day. The Chief and Chief E.R.A were the only persons besides the C.O. who did not keep a regular watch; everyone else was two hours on, four hours off, excepting some lookouts who were one hour on, three hours off. In that off-period a man had to do all his eating and sleeping and the maintenance work on the equipment for which he was responsible; frequent alarms and excursions called all to Diving Stations. Besides his actual time on watch a lookout had to spend at least ten minutes in accustoming himself to the darkness of the bridge before he took over. Sometimes the Chief and Chief E.R.A. would have an easy time; more often maintenance work kept them busy, somtimes twenty-four hours or more on end. Moreover the Chief was expected to play "Ukkers," a particularly vicious adaptation of Ludo, at any hour of the day or night with any officer of the watch who did not feel like sleep.

"Silent" Harris preferred chess and got me to play once or twice, but chess was not a game for submarine patrol. Always, subconsciously, even in your sleep, you were listening for a change in the beat of the diesels as the helm was put over, some extra orders down the bridge voice pipe next to the wardroom, or the buzzer which called the C.O. to the bridge. Ukkers was the perfect game for submarine patrol; sufficently absorbing without undue concentration; infuriating when your piece was Ukked on the threshold of home and safety; most satisfying when you Ukked your opponent at a similar stage—no quarter asked or given. Fore and aft in every mess of every submarine on patrol, Ukkers was played and doutless a psychologist could find the reason why; we took to it naturally.

Similarly, early in the war, we all started eating sweets—it may have been because we could not often smoke—and eating them in quantity like children. Later on the doctors, studying why and how we lived, prescribed sweets and they were issued as rations; but we had already taken to them naturally, without thought in response to a natural craving.

Suddenly the peace of that lovely night on the Adriatic was broken.

There was a slight tang of funnel smoke in the air. An order was called down the voice pipe. In seconds the wheel went hard over to steer down-wind. The battery charge was broken off. The tail-clutch was let in. Both engines were now propelling the boat, the crew was at Diving Stations and on the bridge binoculars were trained up-wind.

The first thing on a night sighting was to turn stern

on; it gave you time to turn either way or open the range as you dived. If it turned out to be a target, you could always turn in again after judging its course and speed; if it were a patrol, you would need every second to take avoiding action. Supposing the visibility was 1,000 yards—often it was less—and a destroyer was coming at you at twenty knots, he would be there in 90 seconds. He would probably see you at 500 yards range if you remained up, which gave you 45 seconds, about the time it took to dive if you remained stopped. But you never stopped if you could help it; you kept steerage way so that by turning away and speeding up you reduced the relative speed of closing and got a chance to see what it was. It was no good diving at night and, except in bright moonlight, rendering yourself blind on every sighting because the object might well be a worthy target. At best you surrendered the initiative and, anyhow, you had to stay up some time to charge.

To detect a ship by smell was rare, it only happened to me twice; on this occasion it turned out to be a small torpedo boat, whose silhouette was low and hard to see. We had no difficulty in avoiding it, but it proved a nuisance as it was around all night and later, when the moon rose, had to be given a wider berth. Consequently, when we dived at dawn we were farther from the entrance to the islands than I had planned and proved rather late for our steamer.

I had decided to intercept in Zuljana Bay, opposite the Mejet Channel, which we entered submerged just as it was growing light. Having sighted a floating mine we went deep and ran in under any possible mines until four miles inside the islands, when we came back to periscope depth to close the mainland. The shore was steep and it would be hard to pick up a ship under its shadow.

Shortly afterwards we sighted our steamer. It was one of those passenger-cum-cargo boats which look like an ocean liner except in size. Through the periscope it is very hard to judge size and this type of ship is particularly deceptive. Having been delayed we were unable to get in to good torpedo range. She was unescorted and the A/S air patrol had recently passed and should not be back for some time. It was an occasion to stop her with the gun. Up we came 3,000 yards on her quarter, and before she knew what was happening our 3-inch shells were crashing into her bridge. She soon caught fire, but before we could manage a crippling shot in the engine room she had managed to beach herself by the tiny village of Padobuce. She was being used as a transport and many men were jumping overboard. We secured and dived, closing her submerged, and put a torpedo into the stranded ship from 1,000 yards. She went up in flames and the smoke was still visible from far to seaward next day.

There was an interesting sequel to this attack. Twelve years later, I was talking to Captain Orhailovitch, the Yugoslav Naval Attaché in London, and the conversation veered to coastal artillery. I remarked that I had been shot at on occasion by Yugoslav coast artillery—manned, of course, by Italians—when patrolling the Dalmatian coast during the war. He then asked if I had been in the submarine which drove this steamer ashore. It transpired that he was the leader of a band of partisans in this mountainous area and they had been up above Padobuce on this day. They had watched the whole affair, descended upon the Italian soldiers, who were wet and unwarlike, and then captured from the wreck a tremendous stock of rifles, machine guns and ammunition.

We remained in Zuljana Bay all day, hoping for something else to come along. Although much smoke to the northward gave us hope, the shipping had evidently been stopped; the only thing which came along was a 300-ton auxiliary schooner. This we had to let go as by this time A/S air activity was intense and she had an air escort, which refused to go away; we could not therefore surface to use the gun. She was no torpedo target and so she went on unscathed.

In the evening as we started to withdraw to seaward to charge, four torpedo-boats arrived and started a very well organized hunt. One boat in particular appeared to have got our scent and hunted round us for a long time. This was very annoying, as I did not want to be caught amongst the islands when the moon came up, and we could not get out to seaward whilst dodging this party. However, as dark came down they formed up in line abreast and swept out between Glavet Island and Golinut Point. This was most convenient; *Safari* surfaced and fell in astern, provided with a first-class guide through any possible minefields. It was amusing to see them flashing signals to each other, oblivious of the fact that the submarine for which they were hunting was following close astern of them.

Having stirred things up on the Yugoslav side we decided to have a go on the Italian side of the Adriatic. The water that side was generally shallow, mines being a very real menace, and there did not seem much future in inshore work. Enemy shipping was hugging the coast, but I hoped that some would be tempted to take a short cut across the Gulf of Manfredonia; I spent the next day there, to no avail, and it was evident that we should have to get closer inshore. Gargano Head appeared the best bet, as you could get within three miles of the coast before the water shoaled to ten fathoms, our minimum operating depth.

Accordingly at dawn the following day we dived on the ten-fathom line and hazily in the coastal morning mist a good-sized ship was sighted under Gargano Head. There was not much time to make estimations and I gave her about ten knots. The nearest we could get was 5,000 yards and in view of the range decided to fire four torpedoes, spread so as to cover some error in speed estimation.

She was, as it turned out, doing between eight and nine knots, and was also an exceptionally efficient ship. She sighted the first torpedo missing ahead—in the glassy calm the tracks of our torpedoes showed up like broad silver ribbons—and put her helm hard over in time to avoid the later ones. At first it looked as if she was going to ram the cliffs under her lee. However, she straightened up as we surfaced to see if we could do any better with our gun.

Hardly had we opened fire than she very sportingly replied, with an alacrity which would have done credit to a warship. She had two guns, the after one of heavier caliber than ours, the forward an A.A. gun of small caliber. It was difficult shooting as the ship was hard to see in the mist against the cliffs and too difficult for our gunlayer. Infuriating as it was at the time, this was really an amusingly ineffective little battle. Occasionally one of our little shells would apparently go home, when the enemy would cease fire and start to beach herself. Then she would regain courage and reopen fire as the following shells went wild.

Her shooting was even worse than ours and the after gun appeared to be using black powder which enveloped the target in smoke.

By this time we were in water too shallow to dive, an air patrol would be along at any minute, our ammunition was disappearing at an alarming rate and there was no future in continuing. So we had to give the *Valentino Coda,* a very gallant ship, best and slink away to deep water.

Encouraged by our retreat, she actually put one shell within fifty feet of us. We had intercepted her S O S, which included the words: *"Salve carta."* I noted in my patrol report: *The literal translation of the latter, giving rise to ribald speculation as to what paper had been saved, provided the only bright thought in a very distressing morning.*

Before we reached deep water we put over a dummy periscope. These dummy periscopes were a brainwave of Shrimp's. They were perfect copies of a periscope, but made of wood and weighed so as to float vertically showing about three feet. The idea was that they would be seen and reported and the Italians would waste much fuel and energy in rushing to attack them. The sailors had painted on extremely rude messages to Mussolini. Had he obeyed the exhortations, even that amply proportioned man must have suffered intolerable discomfort.

We returned to the Yugoslav side and made for the Sibenik approaches. The M.D.U. picked up a minefield off Komorica Island on the morning of the 5th and we ran in deep under it and so to the most lovely inshore waters amongst the islands. At 09.40 smoke was sighted off Mulo Island and this turned into a small steamer of under 1,000 tons, her decks crowded with soldiers. She was on the small side for a torpedo target, and at 10.21 we came up on her quarter at 1,000 yards range. The first shell was away about 45 seconds from breaking surface, but to my surprise there was an extremely alert shore battery, which must have heard of our inshore gunnery, and very soon shells were pitching all around us. Our shells, however, were all hitting about the water line and as our target turned stern on three went in around her rudder; she ran up on the reefs of Trara Island. Men were leaping off her into the water, which was black with bobbing heads. By this time the shore artillery was putting up a very creditable performance and we secured and dived. It was just under three minutes from the submarine breaking surface to sinking out of sight again, during which time we had got off twenty rounds, all hits. In this action we had had to leave the telescopes shipped as the crew scrambled down; the enemy shore batteries at point-blank range had demanded it. We would surface and get them down as soon as convenient and the E.A. would strip them and dry them out. The Germans had the luxury of watertight sights and also a gun designed for submarines with stainless steel mechanisms. When the designer produced *Safari*'s gun to shoot at Zeppelins in World War I he little dreamed how it would end up. But despite the constant abuse it got, it commanded our very real affection.

Our target had run up really hard on the reefs, but I felt that we could afford a torpedo to make certain she could never come off. The trouble was that there were other reefs between her and us and we had to make quite a detour to find a clear passage for our torpedo. The next twenty-five minutes were spent maneuvering round the navigational hazards to open the target up for a shot. It was mirror calm, the enemy battery knew just where we were and at that range on such a day anyone could see a periscope, even if it only broke the surface an inch or two; and they expended a lot of ammunition shooting at it, as it had to be used a lot for navigational reasons. At last we were lined up and away went the torpedo. However, it was a rogue, the gyro failed, and it came circling back at us.

Normally one would go deep to avoid being savaged by such a rogue; it is a matter for some consternation when you are being chased by your own torpedo. However, we had not got the water to go very deep and I felt very thankful when the torpedo went up on some rocks.

Tubby Linton (Commander J. W. Linton, V.C., D.S.O.) had a satisfactory experience with a circler. He had fired several torpedoes at a convoy, with good effect, but one circled. As *Turbulent* went deep an Italian destroyer, racing down the torpedo tracks to depth charge, ran into the circler and was sunk.

I now had to decide whether to maneuver around again into a firing position and expend another torpedo; I was a little worried about our position with no sea room to maneuver should we get another rogue, or should an aircraft turn up. A careful examination suggested that our victim was a fairly certain loss, but the decision was precipitated by sighting smoke amongst the islands and we could not afford the time for another shot. In the event, she did prove a total loss.

As we withdrew, we fired one of Shrimp's dummy periscopes out of the tube before reloading. I know not whether the enemy used up any ammunition on this, or, indeed, if they saw it, for it took time to drain down the tube and fire it again. We had opened the range considerably and my ambition was now elsewhere.

The smoke had developed into another ship approaching and we were off again to the attack. I fancy she must have been warned, for she doubled back amongst the islands and escaped.

Sibenik was a defended naval port and apart from the shore batteries we were certain of a hunt being laid on, so we headed seaward. The afternoon was occupied with avoiding two aircraft and a torpedo boat, who hunted us assiduously and on occasions uncomfortably closely.

The next day, October 6th, found us off Promontore on the approach to Pola, another naval port. The water was unpleasantly shallow and I knew that if we got an attack we should have to make to seaward at once. We could not afford to stay in the area once our position was disclosed.

It happened to be a good submarining day, with a nice chop on the water, which should have been fruitful of targets. Nothing turned up for some time and then only a small coasting steamer. I broke my rule to take anything that offered and let her go by, hoping for a better target later. We were short of ammunition. There was a mirage that morning and at first she had presented an extraordinary sight through the periscope, her bridge distorted as it came over the horizon and looking like a house. As she got closer, so she appeared smaller.

I paid for my greed, for nothing else turned up that day, and subsequently the weather unsuitable for Promontore.

We had been unmolested all day, which was surprising, but that night we ran into two patrols which proved annoying. The following day, patrolling the Ancona-Silba route, we again drew blank. Hopes were raised by considerable activity from patrols and minesweepers, but no targets turned up; doubtless retribution for not taking what was offered the day before.

It was now time to start working south again and on the morning of the 8th we closed the coast once more off Mulo Island. While still too far off, a considerable convoy passed inshore of the islands, but at least they showed us the route ships were taking and we pressed on in. Shortly after a motor A/S boat came out of the Drvenik Channel and established patrol to the seaward of us; at 11.30 she was joined by another. At 15.31 a torpedo boat came out from behind Smokvica Island; she had a small coaster under her charge, but smoke from the Sibenik direction had already indicated the approach of a better target.

I noted in my patrol report: *No rock or islet appeared too small for steamers to get behind and the most fantastic course was pursued under the cliffs.* This was to avoid coming out in the open. However, where we were there was a short stretch without cover, hence presumably the enemy patrol. Having seen her little charge into the Drvenik Channel, the torpedo boat came out and established patrol about three cables inshore of us, so we were sandwiched between her and the two motor A/S boats. Finally a flying boat swept up and down for good measure. It was as usual a glassy calm. At 16.20 the smoke developed into a steamer of useful size, which came out from behind Smokvica Island and we started the attack.

The torpedo boat was a nuisance as she beat up and down just to seaward of the target. We were now committed to the turn in to fire; as we swung slowly, the small periscope barely breaking surface, the torpedo boat turned and came back towards us. If we went deep now we should miss the attack, we could never get up in time. The only thing was to stop the starboard motor—we were only on one—and she should just pass clear ahead. She did, so close that you could hear the thrash of her propellers throughout the boat, and it sounded like a train passing over the foc's'le. Had the officer of the watch looked down he must have seen our hull through those pellucid waters.

As she passed the sights came on the target and we fired just under her stern. We went deep and heard our torpedo crash home from a range of 1,000 yards. It was nine minutes since our target had come into sight round Smokvica Island.

This was not a valuable target and estimations were easy as you could get target speed by plotting her along the coast. But of all the attacks I ever did this one gave me the most satisfaction.

Nearly always, when analyzing the attack in your head afterwards, you could see some way it could have been done better. But this time, limited to our slowest speed on one propeller by aircraft and anti-submarine tactics, we had slowly swung onto our firing course, with two A/S boats just to seaward of us and another between us and the target, a flying boat overhead and a flat calm day. Further, we had been patrolling there for hours and there was a shore battery and lookout on the top of the cliffs.

In blowing my own trumpet, I must point out that it was the fact that it was the only attack I ever did which seemed completely satisfying that made it so memorable. However, at the time it was no moment for preening oneself and we were getting out of it as quickly as possible.

It did not take long for the torpedo boat to whip round and depth-charge the tell-tale stain in the water where we had fired and very prompt she was. Down came the depth charge and the attacks took their familiar pattern. Lights went out, paint flaked off, and we shuddered to the shocks. The wireless set also suffered considerable damage, but the Petty Officer Telegraphist would fix that up in due course. We did suffer one small, but rather serious, bit of damage. The high-power periscope lens starred and this meant that we were seriously handicapped for long-range vision for the rest of the patrol. Amongst the depth-charge explosions were a steady succession of little bangs. It appeared that the ardent gunners of the shore batteries were joining in the fun and these were their shells going off.

We had no difficulty in shaking off the hunt and when we came up that night we left behind another dummy periscope, hoping that it would waste some more enemy ammunition next day.

We had a nasty turn that night as we withdrew amongst the islands. We had noted the enemy patrolling to the east of Sveti Andrija Island and were passing very close to the westward. By keeping close in to this steep island I reckoned to guard our silhouette from showing against the horizon as the moon rose. But a torpedo boat was lurking under the shadow of the cliffs and came out at us. We got down just in time. She was not very clever in hunting us, but it wasted a lot of the night, and when dawn came we were still twenty-three miles short of where I had wanted to be.

A flare had been fired from the island just before the torpedo boat arrived and possibly we had been sighted from the shore. One could not be certain, in these restricted waters, of seeing the whole time without being seen. In such circumstances everyone is keyed up, particularly the vital lookouts, and nature seems to relax slightly the faculties of the human body. It had been a close call, but we were clear of the islands now, and could look back at the searchlights playing astern of us with amused satisfaction. They had lost the scent.

Still they had served a purpose and the afternoon of the next day was well advanced before we got in close to Kolocep Island, the scene of our abortive attack on Gruz earlier in the patrol. As we ran in we could see lots of smoke approaching. In due course a very puzzling picture was displayed through the cracked periscope. It turned out to be one tug with two lighters, and two others towing a dredger. We could not intercept them before they reached Kolocep Island. The tugs were armed and we had only fourteen rounds of H.E. left; they must now be covered by shore batteries. They were too small for a torpedo target except at point-blank range and we had been unable to get in close. Three armed ships covered by a shore battery gave too long odds for even *Safari* and it was an occasion where regretfully one had to allow that discretion was the better part of valor. The little convoy turned in for Gruz unmolested.

We cruised on down the coast, looking into Dubrovnik and Kotor harbors, both empty, before withdrawing for the night to charge. For once in a way, this our last night on patrol was undisturbed by even a single patrol craft and the next morning found us closing the cliffs in good time. We were going to spend our last day on the Dubrovnik-Kotor route.

At 09.00 we sighted smoke to the southward and ran in to attack. It was hard to see under the cliffs with the high-power periscope damaged, but we could make out two torpedo boats to seaward of a convoy of three ships. The torpedo boats were exceptionally well handled. Actually, although their A/S equipment was indifferent, the seamanship displayed by these torpedo boats on the Dalmatian coasts had throughout been of a high order. They were handy little shallow-draught craft, too shallow to torpedo. Presumably realizing that their A/S equipment was rudimentary, even by Italian standards, they used a method of physical obstruction which was extremely well thought out. These two were weaving about on and abaft the beam of their charges at considerable speed. I liked escorts to proceed in a traditional screen, dispersed in an arrowhead ahead of their charges. Then you could concentrate firstly on getting through the screen to find a clear position on the beam—and particularly just abaft it—to fire your torpedoes in comfort. There is nothing more demoralizing when firing torpedoes than to have an aggressive-looking escort pointing at you; it is apt to make you hurry your shot. The submarine would not be detected till after she had fired—a ship would be torpedoed before retribution could be dealt to the attacker—but the submarine, not unnaturally, was not keen on retribution at any time, before or after.

In this case the two torpedo boats were being handled as if submarine officers themselves were commanding them and a close attack would have been extremely difficult and chancy. However, I had a perfect plot of the convoy's advance up the coast and knew their course and speed so that a relatively long-range shot should hit. We fired our last three torpedoes at the leading ship from 2,000 yards; 500 yards outside the nearest escort. One minute, twenty-five seconds and one minute, thirty-seven seconds after firing we heard torpedoes go home.

We had not waited up to see the result. It had not been a very satisfactory attack; nothing much over 1,000 yards was as it meant relying rather a lot on the torpedoes; but it had worked. By the time the first depth charges came we were very deep and the attack, I noted in my patrol report, *was never dangerous*.

Three and a half hours later they gave up. There had

been one anxious moment when we had been forced to use the ballast pump to correct our trim and one of them had got a bit close, but otherwise we had not been unduly troubled.

That night as we surfaced and headed for home we could see searchlights and aircraft flares astern. The enemy was evidently laying on an intensive search. I felt that we had done what we had been told to do; the enemy A/S forces were well and truly stirred up. We put over our last dummy periscope. The messages had been carved onto this this one and Hitler was invited to share with Mussolini a discomfort which his meager proportions could never have accommodated.

Everyone was feeling pretty happy. We had four ships in the bag and, unlike most patrols, there had been hardly a dull moment. Of course we should have had another couple; the *Valentino Coda* had got away with it, and on her we had expended valuable torpedoes and ammunition; the consequent necessity to husband these had weighed heavily when letting that coaster get away off Promontore. And then Gruz had proved a bitter disappointment after all the planning and practicing to get out astern. But disappointments are necessary to appreciate one's little successes. The weather had been lovely and for me the navigation in beautiful scenery had been great fun, so much so that one was tempted sometimes to be unwise.

I remember particularly one fat and pompous Italian official, bedecked in blue and gold, being driven in a motor boat to an island. We examined him and his boat's crew through the periscope; it would have been such fun to bob up and pinch him and leave the motor boat's crew to tell the tale to the annoyance of the Italians and the pleasure of the Yugoslavs. But I managed to resist the temptation; it would have given us away and scared off any possible targets.

It had been amusing seeing all the Italian soldiers jumping into the sea as we shelled their transports. Torpedo attack was a rather serious business, only the C.O. could see what was going on, but at gun action more could join in and tell the tale in the mess afterwards. For it must be remembered that many of the crew on patrol, the engineers particularly, never saw the open air throughout; at best, they could only have a short breather on the bridge when their turn came, because only one person apart from the lookouts could ever be allowed there. You could not afford the delay whilst extra people got through the narrow conning-tower hatch when one had, as so frequently happened at night, to crash-dive to avoid a patrol.

The feeling of elation nearly proved our undoing and only luck and our routine zig-zag saved us. Going out through the Straits of Otranto there must have been some unconscious relaxation as we left confined waters. A U-boat spotted us and, unseen, attacked us.

She missed.

Maybe she had had the advantage of the light horizon, but it should not have happened. It was a lesson we did not forget—you could not afford to relax on patrol, from the moment of slipping to securing again. But it had been an enjoyable patrol, my most enjoyable; the opposition had been keen enough to be stimulating; and we had had luck at the end—you needed some luck to survive.

Two days after we had got back to Malta we were off again to intercept a convoy off Pantellaria and thirty-six hours later we had got another ship. Malta provided good hunting, if little food.

13

THE NORTH AFRICAN LANDINGS

The submarine contribution to the North African landings,
apart from the cloak-and-dagger operations landing agents
beforehand, was to cover the invasion in case the Italian
Fleet ventured out. I had by now spent a good deal of time
in patrolling on Thin Red Lines, Iron Rings, Dunkirk,
Malta convoys and so forth to intercept German and
Italian Fleets which did not materialize and I viewed the
prospect without enthusiasm. We were, with a number of
other boats of the Malta flotilla, strung out between Sicily
and Sardinia and, as usual, nothing came our way. However, P.46, later to be called *Unruffled*, a name which aptly
described her C.O. (Lieutenant Stevens, D.S.O., D.S.C.),
got in an attack on a new cruiser of the "Regolo" class.
She winged it and we looked on enviously at the clouds of
smoke over the horizon and listened, not so enviously, to
the depth-charging which was the inevitable sequel.

It was a Sunday and that evening as we were having
our Sunday Service in the control room, Paris, the Petty
Officer Telegraphist, brought me a signal from Shrimp
Simpson. It read: *Damaged enemy cruiser N.E. of Cape
St. Vito in tow with eight destroyers, six E-boats and
aircraft in company. P.44 close immediately. P.211* (Safari) *proceed to C. Gallo to intercept.*

In his covering report on these operations, Shrimp
said: *In two years of operating the Tenth Flotilla I must
remark that I have never felt more conscious of my
armchair directorate than in making this signal to P.211
and P.44. I had the advantage of knowing that both
Lieutenant Barlow (P.44) and Commander Bryant had
experience and a sense of humor.* It was a tremendous

198

screen for a single ship and there must have been nearly record odds against the submarine.

It was nice to be released from the boring patrol line, but the prospect of being mixed up with this party on the surface at night in inshore waters was a bit sobering. I reckoned that our interception could wait a few minutes whilst we finished the Service and maybe a little more fervor went into the prayers.

I dare say that many Services have been held in stranger places, but no one in *Safari* would have missed our little Sunday Service in the control room; the officer of the watch scanning round on the periscope, the planesmen controlling the depth, the helmsman his wheel, an occasional trimming order. One particular prayer—it is not to be found in any prayer book and I forget where I found it, though I believe it is called the Knight's Prayer—was particularly pugnacious and that we looked upon as our own. Everyone who could crowded into the control room, oil-stained and unshaven, and just outside the Roman Catholics, the only denomination who could not join in, would collect for the sermon. I regret to say that this was a bit secular; it covered what we had done the previous week, the mistakes we had made and what I intended doing the following week, together with any general information. On this occasion I read out Shrimp's signal, which was greeted with the usual imperturbability. We then surfaced and worked up to full power as we made for Cape Gallo near Palermo.

Sunday was reckoned a lucky day in *Safari*, we had once sighted a ship during the Service and had to break off to sink it, but on this occasion we never found the cruiser. It was before the days of radar as far as *Safari* and the Italians were concerned. Night work was just a matter of seeing without being seen and, as we closed Cape Gallo two hours later, we had to cut down our speed or the wake and bow wave would have given us away.

It was a dark night, it was hard to see under the cliffs, and we were coming in from seaward. We were very close to the first destroyer when we saw her and had to dive in a hurry. From 19.45 to 01.00 we were in amongst the screen, occasionally diving for a few minutes when one got too close, most of the time on the surface. First we had to work through them to get under the cliffs ourselves, thus being able to see better to seaward, hoping to find the cruiser on the way, but we were continually thwarted. The screen was weaving about, fourteen of them covered a good deal of sea, and we had constantly to take evasive action. For over five hours there were seldom less than two destroyers in sight. We did finally get through under the cliffs but we never found the cruiser.

It must be remembered that visibility on such a night even with excellent binoculars was not much over a mile under the cliffs; we were frequently within 600 yards of destroyers, our speed reduced to avoid wake; our target could have been anywhere within an area of about seventy-five square miles and every time we were forced to dive we lost distance. Surfacing again in such circumstances is not without interest; you could not range, you just judged from the propeller noises how far away your nearest opponent might be—and part of enemy hydrophone technique was to stop and listen; if they did that you could easily come up alongside one unless you kept tabs on everyone in the vicinity. The Asdic operators had a tremendous responsibility.

By 01.00 it became evident that the cruiser had made her escape to Palermo and even though her screen failed to see or detect us, they had served their purpose. We had had a very strenuous five hours. Had we allowed one of those destroyers to see us I should probably not be writing the story. Our eyes were nearly hanging out; failure is so often harder work than success.

It was a great relief not to be sent back on the patrol line; all our submarines were concentrated in the Central Mediterranean. The initial landings had been achieved but the reactions of the French in North Africa were still unknown; we were despatched to Susa, east of Tunis, to report the situation.

We threaded our way through the minefields of the Sicilian Channel, an area where the turtles which so closely resembled mines awash would collect and cause much unnecessary anxiety, and then made off on the surface for Susa. The French tricolor was still flying over the citadel as we closed submerged and there was no sign of activity; it was rather hard to know how to collect information.

An Italian auxiliary brigantine of some four hundred

tons, carrying stores to Rommel's army, blundered into our deliberations; and, in due course, down she went. We picked up a couple of chaps swimming in the water and went alongside a boat to deposit them; we demanded that "El Capitano" should come on board. The whole boatload immediately leapt aboard and eventually No. 1 picked out the captain; the enthusiasm of the rest to join us necessitated their being pushed back into the water.

We had given them time to take to their boats before opening fire, an old-fashioned courtesy seldom possible in these days of air patrols, and presumably they thought us nice chaps. In any case, the Sicilians had no enthusiasm for the war, the Germans by this time had made themselves far more unpopular than anyone else, and the little boatload gave us an enthusiastic send off as we left them to row into Susa. I thought the captain might give us some useful information. As he went down through the conning-tower hatch, Devlin, the navigator, noted some papers in his breast pocket and fished them out—they included the Italian recognition signals for the next week and also route orders and some very useful navigational data which we signalled back to Malta.

Our next orders were to move east with all despatch; a German petrol ship had been reported making for the battle front. The Eighth Army had won Alamein, but had not yet reched Benghazi. Our boats had kept Rommel woefully short of petrol—I believe that shortage of petrol had a significant effect upon the battles—and the Germans were seizing on our preoccupation with the Algiers landing to run in a ship.

Normally one would not have gone on the surface by day in these waters; but reckoning that everyone was fairly well occupied elsewhere, a homemade Italian Ensign fluttering bravely and armed with recognition signals, Chiefy Harris and his engine room were soon coaxing every possible revolution out of the diesels as we made off on the surface to the eastward.

On the second morning as dawn broke we were closing Ras Ali in the south-east corner of the Gulf of Sidra when we spotted a ship making away northward towards Benghazi. This was doubtless our quarry.

Our approach must have been reported by the numerous transport aircraft, the position checked against enemy submarine dispositions, and the ensign established as bogus. We set off in chase. We would have to work round ahead of her to get in an attack, keeping below her horizon, then dive and wait. It was an exciting chase; we were near the battle area, transport planes and landing craft were frequent and it could not be long before a Ju.88 was despatched to deal with us.

Ju. 88

We had to be satisfied with just keeping her mast heads above the horizon; occasionally her crow's nest would come clear, which meant that anyone in it could also see our bridge. She was pursuing a most erratic course and judging the alterations with just those two masts to go on was not easy. Every minute counted; at one time it would seem that we were doing nicely, then an alteration of course would throw it all out.

I learned later that the operations room at Malta was following all this from the German signals; the ship was of vital importance; loaded with cased petrol she not unnaturally had the wind up and was calling plaintively for help, but the Italian Fleet was elsewhere. By now she must have been receiving reports of our presence; we could not afford to waste time by diving for the innumerable transport aircraft.

At last, towards noon, just as we were working into our position to dive ahead, she turned right round.

For nearly two days the engine room had been doing virtually a full power trial and now all was set at nought. The A/S air patrols arrived; we could not continue the chase and were forced to dive. I reckoned that she would make back for Ras Ali, where there was a small stone landing pier on the desert beach. The North African desert shore is not a nice place to close at night; it is low and shallow for a long way to seaward so the soundings give you little help.

There was a moon that night, and choosing the time when it would be to the southward, and therefore helping us, we closed the coast. The water became too shallow to dive, but hidden against the sand dunes we found her. She was lying at rather an awkward angle and we had to creep rather close inshore to get a shot; she appeared to be surrounded by E-boats, small dark shapes in the moonlight, not nice things to encounter in water too shallow to dive. The sights came on, the torpedo fled the tube leaving a silver ribbon on the dappled waters.

We had to wait and see if it ran before retiring, but run true it did. Suddenly it was broad daylight. The ship went up in a sheet of flame, and here we were, right into the enemy shore in shallow water infested by E-boats, plain for all to see. The tail rattled as the helm went hard over when I called for emergency full speed. The boat turned sluggishly in the shallow water and we felt terribly naked in that brilliant illumination.

The anti-climax was that no one took the slightest notice of us, there was nothing to worry about; the "E-boats" were only landing craft. But for those who like fireworks, it was certainly a rousing sight.

I thought of our prisoner who had apparently become very depressed. He was living in the E.R.A.s' mess and spent all his days sleeping under the table; I thought a little fresh air and a pyrotechnic display, especially as he had no love for the Germans, might cheer him up. I asked him to come up as we headed for deeper water, but his depression was too deep to be relieved. It turned out that his trouble was constipation; there was a language difficulty but things can be conveyed by signs. This was well within my medical repertoire. I prescribed a "number nine"—popularly supposed, like faith, to move mountains. The depression continued. I prescribed two number nines. Then three. No relief; something that could not be cleared by three number nines was beyond my medical competence; the possible effect of building up number nines further was alarming. He must wait for proper medical attention when we got in; meanwhile he continued sleeping under the table.

When we got in he was sent up to the interrogation center and a couple of days later I met an officer who worked there and enquired after my friend. He said at first they could get no information out of him, he could only ask for a purge.

The doctors purged him and once more he came up for interrogation; as usual, they first asked him how he had been treated.

He said: "The Captain he was very kind to me; he treated me as one gentleman to another gentleman; he gave me these," and putting his hand in his waistcoat pocket produced the six number nines; he had kept them as curios.

Possibly he thought they were not meant to be eaten, except by horses.

The landing craft were to cause some amusement in the next couple of days. The bigger ones were called Siebel ferries and they had a formidable armament. Some carried a German 88mm. and all seemed to carry Bofors, quite a lethal weapon, even though smaller than our 3-inch (75mm.), and a quarter of a century later in design than that ancient model. Like us, the landing craft presented a low silhouette and were hard to hit; we had some stimulating exchanges of cannonry with them. Their automatic armament, fitted for use against attack by aircraft, used fixed fuses, which exploded at about 2,500 to 3,000 yards. One had to keep outside that. Between us and the landing craft would be a scintillating wall of balls of cotton wool, with the water boiling as the fuses exploded short. There was still some interest in their fire, as not all fuses explode to order.

We were not very clever with them; they could absorb quite a lot of our 3-inch and we had difficulty in hitting them at all. We were also short of ammunition, normally on such a patrol every nook and cranny, even the passageways, would be strewn with ammunition. But we had started this patrol to attack the Italian Fleet; loose ammunition is a hazard when you are being thrown about by a depth-charge attack and we had taken little beyond the designed stowage which, although it obeyed the explosive regulations, was otherwise inadequate. However, we did set a couple on fire, but what with their guns and A/S aircraft always turning up at an awkward moment it was not very satisfactory. They were too shallow draft to torpedo normally, but we did have a satisfying crack at them at Ras Ali pier the morning after getting the petrol ship. She had capsized and sunk; her hull still showed above water and from it came little spouts of flame all next day. The sea was also strewn with 50-gallon drums, floating awash so that they were difficult to see and a danger to the periscope.

In that shallow water and against a bottom of silver sand, a submarine would normally show up clearly to aircraft, but there was a nice chop on the water and we managed to get in to 4,500 yards before it became too shallow. Ras Ali pier was packed with landing craft; we fired a torpedo set very shallow to run over the shoals, it ran dead true to the pier and there followed a truly remarkable explosion; there must have been some ammunition lighters amongst them. When the explosion died down you could see lots of little black figures scurrying up the sand dunes. There had been a tank down by the pier but when the explosion died away it had gone. *Safari* claimed to be the only submarine which had torpedoed a tank on dry land.

We coasted along the shore looking for targets; it was amusing surveying a hostile army through the periscope; but infuriating that we could not do anything about it. It would have been a waste of ammunition to bombard with our little gun. El Agheila drew blank, but that evening we found a large three-masted schooner sheltering in El Brega. It was a narrow reef-ridden entrance, with a nasty quartering swell, and what landmarks there might be were hard to pick out in the moonlight. The first run in we nearly piled up on the rocks.

I see in my patrol report that I said: *By violent use of helm and screw, holding my breath, trunk twisting and wrenching at the bridge, and other well-known devices for reducing turning circles we got out to sea for another run.*

Golfers who have tried to correct a ball slicing out of bounds by facial contortions will appreciate the technique. However, all was well and on the second run in our torpedo did its stuff. But we were running short of fuel, nearly all our ammunition was expended and we had to turn for Malta. Pausing to sink a light float which someone had placed off Ras Ali to guide in landing craft, we decided to have another shot at torpedoing landing craft. We bumped along the shoals at periscope depth striving to get close in to the beach, but the weather had blown up, and although we fired a torpedo at one, it could not compete with the sea when set shallow. We had plenty of torpedoes left, but it was obvious that they were useless in the circumstances.

As we coasted along, the ruins of Roman civilization contrasting with German fighter aircraft, we looked hopefully for a receptacle for our last rounds of ammunition. A tank landing craft towing a lighter provided the opportunity, but a Ju. 88 on A/S patrol—air patrols were by now regular—prevented us engaging at the most favorable moment. The Ju. 88 passed on and up we came. She had a better gun than us and shot quite well, I noted several shots within fifty yards of us. We managed to start a small fire on board her before we ran out of ammunition and so we pushed on back to Malta.

We had steamed 2,800 miles; our bag was not very big, though varied, but some 5,000 tons of petrol and a lot of other stores would not reach Rommel's army.

14

ROUGH SHOOTING ON THE DESERT SHORE

Malta was relieved soon after Operation Torch, the landings in North Africa, but it was to be some time before she ceased to be on short commons. *Maidstone* and the Eighth Flotilla moved to Algiers after the First Army and the Americans were established, though the Germans were still far from giving up the struggle in North Africa. While Rommel's Afrika Korps retreated from the east through Cyrenaica and Tripoli towards Tunisia, with the Eighth Army in hot pursuit, the Germans threw everything they could muster into Tunisia to hold back the First Army and the Americans pressing in from the west. The job of our submarines was to disrupt the supplies to the retreating Rommel in the east and to the forces the Axis were building up in Tunisia on the west of the battle front. A lot of these supplies came by air and on patrol one would see a constant stream of transport planes and gliders, but they were still attempting to get things through by sea. For some reason our submarines struck a bad patch soon after the landings in Algeria and, though they were sinking ships, somehow there were far too many misses. The German losses on the run from Italy to Tunisia were nothing like as heavy as previous form had suggested they would be.

Safari remained at Malta for a time and boats from the First Flotilla, based on Beirut in the Levant, came to back up the Malta flotilla as the scene of operations moved west. These reinforcements were very welcome, and particularly the bottled amenities of life they were able to

bring with them. With events moving fast the Central
Mediterranean ceased to be the private hunting ground of
our submarines. Surface ships started to arrive and join in
the hunt, staffs started building up and the ether became
correspondingly saturated with signals. Whereas staff officers spend much of their time making signals, other staff
officers are detailed to cut signalling down; one of their
techniques is to monitor signal traffic. They intercept
signals on the various wavelengths, decipher them, pick
out the ones which do not seem really necessary and the
Command then administers reproof to the offending originators.

Turbulent was joining Malta from Beirut and Simpson sent her a signal giving her the route. One had to make
submarines on passage travel to a definite schedule on a
definite route, so that there would not be unfortunate
encounters with friendly forces, over the sea, on the sea
and under the sea.

Having given a series of positions and times he ended
up: *and bring plenty of booze so we can have a good
time.*

This signal happened to be monitored and Shrimp
was taxed by the Flag Officer with frivolous use of the
ether.

Far from being abashed he stood his ground and said,
more or less: "Sir, I would have you know that in all the
time I have commanded the Tenth Submarine Flotilla,
never have I known anything like the disastrous series of
misses that have occurred during this last month. This has
coincided with the Lazaretto's supply of refreshment being
completely exhausted. The two matters are not disconnected. I consider that anything to relieve the staleness of
my overstrained C.O.s is a matter of the most vital
importance."

Of course the relations, as always in the Royal Navy,
between the Flag Officer and one of his Captains were of
the most cordial. But there was more than good-humored
badinage in this statement. Malta at the end of the siege
was dreary; men who are subjected to considerable strain
do not readily relax and regain their resilience when all is
dull and depressing; they go stale. A stale C.O. would be
that second or so slower, the second or so that makes the
difference between success and failure. Submariners do not

drink at sea, except possibly a tot a day; if a C.O. drank heavily in harbor it was usually a sign that his nerve was going. I do not claim that alcohol was necessary for all in harbor; I personally used to go virtually teetotal and stop smoking for thirty-six hours before going on patrol to make sure my night vision and reactions were keen. But most of us needed something to help us unwind when we came in from sea. Alcohol could serve that purpose; so could other things, but they were neither available, nor easily transportable and accommodated.

The air raids died away. For some time our mounting force of Spitfires had made the enemy decide that bombers were unprofitable and the raids had been conducted by fighter bombers. One was apt to meet these as one entered or left by the swept channel, or rather the skimmed channel, for resources still did not enable us to do a thorough sweep and it was unsafe to dive. We were shot up on leaving the breakwater as we left for one patrol; no damage was done but our escorting minesweeper bagged one of our assailants. As we rounded the east end of the island I saw a fighter coming low at us from under the cliffs. Austin, the signalman, remained up with me to man our two .303 Vickers machine guns, the only anti-aircraft armament we possessed and not very lethal weapons, but even so I should have got this one. She came low, pouring out cannon fire, luckily badly aimed, and as she swept across our tail, only a few yards away, I gave her a burst of .303. You could not miss at that range and I stopped to watch her fall; it was sheer stupidity—I should have emptied the pan. A few rounds of .303 were not enough and, wobbling a bit, off she went. She did not try another run.

We spent Christmas 1942 on patrol in the Gulf of Hammamet, the third Christmas I had spent on patrol. We had taken a Special Boat Party—brave men who used to land from submarines in collapsible canoes, and even return in them sometimes. The mission was to blow up the railway close to the west of Hammamet. We only had a couple of nights before the moon rendered the operation impossible and as it happened the weather was unsuitable for canoeing on both.

This was just as well, for unbeknownst to us the Cs.-in-C. in Algeria and the Middle East were conducting a lively discussion by signal as to whether the railway should be blown up or not. It might come in handy for Monty and his Eighth Army when they got that far.

And so we settled down to interrupt Rommel's sea supplies. He was being kept short, few steamers of any size could risk the run to the east. *Safari* had got one out of the last major convoy which attempted to run to Tripoli, and I believe the last sizeable petrol ship to try and deliver direct to the desert shore. It was mostly small stuff now, though we did sight a sizeable ship hull-down the second day out, but we were unable to get within range. Her air escort kept us down so that we could not use our surface speed.

As she disappeared over the horizon towards Suza we sighted and heard a large explosion in her direction, and thought that she had probably been mined. We had not long to wait for something else, in fact two targets arrived at once from different directions, so as to cross close to where we lay in wait about three miles off the little town of Hammamet. Northbound came a very shabby tug, escorted by an equally shabby minesweeping-trawler, and southbound a heavily-laden auxiliary schooner. The northbound ships were on their way home so I decided to take the outward-bound schooner first. Soon after the tug and trawler had passed we surfaced and opened fire on the schooner. It only took a few rounds to touch off her cargo of petrol and her crew had barely time to get clear in their boat. The minesweeping-trawler turned back very sportingly to give battle and I had visions of getting the lot.

However, I knew that there was a torpedo boat just over the horizon; and the Ju. 88 which had been patrolling to seaward of us, no doubt attracted by the smoke and flames, now turned in to close. There was nothing for it but to dive and retire, which was to prove a wise precaution for two torpedo boats arrived very promptly to hunt us and deeper water was welcome.

We got a signal from our motherly S.10 that evening telling us to keep at least twenty miles off shore. His bush telegraph had told him that they were laying on a hunt. Our Captain (S) always kept us marvellously informed of such things and, looking back, perhaps we were not as appreciative as we should have been. Usually one knew very well about the hunt, which you yourselves had stimulated, and like a child reckoned that you could look after yourself without being fussed over. I had not yet learnt, as I was to do when I became a Captain (S) myself, how anxious he felt for his children. One always felt that where the heat was laid on, there you would find a target; or at least if one withdrew, a magnificent target was bound to come along where you had been. In this case it was to be another day before we got back on the job as we were sent off on one of those chores which fell to the submarines— to search the seas off Pantellaria, where a luckless aviator had come down and might be in his dinghy.

We returned to the coast on a day of blinding rain squalls and we sighted a ship in one of them, though we were unable to make out what it was as we ran in to attack. Fortunately the rain lifted conveniently to reveal a small tanker and we were soon on the surface engaging her. We had only scored six hits when the Ju. 88 on its tramline patrol some four miles to seaward of us, came along. I did not think it would see us against the sand dunes inshore, but it meant ceasing fire till it was past; I sent the gun's crew down in case we had to dive in a hurry. It was an interesting couple of minutes. After it had gone we re-opened fire on the tanker and she drifted aground, where we filled her full of holes. A new gunlayer had joined the boat and I was anxious to see his work. Not only had he been trained, but he was a natural shot. Thenceforth *Safari*'s performance, and my confidence in giving battle to armed adversaries, increased enormously. His predecessors had been splendid men and had accounted for quite a lot of shipping, but training makes a world of difference.

The following day we had to consider whether to engage a novel target; strung out along the shore came a long camel caravan; it seemed that poor Rommel must indeed be hard pressed for transport. It would have been extremely distasteful to shoot up animals and, although such squeamishness is misplaced in war, a muster of our ammunition reserves established that we could not afford to expend shells on such a meager target. However, we were being accorded considerable honor by the opposition and no less than five torpedo boats collected in the area. If only non-contact pistols could have been made to work we could have retaliated, but as it was they could harass us unscathed and we sneaked away to the Hammamet area.

Light was failing the next evening when, after a blank

day, a small ship was sighted approaching from the north. As we closed submerged, periscope visibility shut down before I could make out exactly what she was, except that she was a naval vessel. We surfaced and followed her around, keeping her silhouette against the glow of the setting sun to the westward. With so many torpedo boats in the neighborhood we wanted to make a quick job of it. We were able to close to 500 yards on her starboard quarter unobserved before we opened fire. Shells were raining into her before she could man her guns. A boat left almost immediately and as men started jumping overboard we ceased fire. But not for long; some of her crew stuck by their ship and I could see men manning the for'ard gun. They quickly desisted and jumped overboard as we re-opened fire, our new binocular sights proving their worth.

She was a stout vessel and refused to either catch fire or sink; after we had expended forty-one rounds we ceased fire. She was a shambles and there was nothing more to fear from her guns. She proved to be one of the Italians' latest magnetic minesweepers with a crew of twenty-four and carrying fifteen service passengers in addition. Many of these were now in the water, and although Hammamet was only a couple of miles away it was a long way to swim. Whilst the lookouts strained their eyes through binoculars for the patrols which would not be long in arriving, we started picking them up in the glassy calm, pitch-black night, pausing in the operation to ease a torpedo into the derelict to hasten her end. She disappeared in a welter of debris. We turned northward to make our getaway on the surface.

They were an oddly assorted lot, our prisoners; four wounded, two seriously, but with one thing in common, a bitter hatred of the Herrenvolk. They said that the Germans had told them that it was better to shoot yourself than fall into the hands of the brutal British, and some, indeed, half expected to be shot.

I asked the captain, a Lieutenant of the Naval Reserve, when he thought this rather stupid war for Italy would be over.

He replied: "For me today—for Italy tomorrow."

Ronnie Ward, our No. 1, had frisked an automatic off him. It was a small Beretta and I asked him what was the

Beretta .380 Mod. 1934

use of such a little thing. As far as I could gather it was issued so that he could encourage his crew.

I then went along to see the wounded, who were in the after end and under the care of the Chief Stoker. One man had a hole in his thigh where a 3-inch shell had gone through taking out a large bite of flesh. How he had managed to clamber up the casing and get through the conning-tower hatch with that great wound has always defeated me. Someone had already got on a most seamanlike tourniquet with a length of 2-inch hemp and a large spanner. I suggested that it might be unnecessarily powerful and possibly a somewhat gentler application might assist circulation to the lower leg. He looked at his handywork doubtfully.

"At any rate, it has stopped him making a bloody mess of my deck," he said.

The party included army gunners, electricians, motor mechanics and seamen. During the garrulous period which always follows rescue, we got a lot of information about Italian magnetic-minesweeping technique which may have been useful in due course to our mining experts. But they were too many for our hospitality and we set sail for Malta to dispose of them; I was not certain if they would be welcome because, although Malta had been relieved, there was little shipping space to spare, and not a great deal of food.

We got in the next afternoon, fuelled and ammunitioned, and were away again by the evening. *Turbulent* had arrived and it was grand to meet Tubby Linton again, my fellow old stager of the Mediterranean submarines and a friend since our cadet days. He had brought the booze and a whisky and soda was something I had only dreamt of for some time.

Christmas Day found us off the Tripoli coast, but shipping seemed to be observing the holiday. The railway runs close along the coast here, we could see the smoke of an occasional train above the sand dunes. We sought to relieve the tedium by a little train strafing, which was a popular sport with some C.O.s. Personally I regarded it as a rather extravagant way of expending precious ammunition; it would need an awful lot of ammunition to really destroy a train and a small schooner would carry far more stores than a goods train.

Along the coast of Italy the railways often run very close to the shore, dodging in and out of tunnels through the cliffs, and the classical way of dealing with them was to send a canoe at night, with a Special Boat Party. They would place their demolition charges just inside a tunnel, so that the engine would blow up in the tunnel and block the railway for some time. The Italians reacted unfavorably, sentries were placed all along the beaches by the railways and the Special Boat Parties became a one-way traffic; we had more or less to give it up. The amount of manpower held down guarding the Italian railways must, however, have been terrific.

The submarines then shelled trains and bridges, but though they achieved some success, a small-caliber shell does very little damage to masonry; I reckoned it was too unprofitable and preferred to keep my ammunition for ships.

However, this particular patrol we had taken in a very large supply at Malta; you had to walk on ammunition in the gangways, and it would have improved comfort to expend some. Going out on patrol, the gangways were paved with cases of tinned food and stores, reducing what head room there was, so it became progressively more comfortable as you ate your way through the paving of the gangways.

But in spite of strenuous efforts, we just could not find a place where the railway was not protected by sand dunes and it proved a very frustrating Christmas Day, though the wiry pork which represented the finale of the Lazaretto pig farm was very much appreciated.

Boxing Day* was no more satisfactory, in fact rather less, for although no targets came into sight, five E-boats put in an appearance and harassed us considerably. There is little future for a submarine on inshore patrol at night in moonlight with a number of E-boats about; they can see you as well as you can see them, and we were driven off shore.

We were back again before dawn and intercepted a petrol schooner of useful size. Four hits and she went up in a spectacular blaze which, strangely enough, two fighters passing high overhead failed to notice and left us undisturbed. We started to pick up some survivors, but the air escort, which had been ranging ahead, appeared after we had only picked up a couple and we had to dive and get clear. These two appeared even more certain than their predecessors that they would be shot. It was obvious that the Germans, not without reason, were beginning to have doubts about the enthusiasm of their Italian allies and were stimulating them with tales of horror about what the British would do to them. Once reassured they worked well and happily in the boat and were to be christened in due course, like all true submariners, by being bombed by their own side.

The most versatile survivor to be picked up out of the water by one of our submarines was a certain "Willie Wop," a pilot in the German Air Force. Having come down in the sea he was picked up by an Italian ship, homeward bound. That night his new transport, which carried a couple of sizeable guns, met up with John Bromake in *Sahib*, who put it down in the best style. They were so taken by surprise that they fired the only gun they got into action on the disengaged side.

Amongst the survivors to be picked up by *Sahib* was

*The first week-day after Christmas.

Willie Wop, who thus in twenty-four hours had travelled
by air, by surface ship and by submarine, with a couple of
bouts of swimming thrown in. The German air-transport
timetable he carried had also survived the wetting and it
was passed to the R.A.F., whose fighters were able to keep
some very profitable assignations with the German air-
transport fleet before they changed their route and timetable.

The Christmas holiday being over, things started
moving again and along came an armed yacht, doubtless
having been despatched with the unenviable task of dealing with us, apparently without the help of an air escort.
We were on the point of surfacing to give battle when her
air escort arrived in the nick of time and we had to take a
less martial attitude to the situation. The trouble with these
auxiliary A/S vessels was that they were practically impossible to torpedo; as long as we were submerged they were
fully capable of destroying us and we had no alternative
but to creep away.

At noon we received a signal ordering us to intercept
a steamer which should pass some ten miles to seaward of
us and off we set submerged and full of hope. The steamer
failed to arrive and it was infuriating to see the masts of a
large three-masted schooner passing hull down inshore of
us near the billet we had just left. She was obviously bound
for Tripoli and when, in the first dog watch, it became
evident that our steamer had gone elsewhere we surfaced
and set off at full speed to try and intercept her before she
got there.

There was a quite a bit of cloud about, not pleasant
for surface work in these waters, and before long the
inevitable happened. A Caproni came out of a cloud and
spotted us before we could get under. We were well clear
before her depth charges came down, but it was a couple
of hours before she moved off and we could continue the
chase.

Our rather ambitious program soon had to be altered;
we were evidently getting unpopular and a large-scale
search was laid on which we ran straight into.

Once again we found ourselves the hunted.

It was dark by now and we were close inshore again;
we could see the glowing exhausts of low-flying aircraft
and they were signalling to the surface ships who had

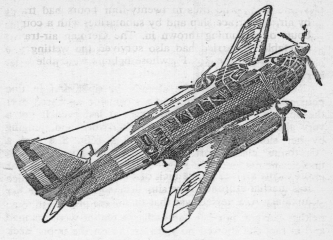

Caproni 314

come to join in. What made it more troublesome was that they kept firing flares which lit up the sea like starshell, though doubtless the illumination looked far more effective to us than it actually was.

We had used up a lot of battery that day in running out to the reported steamer and once we dived it would have been difficult to come up again, for it was close to moonrise. I did not fancy being kept down all night and facing the next day with a flat battery. The thing was to get clear of the coast so as to have some sea room before the moon came up.

We ran dead slow on the diesels, to avoid the telltale wash, and nosed our way seawards. Luckily the signalling told us where the surface ships were, but each time the glowing exhausts of an aircraft came near there was the nasty suspicion that she would drop a flare and show us in our nakedness. It was an anxious hour, but as the moon rose the hunt started to drop astern, we could crack on speed, and an hour later we were charging happily. The battery was well up before an aircraft, making a wide cast, put us down for a bit in the middle watch.

As dawn broke we were closing the little port of Zuara, with considerable anticipation as there was smoke inshore. It was reasonable to suppose after the night's activity that there would be some shipping moving. This smoke turned out to be an escort vessel and, inshore of her, a homeward-bound schooner with an air escort. They obviously were not taking any chances and we had to let her go.

But more smoke was already in sight and in due course the masts and funnel of a steamship appeared over the horizon. It was a torpedo target at last even if not a very glamorous one. She was weather-worn and, judging by her slow progress, in need of a refit. She had a "Crotonne" class escort vessel which circled us in a most unpleasant manner at a range of about 300 yards. I was able to take a good look at this escort, as there was a nice ripple on the water, and I was relieved to see that her circling in our bit of the ocean was quite fortuitous; neither her gun nor her depth-charge chutes were manned and in fact she showed no signs of life on the upper deck at all except on her bridge. Nevertheless, it was prudent to suppose that her detecting gear was manned and our advance was delayed.

Her charge was zigging strenuously inshore of her and there was no chance of attacking on the landward side, as she was keeping close in to the shoals. In due course the "Crotonne" went on her way, but she had delayed the attack, and before we could press it home our target did a smart alteration to port and went into Zuara. Her escort did not go in immediately and patrolled up and down off the port. Conditions were favorable for a torpedo to run at shallow depth and I proceeded to try and torpedo her.

In the perisher days, when your confrères wanted to reduce you to a state of exhausted frustration, they would devise an attack on an escort vessel beating up and down on patrol. It had always been my ambition to bring off such an attack in action, and though by now I should have been wiser, once again I started the frustrating business.

Everyone got hotter and hotter, but whenever things seemed to be going well she would make a large alteration of course and we would have to start all over again.

At last it looked as if we were going to make it; she stopped and I could see her officer of the watch on the bridge resting his burning forehead on the binnacle, the most wonderful picture of a hangover.

Slowly *Safari* swung to bring her sights to bear. We had been pointing astern of her.

With thirty degrees to go, the captain came on the bridge, the officer of the watch sharply raised his head, a swirl of water appeared under her stern, she got under way and went into Zuara.

There was nothing for it but to wait till her charge came out again and for the rest of the day we shared the approaches to Zuara with two aircraft, who were joined by a couple of E-boats. We found it prudent to withdraw a bit.

Towards evening much smoke and aircraft activity over Zuara indicated that our friend was leaving and proceeding westward. A moonlight night in shoal water, and a target with surface and air escort, did not recommend a night surface attack; I decided to shadow her through the night and dive ahead of her at dawn.

Accordingly we worked ahead of her and through the night endeavored to keep her in sight. We lost her passing Jerba Island, but in the morning watch found her again and at daybreak dived ahead of her. We could not see her through the periscope at first and it was forty anxious minutes before we picked her up.

I was getting very puzzled and anxious for she should have arrived, but nothing appeared on the expected bearing. It became obvious that something must have happened to her. It was quite light before I found her again; she had done a very large alteration away, leaving us very broad, and it was obvious that we should have to get a move on if we were going to intercept her.

This was no time to husband the battery and we spent the next hour and half going flat out on an intercepting course. The "Crotonne" escort, with which we had been playing games the day before, for some reason now turned back and we were left with only a screen of four E-boats and two Ju. 88 aircraft to compete with.

In my endeavor to press in, I may have underestimated the E-boats and used rather too high a speed too close in to them. All was going well and we were by now in an ideal position; we were inside the two E-boats on my side of her and only had to wait for her to steam about three quarters of a mile to get a copy-book shot at six hundred yards.

Suddenly our target appeared to smell a rat and did a very large alteration of course away. Our only hope was to swing rapidly and fire a long-range shot from her quarter. We knew her speed exactly, we had been plotting it all night, but I had little confidence of a successful attack when I sent the torpedoes off to run 4,000 yards to catch her up on her quarter. Furthermore, a Ju. 88 was passing as we fired and, before we could clear the tracks, she put down a stick of depth charges which broke some lights and shook us up quite a bit.

I felt fairly sure that she would warn our target so that she could avoid the topedoes, which would take three minutes to arrive. However, it appeared that our friend was too busy trying to sink us to warn his charge; much to my surprise we heard an explosion, as of a torpedo hitting, at the end of the correct running time. It might have been a depth charge dropped at random, and twenty minutes later we ventured up from the depths to survey the situation. It was most satisfying to see our steamer stopped and down by the stern. As I watched, her bows reared up till they were above her funnel and she slid under by the stern. It had been a very lucky shot, but I think well earned. We had started to attack her twenty-seven and a half hours before; it was the longest attack I ever did.

Now it was time to return, and the following morning we slid into Lazaretto Creek and secured alongside. Measured in tons our bag of five assorted vessels had been small, but one could not assess the value of such a patrol in tons sunk. For two or three days, until they had collected a sizeable antisubmarine force, communications were stopped. The enemy had expended a lot of fuel and effort in chasing us, they had been forced to give even a single schooner a surface and air escort, and quite a bit of Rommel's petrol had gone up in smoke.

When we got in I was told that we were to start for Algiers, to rejoin our proper flotilla in three days' time. This was greeted with enthusiasm; tales of the flesh-pots of Algiers had already reached us. I fell-in the ship's company and, since Malta was no longer dry, suggested that the port watch should have a bender that night, the starboard watch the following night, but the third night I wanted everyone to be on the wagon as we were sailing the following day. That routine was faithfully observed. We threw a farewell party in the wardroom of *Safari* the first evening in. It went on for a long time and when it was over I realized that walking back to shore across the narrow planks connecting the submarines was going to be a delicate business. Falling off a plank is no joke; people have been badly injured, even killed, by so doing. I asked the duty watch to put on an extra man rope and meanwhile stayed down a bit gossiping to the one remaining guest. In due course, it was reported that all was now ready to essay the crossing. I climbed up the fore hatch to find that the duty watch had rated my chances of walking the plank even lower than I had and an absolute network of heaving lines had been rigged on both sides of the plank. Solemnly and slowly, fixing a window of the Lazaretto with a glassy eye, I made the passage under the sympathetic gaze of the riggers. Looking back, this was a most regrettable occurrence by all the standards of discipline; but in a submarine in war discipline was not of the textbook variety; we knew each other too well.

I had enjoyed being at Malta, or at least, operating from Malta; but I left with no real regret. By now I was so much older than my brother submariners—there is a big gap between the early twenties and the middle thirties—and the little flotilla staff were all too busy to be much company. It was lonely in harbor for a relic of an earlier generation of C.O.s and I was tired of walking by myself across the fields and terraces of Malta. I used to look forward to going on patrol to relieve the boredom.

On the 2nd January, 1943, we bid farewell to the Tenth Submarine Flotilla with pleasant anticipation. It had been an honor to serve in it, if only as a lodger. As I said goodbye to Shrimp I noticed how grey his hair had gone since he had been our Commander (S) in the old *Cyclops* at Harwich three years before. On him had fallen most of the strain.

15

ALGIERS

We got a signal from S.8 as we closed Algiers saying that Captain (S) would meet us off the breakwater in his car. Sure enough, as we swung round the breakwater head, there was Barney in a water-jeep. Jeeps, let alone amphibious ones, were a complete novelty to us. Transport in Malta had been limited. At the Lazaretto we had had a very small motorcycle for running emergency messages to the dockyard. This was rather more luxurious transport than Lord Gort's; the Governor rode around the island on a push-bike, much to the distress of his staff, some of whom lacked his athletic zeal and figure.

Gort not only set the example of Spartan transport, but also Spartan living. Those who, on being bidden to a meal, imagined that rationing for the Governor would be eased, were due for a disppointment, particularly as the Palace could scarcely patronize the black market. I remember talking to a lady the day after she had been to dinner with the Governor. She was bitterly regretting that she had refused a second helping of minestrone soup; she had not realized that it was not only the first but the only course on the menu.

Having so recently taken considerable interest in such simple fare as a slice of toast, Algiers was indeed a wonderland and Barney's amphibious jeep the first wonder. It was good to see his smiling, welcoming face again. Suddenly the smile shut off; the jeep abruptly turned for the shore getting lower and lower in the water. It only just made it before it decided to become a submersible; the bilge pump had failed.

The Eighth Flotilla had done most of the landing and

taking off of agents before the North African landings and as a mark of appreciation the American General Mark Clark had presented the flotilla with a couple of jeeps complete with drivers, named Jo and Bo. Their main duty was to restore the morale of jaded submariners by taking them around the local countryside. Jo and Bo should have been able to write a very comprehensive drinking guide to Algeria.

Amphibian Jeep

Barney had apparently reckoned that my morale would need some boosting and I found that not only was there champagne laid on, when I went down to his cabin to report, but he had collected some young women. They had jobs in the Ike Eisenhower personal organization; two had been his drivers during the planning stage in London and all had moved on out to Algiers with the boss, having their transport sunk under them on the way.

Actually the champagne was no particular achievement; at that time it cost about half-a-crown for a bottle of the orthodox shape, with the orthodox cork and tinsel.

It was sweet but pleasant. The young women were, however, no mean achievement; they were in very short supply and the demand was unlimited, with two armies and corresponding naval and air forces collected round. But *Maidstone* had one thing to offer which was still practically unobtainable in Algiers and that was a civilized hot bath. However short the supply, there were always young women available for the parties given in H.M.S. *Maidstone*.

I particularly remember one party given in Barney's cabin. Our host had to depart, as captain of the ship, to deal with an air raid which was taking place. It must be realized that to the submariners the depot ship was just a hotel and service station; their responsibility was in their submarines. The fact that the depot ship, which had quite a heavy anti-aircraft armament, might be in action during an air raid was no concern of the submariners. There was, therefore, no need to break up the party and the vibration and roar of the guns and bombs merely added local color. However, it was not safe to go outside till all was over what with all the falling debris, and the breaking up of this party was delayed. Amongst those present was one of Ike's drivers, who had fetched a new car for the personal use of the great man from Oran earlier that day and had parked it down by the quay.

On this particular raid the Axis had tried out a new form of circling torpedo, dropped by the aircraft in the harbor, the idea being that it would circle around until it found something to explode against; it was hoped a ship. One of these had ended its wanderings against the quay immediately under Ike's new car, which ceased to be of practical value. When the raid was over, Kay had to report to the Supremo that the new car was a casualty and that she and others had been drinking in the *Maidstone* when it happened; it was unfortunate that our C.-in-C., Admiral Cunningham, was present. I suppose that if *Maidstone* had been hit whilst a party was in progress it would have looked in the press as if we were not taking the war seriously. Such parties were banned in future.

Soon after our arrival I was bidden to lunch with the C.-in-C. His reputation in the Mediterranean was legendary; as far as I could gather from the locals the French regarded him, as history may well do later, as a second

Nelson. When in 1940 Britain looked to all Europe like a busted flush and it appeared only a matter of time before Mussolini's much-vaunted fleet, linked with the German Air Force, drove the Royal Navy from the Mediterranean, A.B.C. took the offensive and had kept it up. Now the tide had turned. He was a man with an incredible memory; he knew the name and idiosyncrasies of one and all of his C.O.s, however humble, apparently carried in his head the position and mission of every ship of his fleet. He managed with, by modern standards, an extraordinarily small, but highly efficient, staff. It was the perfect arrangement from the point of view of the fighting ships; in my experience large staffs only lead to confusion.

I always remember one piece of advice he gave me on this, the first of several occasions, when I lunched with him. He had asked me what I thought of the Americans and I was obviously searching for a suitable answer. At this time the Americans in North Africa were a very unseasoned lot compared with the magnificent fighting men they had in the Pacific. They were finding, judging by results, that it took a great deal more than magnificent equipment to compete with the Germans. In view of their indifferent showing many of us found their accounts of their own achievements not only difficult to believe, but in most indifferent taste.

A.B.C. must have read my thoughts for, before I replied, he said: "Just because they speak, more or less, our language you must not judge them by our standards. You must remember that you have far more in common with the Italian and the Greek; the Americans are a different civilization."

It was quite true; it was because the tale in the bar was being told in English that it seemed in such sorry taste. Their senior officers suffered no such illusions; every failure was ruthlessly analyzed and whereas it was true that everything seemed to have to be learnt the hard way, regardless of expense, the lessons were grasped. They learnt quickly, with no sentiment for the love of yesterday; they learnt quicker than we did.

As the weeks went by you would occasionally see men of the Eighth Army in Algiers. They were unmistakable. Lean and hard, their complexion a sort of transparent bronze, they carried themselves with the unconscious confidence that became a member of what was probably the finest fighting-army of the war, on either side. It always gave me a thrill to see one of them.

8-cyl. Bugatti

When I was in from sea, Barney used to provide me with an 8-cyclinder Bugatti which had been commandeered from somewhere; it had seen better days, but it was great fun. In that I would range far and wide, dining and wining, and life in harbor became fun again. By this time I, and undoubtedly lots of others, had developed two distinct personalities; the one suited to life on patrol, the other to the routine of civilized existence.

To the former, days were twenty-four hours long, routine revolved round the charging cycle of the submarine battery. Sleep was a thing to be taken whenever minutes could be spared. Even if you did not feel like sleep you would take some in case of need. You liked to keep yourself topped up with sleep for you never knew when you were going to get the next chance. And all the time on patrol, waking or sleeping, you were subconsciously listening. The ward-room was next to the control room, there was no door, and when in your bunk you could hear everything that went on in that nerve center; beyond the control room was the engine room, so that you could hear the diesels when running on the surface.

One slept a deep dreamless sleep when all the noise was normal, but the slightest change in the beat of the diesels, some out-of-routine order down in the voice pipe from the bridge, and you were wide awake in a trice. I used to wear very short sea boots, the only things I ever took off to turn in, and I would leave them beside the bunk. As I swung my legs out they would drop straight into the sea boots and one could start for the conning-tower ladder in one movement. Somehow one was half-way up that ladder before the message came from the officer of the watch calling you to the bridge. It could have been telepathy, or it could have been some change in the routine noises.

Every hour of the twenty-four was planned and except when on passage there was always something to think about. One read a lot when things were quiet. I used to take a mixed bag of books on patrol, a selection of thrillers, one or two books about fishing and one or two historical books. But I never gave them more than half my attention; at the finish of the book I probably would not remember its name or what it was about. I even found as time went on that I had become a non-smoker on patrol. One could not smoke when diving and even after surfacing at night I was usually too occupied to smoke for some time. Normally I was a moderately heavy pipe smoker and at one time I used to look forward to that time of the day when I could smoke. By this stage of my submarine career, however, I had ceased to want to smoke at sea. I was getting old for the game, my night vision was not so good as a younger man's and I cut smoking to improve it. And yet in harbor my other self would crave tobacco. As I crossed the plank on return from patrol, I would start fumbling for a pipe and tobacco to which I had not given a thought for many days. The dangerous time, I always reckoned, for a submarine's crew was the first twenty-four hours of patrol before everyone had changed over to their keyed up submarine selves. Luckily you were unlikely to run into trouble the first day out.

I think most people used to avoid the flesh-pots for the last day or two before sailing; I suspect that many, like myself, did not feel very settled and happy for that last day. I would not even take salt at breakfast before sailing, in case I upset it—bad joss. It was a relief to get out to sea, for then everything settled into routine and you were occupied and happy. I did three and a half years in command at sea, with a short break to stand by *Safari* whilst she was being completed, and I believe I did considerably more patrols in command than any other C.O.

A great deal of attention was given to studying the C.O. and how he was standing up to it. At Malta, Simpson worked the routine with some of his boats, when things were tough, of standing down the C.O. for a patrol to rest him and sending the boat with a relief C.O.—a routine I would not have accepted myself.

But no one found it necessary to give any of the crew a spell. Late in the war, when I was captain of a flotilla in the Pacific, I would go through the crew with a C.O. when a boat had notched up a score which qualified for decorations. Scattered amongst these crews, not many of them, for our losses had been too great, were men who had been right through the war in submarines on patrol. Usually you would find that for some reason they had left one or more submarines shortly before they were lost. Such men had sought no advancement, so they were not withdrawn for courses or for training others; usually fortune had not drafted them to glamour boats where decorations were strewn around. They had gone on, year after year, never seeking a safer billet, which they would have been given, if they had wanted it; some even deliberately avoided advancement so that they could serve on in submarines.

The Americans, who strewed medals around generally, did produce a submarine decoration which I think we might well have copied. The Admiralty were generous to the boats that sank things, starting with the C.O., and the submarine service was a much decorated one. But for most of the crew of a submarine it was just the luck of the draw whether they arrived in a glamour boat; the devotion of all was the same, whatever the boat, and the risks they ran were the same.

I said I was getting old; at 37 Tubby Linton and I were a dozen years older than many of the Mediterranean C.O.s of this time and it so happened that *Turbulent* and *Safari* were in Algiers together before his last patrol. We discussed our senility—we would not have admitted it to anyone else—and confessed to each other that maybe we were getting a bit over-cautious, but consoled ourselves that guile compensated for a good deal.

Actually the only real handicap of age that I felt was that my night vision could have been better; I had good eyesight, but in pre-radar days a C.O. needed outstanding vision for night attacks. I therefore concentrated on day attacks and managed to fill the bag reasonably, though not so well as I might have had I been younger.

Before the war I had been a great protagonist of the night submarine attack; as I have said before I had *Sealion* equipped with the first practical night sight to be carried by a British submarine; but in the event I found that my age prevented me from exploiting the night attack and nearly all my sinkings were by day.

The Eighth Flotilla, running from Algiers, concentrated mainly to the west and north of Sicily; the Naples approaches were one of the most fruitful areas. Strangely enough, for there was deep water, several of our boats were lost off Naples and Barney did not like his boats going there. I never found it a lucky billet, but not because of enemy action. There are two entrances from the southward into Naples Bay, the Bocco Piccolo and Bocco Grande. One had to withdraw a bit at night, the patrols were too thick, but whichever of these two entrances I chose by day always seemed to be the one they were not using; I would have the infuriating experience of seeing the mast-heads of ships coming and going by the channel I was not covering. We did, however, catch one convoy at dawn leaving the Bocco Piccolo and got a good ship; it was a short way east of this channel that *Safari* got a right and left, torpedo and gun.

I had got browned off at apparently always picking the wrong hole, but had noted that some ships were keeping very close along the Italian coast after leaving the Bocco Piccolo, the eastern entrance. I therefore established patrol to the eastward. Sure enough, along came two ships, a tanker leading followed by a coasting steamer, and wonder of wonders, for once unescorted. I suppose that there had been some slip up in the provision of escorts and they reckoned to pick them up later on. There were regular air patrols and the routine A/S craft which were always operating off the two Boccos, but even the aircraft patrol was temporarily out of sight.

We put two torpedoes into the tanker, which for once in a way settled very quickly, and hardly had they detonated when we were on the surface and engaging the coaster with the gun.

She turned to run for it, the little seaside town of Positana being only about a mile and a half away. We only had two and a half minutes before we had to dive again for the air patrol coming back, but we managed to get in twenty-six hits. The next few minutes were spent going deep and getting clear of our diving position to throw off the aircraft. When we came up again to periscope depth I had the satisfaction of seeing the coaster on her beam ends before slowly sinking.

This attack was to provoke a signal in verse. There was a very efficient system of monitoring Italian signals and from these the flotilla staff would glean quite a good idea of what was going on. The submarines themselves, except in the case of reporting major warships or in an emergency, never broke wireless silence; they did not want to give their presence away. But the Axis, not without reason, were very submarine-minded and were continually reporting real or imaginary British submarines. The Captain (S) could not know if the reported submarine was real or imaginary, but if the position was in one of his boat's operating areas he would presume it real. He then did not know whether or not his submarine knew she had been sighted; if she did not, as could be the case in an aircraft sighting, she would have no warning that unpleasantness was perhaps being laid for her. To make sure that the boat would not be taken by surprise, he would make a signal: *You may have been sighted at . . .*

The opposition had already had reason to complain of *Safari*'s presence on this patrol, and had been making a number of submarine reports to their shipping. Barney was getting rather bored with informing *Safari* that she might have been sighted. Usually the submarine knew very well why the Axis were howling, having given them something to howl about, and, as I have said before, may not always have been as appreciative of mother's care as she should have been. I think possibly, too, because he mistrusted Naples, Barney was particularly anxious about our welfare. The loss of their tanker and coaster, right under the noses of their Bocco Picollo patrols, had aroused Italian wailing on the ether; a signal from S.8 followed. When deciphered it read:

Ben, Ben,
Sighted again.
13.40
Very naughty.

It was during this patrol that *Safari* was named, and as it was an extraordinary coincidence is worth recounting. By now patrolling was a much more gentlemanly occupation than it had been in the early days of the war. Excellent tinned food; a proper cook and fresh baked bread; and an interesting daily W/T news service. Shortly the *Daily Mirror* was to provide the submarine service with its own newspaper, called *Good Morning,* largely cartoons and feature articles because the date was immaterial. If a boat was going out for say 21 days, it would take 21 editions. These were kept by the Coxswain, and each mess issued with a new edition every morning, and the adventures of Jane were followed enthusiastically day by day. We also had boiled sweets and barley sugar as rations. One early patrol in *Sealion,* before sweet rationing but when they were becoming scarce, we had been unable to buy anything except a superannuated cheap line of licorice allsorts, a sweet I have never been able to enjoy since.

We were still P.211 but it was general gossip that the submarine service was going back to names. On the news service we heard that the edict had gone forth and all submarines had now been given names. Our class would start with an "S." We discussed what name we were likely to be called, the pessimistic felt sure that it would be something dull and unimaginative like *Shakespeare* or *Spencer;* and then we discussed what we would like to be called. We fancied ourselves as a hunter and felt that *Shikari* would be splendid, but there was still an old destroyer claiming that lovely name. From that we passed to *Safari,* and one and all in the wardroom decided that that was the name we should like to have.

When I got in from that patrol and went to report to Barney he said:

"You know of course that you have been given a name."

"Yes," I said. "We heard that we were going to be giving one on the news; *Shakespeare,* I suppose."

"No," he said, *Safari.*"

It took me some time to believe it. Actually one of our class was named *Shakespeare* and no doubt they were very happy and proud of their name; it just happened to be the bottom in our opinion. *Safari* also exactly conformed to our home designed badge, which I have described elsewhere.

The Tyrrhenian Sea was getting very congested and, although the Axis still had command of the air, they no longer had a monopoly of it. At night our cruiser force would make raids on enemy shipping to the west of Sicily and there would be air strikes on Axis convoys. These could be very embarrassing for a submarine shadowing the convoy before going in to attack. Flares would be dropped illuminating both submarine and convoy, and the latter would take drastic avoiding action.

Hospital ships, brightly illuminated, became a familiar feature of the night scene. Hospital ships have to be properly declared, individually-named ships before they are immune from attack. But in addition to their proper hospital ships, the Axis had some odd ones painted white with red crosses, which were not declared. Whether or not these ships actually carried wounded, or whether they were just disguised to get supplies safely through, I know not. We did not attack them, but we got a photograph through the periscope of one of these dubious hospital ships.

We still encountered enemy U-boats and we had a fortunate escape from one. It was bright moonlight, so bright that you could see through the periscope, and we were on the surface charging. Suddenly the officer of the watch sighted a U-boat breaking surface on our port bow, probably breaking surface on firing. He put the helm hard over to avoid, and we never saw the tracks. The Axis used electric torpedoes which, although they had an inferior ultimate performance to ours, made little or no track. One could not always guarantee seeing an enemy U-boat first at night, particularly with a low moon, as a lot depended which had the other silhouetted against the moonlight. In this case our opponent had had the luck of the light horizon and had been able to dive unseen by us; we had had luck in a bit of bad submarining on his part, allowing his boat to break surface. I noted in my patrol report: ... *tracks not seen, but a floating mine bobbed down the side to provide the requisite thrill.* Actually when on the surface at night, whether charging or on passage, one always did a very complicated zig-zag to give you a good chance of avoiding any torpedoes fired at you whether you saw them or not.

I came as near to losing my boat as I ever did on a patrol from Algiers and it was really due to overconfidence. It was not merely the very inexperienced boats which tended to get lost, but also the exceptionally experienced ones, where familiarity may have bred some contempt.

Dawn was just starting to lighten the horizon when we sighted a destroyer approaching and we dived to attack. The light was difficult, but we were maneuvering into a very good attacking position. It was January and water conditions were particularly favorable for the anti-submarine detecting equipment and unfavorable for the submarine. Normally I would have taken avoiding action. But I had an idea that this might be a large Fleet destroyer, which I had always wanted to come up against in a hunt. They drew enough water to torpedo, unlike the smaller ones which normally harassed us and which were immune owing to shallow draft. The silhouettes of the Italian Fleet destroyers and their torpedo boats were nearly identical. About the only difference from the bow was that the Fleet destroyers had a double gun mounting —two guns in a single mounting—on the fo'c'sle. In the torpedo boats it was a single mounting. When the destroyer was about 1,500 yards off and coming along nicely, in the bad light I could not make out her class and, injudiciously striving to make out her identity, I used too much periscope. She had an alert lookout and spotted it. The destroyer turned straight at us.

It was a delicate situation. There was no time to get out of the way, so I speeded up and went straight at her, gaining depth as we went.

She passed right over us, but luckily had not allowed for the speed at which we were closing her and she dropped her depth charges just too late—for her. They shook us up considerably and did a certain amount of damage aft, including a troublesome leak in the stern gland. It also damaged one of our propeller blades, causing it to sing—that is, make a high-frequency noise, which meant that we could not use that propeller near A/S craft for the rest of that patrol.

The leak in the stern gland was troublesome during the subsequent hunt when we were deep. The acoustic conditions were ideal for the hunter and every time we used the main ballast pump to pump out the bilges where the stern gland was leaking, things got unpleasantly close. We could not afford to let water collect in the after bilges for, apart from loss of trim, it would have mounted up and shorted the main electric motors.

In the end we managed to compete by keeping fairly shallow—so that the pressure on the glands was not so great—shutting off the after ends and increasing air pressure in there to keep out the water. I have never been more relieved than when we shook off that hunt. And it all had been caused by overconfidence on my part.

In general the Italians did not keep a very good lookout, nor were their A/S forces particularly efficient. But they had a "First Eleven" which was pretty good by any standards, and this destroyer was definitely in the first team. You could usually tell very early in a hunt if you were dealing with one or more of the First Eleven.

In February, with preparations for the Sicilian landings under way, *Safari* and two other boats were detailed to carry out some surveys of the possible landing beaches. I was not very pleased about this, I rather looked upon Special Operations, that is landing and taking off cloak-and-dagger parties and that sort of thing, as beneath the dignity of a hardened, seasoned boat. It was all right for new boys and boats working up, or if a C.O. needed a bit of a rest, but the hard cut-and-thrust of attacking shipping was more the line of country for a hardened old-stager.

But if these operations may have been rather small beer for the submarine, they certainly were not for the survey parties. Each team consisted of two, one or both being fully qualified navigating officers. They were landed in canoes wearing a sort of frogman suit. However well charted waters may be, except in actual ports, there are always liable to be odd rocks at the actual beach which are not charted. This does not matter for ordinary navigation when your object is not to run up on the beach. But if landing craft, carrying an invasion, are going to deliberately beach themselves, it is essential that they shall not tear their bottoms out on odd rocks before they actually reach the beach.

The object of the C.O.P.P.—Combined Operations Pilotage Party—was to survey beaches in advance. They would go in their canoe, land on the beach and wade up and down searching every foot for possible obstructions, all of course being done in the dark. It was a highly skilled and dangerous job. All the likely beaches were heavily guarded. The C.O.P.P. would have to hide their canoe at a time when a sentry was elsewhere and keep one eye on him whilst carrying out their paddling operations, disappearing under water if he came too close. When the time came to leave they would have to find the submarine again, which would be about half a mile off shore. It all had to be done on a dark night and you could not afford any noise or shouting. We had two C.O.P.P. teams and these were the first action operations of this nature. In order for the canoe to be able to find the submarine again both were equipped with infra-red signalling lamps. You can only see infra-red through a suitable receiver, so that the enemy would not be able to see signalling going on. However, you had to train the transmitter direct onto the receiver, and as neither knew exactly where the other was this proved impossible in practice. I had no faith in this as a method of picking up the canoe and we went to a great deal of trouble to arrange a rendezvous. Any form of accurate navigation in a very wet and unstable canoe was not on.

Landmarks which are conspicuous by day are invisble by night; you have to pick something like an escarpment or the peaks of hills. We went to a great deal of trouble to find a really satisfactory transit on which our canoes could run out to find us; after some more practice at launching, the canoes started on operations on the north coast of Sicily.

Although it fell short of the excitement of the submarine's role of a raider of shipping, such operations were not without some interest and danger, though I do not think that any submarine was ever lost on such operations.

Trimmed right down, to show a minimum of silhouette, the submarine would creep right close to the enemy beach. The final run in would be made at slow speed on the electric motors so as to avoid noise and wash. She would then stop, about half a mile off shore. The fore hatch would be opened, taking care that there was no sound—sound travels well over water and with an off-shore breeze you could hear people talking on the beach, dogs barking and that sort of thing. Silently, every one wearing sneakers to make no noise on the steel casing, the canoes would come up through the torpedo hatch, the final assembly being made on deck. Then the canoes would be put carefully over the side, the torpedo hatch shut and maybe the bow trimmed down a bit to make it easier for the intrepid surveyors to get into their canoes. You had to be very careful about trimming down, as venting a tank is apt to make a noise; a noise like an angry whale blowing would excite the sentries on the beach. A whispered "Good luck," and the canoes would slide out into the blackness to be out of sight in a hundred yards or so. The submarine would then slip out astern to wait two or three miles off shore, till it was time to pick up the C.O.P.P.s again at the rendezvous.

One of our canoe teams failed to return from the night's operations. We had arranged alternative times for the rendezvous; it could be that the team would have to lie up in caves, or even inland, if the interest of the guards had been aroused, and wait for another night to come off. It was always anxious work making these subsequent rendezvous. You felt that your men might have been captured, unmentionable things done to them by the Gestapo and possibly something very unpleasant laid on for the parent submarine at the rendezvous. For three successive nights we kept the rendezvous for our missing team. Actually they had been captured, but suffered no other harm.

We did have one exciting moment with our remaining team. We were attempting a beach rather close to Palermo and had gone into a little bay with rather a narrow entrance. It was a defended area, we had gone submerged during daylight and sat on the bottom till darkness when we surfaced to launch the canoe. We had got the torpedo hatch open and the canoe half out—a helpless position to be in as the torpedo hatch was low down and you could not even maneuver violently on the surface with it open—

when suddenly a searchlight on the headland close to us switched on. It swept round towards us.

Feverishly men tried to stuff back the canoe so as to get the hatch shut while the searchlight swept on. We would be illuminated and revealed like a sitting duck at point-blank range. The glare of the beam had already started to illuminate the men on the casing, you could see their faces from the bridge, when suddenly it stopped, hesitated a few seconds and then swept on back to seaward again. A lucky let off, but we pushed back the canoe and went elsewhere for the night's operations; we had had no idea that we were sharing our little bay with a coastal defense searchlight.

In order to keep our presence secret we were not allowed to attack shipping and as always, when such restrictions were imposed, the sea seemed to teem with targets. There was nothing to do by day except wait for nightfall to continue the beach survey. Most of a submarine's life on patrol was spent in scheming and searching, trying to find a worthy target. But the sea is a big place, even an inland sea like the Mediterranean, and the only place to make sure of finding targets was at the entrance to major ports. There the defenses were correspondingly intensified and it was largely a matter of how close in you could operate to such places and survive till the inevitable target came along. It was much more comfortable to intercept away from such focal spots, if you could only find the game after it had dispersed. Now, of course, wherever we withdrew by day it seemed that a convoy would come lumbering past at point-blank range. All we could do was to make practice attacks, taking the boat through the screen, turning into a firing position and then just not firing. I was criticized for doing this, on the ground that I was taking unnecessary risks, but I considered it worthwhile; it was good training in attack and I never found it possible to be trained too much. In my patrol report I wrote: *It is only to be prayed that when Safari resumes her operational duties such marvellous targets will be vouchsafed to her, if the sanity of her C.O. is preserved that long.*

Boring though it was for us, it was needle enough for our surviving C.O.P.P. team; McHarg and Sinclair were both awarded the D.S.O. In the first wave six teams had

gone out in three submarines. I was very upset at losing
one of my teams, but when we returned we found that
ours was the only one of the six to get back in their
submarines. One other got back to Malta—fifty-seven
miles of open sea in a collapsible canvas canoe—by
paddling. Their hands were in ribbons and both of them
had to go to hospital suffering from exposure. It was
indeed a gallant effort. They had failed to find their parent
submarine. A better form of locating the submarine had to
be devised and this was subsequently done acoustically, by
underwater sound transmission.

Actually this patrol was not completely blank. On one
day of low visibility and rain storms a heavily laden
schooner blundered into us. In such conditions we would
not be sighted and the wretched ship had to take a lot of
pent up frustration; she disappeared, as the German used
to have it, "without a trace." Not a very creditable effort,
even though all may be fair in war. I have a shell-case,
now an ash tray, which was used in that sinking, and I find
it a salutory reminder, when feeling critical of people, of
an unpleasant, brutal episode.

16

MY LAST PATROL

I was feeling rather like the tenth little Indian when *Safari* slid out of Algiers harbor on a spring evening in March, 1943. We had been in the Mediterranean for a year now and that last year had seen the disappearance of the few other pre-war submarine C.O.s still left operating. Allied losses in submarines during the North African campaign had been just on fifty per cent, with the British submarines taking the major knock, and the last few weeks had seen the loss, amongst others, of *Turbulent,* whose C.O., Tubby Linton, had been the last of my contemporaries in the Mediterranean. A number of others had gone and splendid young new C.O.s had taken their place, but my mind wandered back over these others.

Strange how some of them had seemed to see it coming, to have some darkening premonition. Sometimes a change would come over a C.O., he would lose the aura of inner enthusiasm, the carefree confidence that "it can't happen to me"; I used to wonder if it was some sixth sense which detected the Angel of the Shadow of Death over them or whether more prosaically, it was just strain beginning to tell and they were losing the standard of keyed up efficiency which assisted survival. But Tubby had not been like that; he was to earn his posthumous V.C. when *Turbulent* was mined in a well calculated risk to get two Italian cruisers sheltering in Maddalena.

But that spring evening meant more than pleasant weather, it meant that the Mediterranean was warming up, producing temperature gradients in the sea behind which a submarine could take cover like an airplane behind a cloud.

But this was no time for wandering thoughts; the first hours of a patrol, as the last, were apt to be dangerous. True the enemy were not likely to be found so close to Algiers, but air navigation being what it is (or was) there was always the danger of the R.A.F. making a mistake and catching us before we had changed to our second selves, the alert fighting team of a submarine on patrol. Only a couple of patrols before a Wellington had jumped us just after leaving Algiers and, though we got down just in time

Wellington

and her depth charges did no damage, she would never have caught us on the surface had we been at proper patrol efficiency. Only by complete concentration could one sharpen those wits which sense the invisible, or have uncertainty in the mind of the man on the bridge conveyed to you without word or message.

We were off again to the Tyrrhenian Sea, the east coast of Sardinia, where a year before we had made our first sinking. We were a very different crew now, not in individuals so much, though there had been some changes, but as a welded fighting crew. Whereas some of us had grumbled, before we ever saw action, at the loss of sleep entailed by endlessly repeated practicing of breakdowns and evolutions; now, with rising thirty sinkings, recipient of hundreds of depth charges, we swung automatically into our twenty-four-hour day patrol routine; and practiced over again those breakdowns and evolutions we knew so well; but which we could never know too well.

I liked the Sardinian coast and though it was not particularly fruitful of targets, we had had two satisfactory patrols there. In particular the offshore breeze near dawn would bring the most delightful scents of heathland and nostalgic thoughts of rod and gun at home; though in my case it had the slight disadvantage that it was apt to give me a mild bout of hay fever.

On passage you always pressed on for your selected billet, feeling that every second lost might be a chance missed, but in practice there was always a lot of watching, waiting and planning before anything turned up.

Depth-charging and hunting were to the submarine just necessary evils which followed an attack as night follows day. It was something to be endured, but with impatience; absorbing enough, because you needed every wile you knew to make good your escape, so that you could get on with your proper job of hunting ships. The real thrill and excitement came to me, and I suppose others, in the chase, the culmination in the attack; the rest was a comparative anti-climax. If you had made a kill, then it was easy to endure the hammering; if you had missed it always seemed a great deal worse, as indeed it often was. Noise and disorder caused by ships sinking, the picking up of survivors, all tend to disturb the enemy's concentration on the hunt.

You had planned your patrol; preferably the first day or two was spent sniffing round the border hedgerows, before pressing on into the main coverts. You used the first period to check up on patrol beats, the likely strength of opposition and particularly noting the movements of enemy minesweepers—where they swept would be the shipping channels and would obviously be free of enemy mines. We established patrol first in the Gulf of Orosei, and then later we would move into the heavily defended area in the Gulf of Cagliari, at the head of which lay the naval port from which the gulf takes its name.

The first possible target to turn up was a largish minesweeping or anti-submarine trawler, coasting south—not the sort of target you would choose. She probably had a better gun than we had and might be equipped to hunt and depth charge submarines, for which purpose such craft were commissioned, or she might be primarily intended as a minesweeper; we could not know.

She was worth sinking, but was she worth the risk?

She was too small to torpedo. On the surface I had little doubt that we had the edge on her; we would have the tremendous advantage of surprise; we would choose the weather gauge with sun and wind behind us—sun to dazzle him, wind to blow the smoke of his gun back into the gun-layer's eyes. But if an anti-submarine aircraft turned up, the odds would change, we would be forced to dive and immediately the tables would be turned. The air patrol had just passed on southward; it was most unlikely that it would be back for some minutes if it was on its normal patrol for an hour. The only snag was our gun, the breech was only too liable to jam and our strong-arm breech worker, to whose ruthless methods the ill-designed mechanism normally responded, had been left behind sick in Algiers. His relief could scarcely be expected yet to have the same facility for hitting it with exactly the right force in exactly the right place.

The crew were all now standing by for gun action, the ammunition collected in the galley beneath the gun tower. A submarine cook is a versatile man; Dennis Leech, our chef, was in charge of ammunition supply and he turned his hand to many things as well as being expected to produce a meal at unpredictable times. He was almost as used to ammunition in his galley as food. I knew that everyone was going to be very disappointed if we did not come up for gun action, they all enjoyed it and one could feel the expectancy all around. Whether it was a torpedo or gun attack, one's crew was always thirsting for action, rather as if it were purely sport, and yet they knew, none better, the almost inevitable repercussions. Until you gave yourself away by attacking something, you were safe enough, except from mines and U-boats. Nearly any attack meant that you would be hunted; a screened attack meant inevitable depth-charging.

We had maneuvered into an ideal position and I was turning the pros and cons over in my mind as the periscope slid down. Then I caught the gun-layer's eye. If you have met a spaniel's eye as you take out your gun, and he has a nasty doubt whether he has been invited to the party, you will know what I mean. There could be no doubt now of the decision.

"Stand by, gun action. Bearing Green 20. An Armed Trawler. Range 1200. Deflection 4 left."

"Full speed ahead together. Stand by main engines. Take her down."

The boat planes down below periscope depth.

"Stop starboard. In starboard engine clutch. Surface. Gun action."

Ronnie Ward, our No. 1, took over: "Blow twos. Blow fours."

He passed the blowing orders to the outside E.R.A., naming the main ballast tanks by their numbers to ensure that the boat came up on an even keel. Purbrick opened the main ballast blows, the vents had already been reported shut. To the rush of the high-pressure air into the tanks were added puffing noises from the engine room; Shute was blowing round the engines to make sure no water had got into the cylinders.

As the tanks blew, the boat was held down on the planes until the loss of ballast water overcame them. Watson and Mealyer reversed their planes and the boat started bounding up.

"Half ahead starboard!"

The starboard engine started, nicety of judgment being required to open the valve which lets out the exhaust at the right moment. The exhaust pipe was still twenty feet below the surface; if it had been opened before the exhaust from the engine blew it clear, the engine would have been flooded. The engine fired as the boat came up, sucking air from inside until the hatches were opened, but we had a pressure in the boat and wanted to reduce it.

Just before the gun tower and conning-tower hatches broke surface, No. 1 blew his whistle. The hatches were flung open, men scrambled through carrying telescopes and ammunition. It looked a disorderly rush, but actually every movement was made with precision, every hand and foothold of it; everyone knew exactly what to do and they came out in such order that everything would be brought to the ready at the same time.

It had taken about one and a half minutes from the order being given to take her down to the whistle; about forty-five seconds from the whistle to the first round being got off.

The gun had been loaded whilst water was still running out of the barrel; the breech was kept open at sea, to save time, and that meant that the enemy, if he happened to be looking in the right direction, had forty-seven seconds from the time he sighted the submarine breaking surface to the first shell arriving.

I was last up the conning tower, passing orders to get the port engine going as I climbed. Blackburn the Sub. was in charge of the shoot and was already up; Signalman Austin probably had the most difficult duty; he and Devlin, the Pilot, could not watch the action, they both had eyes like hawks and they had to scan the heavens on the disengaged side and astern to make sure that we were not jumped by aircraft.

Tallamy was shooting well. We had come up on the quarter and the trawler's gun was forward, screened by her bridge, so that she would have to turn to bring it to bear; we would maneuver, the engines by now having worked up speed, so as to make it difficult for her.

The first round hit and we were pumping shells into her at the rate of fifteen a minute before she realized what was hitting her. Things had gone well. If you establish hits at once before the enemy knows what is happening, the odds are that she will be demoralized; she made no attempt to fight but turned to beach herself, the shore being only a few cables under her lee. It was touch and go, she very nearly made it. With about one hundred yards to go, Tallamy did it. He had been aiming at the water-line and he got a vital one home in the engine room. She had been getting lower in the water and was now enveloped in steam. We ceased fire. I had spotted the masts of a schooner coming over the horizon to the southward and we were off to get her before the trawler had disappeared.

I have described this gun action, it was typical of any gun action, at length; it took about two and a half minutes. It sounds easy meat, scarcely sporting, but everything depended upon split-second training. If we had given her time to shoot back it would not have been so good.

The one that followed was easy. We slipped down the coast at full speed on the surface, close in so that we should not be seen by our quarry. If she sighted us and turned away, she would have escaped because it was certain that it could not be long now before the air patrol arrived.

The first thing she saw of us was when we came out from under the cliffs. She had not a chance; as long as the enemy avoided the expense of fixing up convoys and sent vessels unescorted, her seamen had to suffer and another load of enemy cargo went down as the first air patrol hove into sight.

All this had taken place close to the enemy coast. One can imagine the outcry if U-boats had cruised about on the surface a few hundred yards off the British coast, shooting down coasters and minesweepers with their guns. But our boats were doing just that, and quite frequently.

All this had only been the hors d'oeuvres and we set off for Cagliari to try and find the main dish. We knew the swept channel and established patrol off Cavoli, a high headland with deep water close in. It was not so deep, as we were to find to our consternation later, as the chart indicated. It was an ideal position; it covered the main approach to Cagliari and water noises on the rocks below the cliffs would confuse the hydrophones of our hunters.

We had not long to wait. On the second day smoke was sighted to the eastward, which in due course turned out to be a deep-laden supply ship, followed by a coaster and escorted by aircraft and one destroyer. It was too calm to be pleasant. It is quite possible for an aircraft to see a submerged submarine in the clear Mediterranean on a calm day, even if the boat is handled discreetly. However, all went according to plan. We had a perfect plot as our target moved up the coast. We went through the usual tense, anxious minutes as we crept undetected across the bows of the escort, the slim periscope breaking the surface to expose only an inch or two occasionally. We turned in to my favorite track at my favorite range—600 yards—for an unhurried shot.

Here I made a mistake.

I fired three torpedoes, one at her bow, one at her middle and one at her stern, expecting to get two hits and a certain sinking. As we took the boat down to get away from the torpedo tracks, I could just see a great column of water tower up as the first hit her bow; there was no second explosion, the second torpedo was a rogue and ran off; the third must have missed under her stern. Knowing her course and speed, I should have aimed all three much closer amidships; the secret of success was to ask as little as possible from our torpedoes and well I should have known it.

Cagliari was not far off and, damaged though she was, that ship got in. I was not to know that till much later, we were busy avoiding the usual hunt amidst the roars and vibrations of depth charges. I noted in my patrol report that the counterattack was *painfully inefficient* and in due course that evening we withdrew to charge and reload. It was April 6th, my wedding anniversary, and I wondered how they all were at home.

The immediate task was to decide where to go next. Normally a submarine gets away from the scene of her crime, but I decided to try a bluff and stay put. As it turned out the heat was not turned on except for A/S air patrols. However, the second day an auxiliary brigantine on A/S patrol came to share our billet. Normally we left them alone. They carried depth charges and hydrophones, and were, indeed, quite capable of dealing with a submerged submarine as long as it remained submerged. They were slow and inefficient, but there was an idea that if one shot them up too much the Italians would think up something better. This one insisted upon patrolling around us and she severely handicapped our lookout; altogether she was a dangerous bedfellow. *Safari* foamed to the surface, the shells poured into her and she was on fire almost before she knew what was happening. There was one brave man on board and two shots whistled over our bridge before she went.

It was a pity, there is always something beautiful and romantic about any vessel which carries the yards of square-rig, even though modern engines have been added as the normal method of propulsion. But war is no time for sentiment, which brings neither profit nor survival.

An amusing interlude to this little action was a motor minesweeper inshore of us. Thinking she might be the next on the list, she hurriedly beached herself. By now the shore batteries were beginning to wake up and we dived.

Again it was a question of where to go next. I decided to try the double bluff. No one would expect us to stay close in to a defended port after giving ourselves away a second time like this. We withdrew to charge and the next day were back again off Cavoli. Fortune smiled, a most satisfying main dish was on the way.

The great advantage of our position off Cagliari was that practically every ship that used the port had to pass us. The swept channel was only about two miles wide, and we were in it. It followed, not so satisfactorily, that the escape channel was restricted, but that was a problem to be taken in its time.

It was a calm bright afternoon on April 10th, 1943, when much A/S activity and smoke over towards Cagliari indicated that something was coming our way. Permitting myself a somewhat generous exposure of the high-power periscope, the picture was unfolded: an armed liner, a tanker and an old-fashioned tramp. Around them was the screen; two large escorts on the seaward side—the ships would hug the cliffs too close for us to attack them from the landward side. There was also a gaggle of motor A/S boats and motor minesweepers—I never counted those, we had to deal with them as they arrived; a horse might just as well plan to avoid individually a cloud of gadflies. Above, two A/S aircraft were quartering the sea around and ahead of the convoy.

CRDA Cant. Z.506B

It was glassy calm and theoretically the Cants— Italian seaplanes—should have seen us as we circled slowly at periscope depth in the center of the channel. In practice, if you went dead slow so as to make no wash and used very little periscope very discreetly they never, or hardly ever, did.

Chiefy Harris passed through the control room on his rounds to see that everything was shut off for depth- charging. There had been a time when this precaution aroused an anticipatory chill; now it was just another routine.

Suddenly Watson, the Coxswain, reported that the hydroplanes had broken down and the outside E.R.A. that the telemotor pressure had failed. This was the hydraulic system which controlled the power operation of everything, hydroplanes, steering, periscopes and vents. Smoothly we changed into hand pump operation but this meant that everything worked very, very slowly; we were fit for little more than to proceed submerged if unopposed. Men, stripped to the waist, sweated on the pumps using up air in their physical efforts that we might need badly later if the hunt were prolonged. It was awkward, but not impossible; we had to go on and pray that we should get things going again before firing.

The engineers located the trouble in time, a faulty bypass valve. I breathed a sigh of relief as we got back into full control as the first of the screen was upon us.

We drifted through the screen, sinking deeper at times to let a vessel pass over; every time I raised the small attack periscope it seemed as if one of them was pointing at us. We swung slowly, trying to keep bows on to the nearest escort. Everything was dead quiet in the boat. One propeller turned very slowly, just enough to give us control; even that propeller was stopped at times when an escort came very close. At last we were through undetected.

First hurdle over and a gentle breeze, just sufficient to ruffle the surface, had sprung up to help us. I decided to try and get all three.

Slowly we swung onto our firing course, resisting the almost intolerable temptation to speed up a bit. One had to point the whole submarine in the British boats to aim the torpedoes. You had to delay the turn to fire till the last possible moment; once committed to the turn, it was difficult to deal with any sudden alteration of course by the enemy. There was always the awful feeling that you might have left it too late. Speeding up increased the risk of detection.

The anxiety passed. We were gaining on the bearing and steadied up with a minute to spare. If only they held their course; if only that escort close astern did not pick us up; if only that circling seaplane did not spot us; then they were delivered into our hands.

It seems peculiar that one offered up little prayers at times like this. Ronnie Ward, our No. 1, was as happy about his trim as he could be at this tense moment. The

Coxswain and Second Coxswain riveted their eyes on the depth-gauge needles—every flicker had to be corrected almost before it started; if we lost depth now it would ruin the attack. In the tube space John McIntyre, the T.I., watched his order instruments waiting for his moment— upon him and his team now depended the culmination of the attack; he was probably going over in his mind if there was anything possible that he could have left undone in the meticulous preparation of his torpedoes.

The seconds dragged by. It seemed that the leading ship would never cross the sights. I had the awful thought that she could be going slower than I had judged and that I should take a degree or two off the firing angle. The periscope was now being shown a fraction of an inch every few seconds, just so that I could see the mast heads through a haze of water. We were within 600 yards and could not risk showing enough periscope to have a decent look.

Austin, the signalman, was reading off the bearing on the periscope ring. Two degrees to go. Then one, and he gripped over my hands to hold the periscope on the firing angle.

"Stand by!"

The stem of the leading ship, the liner, slid across the graticule. As her foremast came in line:

"Fire one—Port 20—half speed starboard."

In seconds now the track of the torpedo would be unrolling across the intervening water. We could not wait for the ships to cross the sights and so we swung to speed things up. As the mainmast crossed the sights:

"Fire two."

The boat gave another gentle shudder as the second torpedo left and we swung faster to port, though as usual every degree seemed to take an age in passing. The sooner you could get away from those telltale torpedo tracks, the better your chance of escape.

The foremast of the tanker came in line:

"Fire three."

Her mainmast:

"Fire four."

But that was all, the boat was getting difficult to control under helm with the loss of trim caused by firing the torpedoes and already the A/S operator had reported an escort pounding in from astern. It had been but a pious hope to think of getting all three. Our position had now been clearly marked and to stay up longer would have been suicidal.

With the fourth torpedo, I put the helm amidships, speeded up and flooded for'ard. Before the periscope dipped I saw the cloud of spray and smoke climb into the air as the first torpedo went home in the liner, followed shortly by the crash of the explosion.

We were going down fast as we heard the second torpedo hit. The noise of the closing escort grew louder.

Blackburn, the Torpedo Officer, counted out the seconds until the third torpedo was due; there was a rumbling crash and five seconds later came the fourth.

The tension of the last forty-five minutes eased; the attack had been successful. It remained to make our getaway.

My escape plan was simple, to dive deep under the target line and then lose our attackers amongst the water noises under the cliffs. According to the chart there was 270 feet of water and we aimed to level off at 250 feet and slow down as soon as No. 1 got the trim.

As we started to pull out, the boat brought up with a shuddering scrunch; we had hit the bottom full and hearty, though luckily there was no rock, at 210 feet. As we struck the first pattern of depth charges came crashing down. I turned to the Pilot.

"I thought you told me that we had 45 fathoms."

Dev looked worried, raced his parallel rulers to and fro, and confirmed the position. I looked over his shoulder and sure enough there it was, 45 fathoms. The chart was wrong.

Things were getting pretty noisy up top, the boat shook to the reverberations of depth charges and we were much too near our firing position to be healthy. We had to try to get off.

I put the motors astern, working up to full speed. The only reaction was a cascade of depth charges; not unnaturally they had heard us. The boat remained stuck firm.

Gingerly we lightened the trim forward and the crew moved aft. I tried the motors astern again, but the reaction was immediate. The roaring crash of a pattern of depth charges; unpleasantly close, a number of lights went out and some of the remaining paint flaked off the deck head. That paint was like the widow's curse, there was always some left.

There was no future in this, we were stuck firm and the only hope of getting off was to blow main ballast. However, if we did that, and the boat came off, we would come rocketing to the surface unless we vented the main ballast tanks again, and that meant bubbles rising up plain for all to see, establishing our exact position.

The only hope was to stay put, hope that the enemy would think that we had moved on, confusing our hull with the other irregularities of the bottom. All machinery was stopped and we settled down to wait till dark to hide the telltale bubbles, in the hope that by then he would have expended most of his depth charges and exuberance.

There was still one very nasty little thought. I wondered if the others had thought of it as well. Submarines have stuck on the bottom before now, never to get off. *Vandal* disappeared off the Clyde in a practice dive in this way and was never found, stuck deep in the mud off Inchmarnoch Water. And there had been others, too.

However, that was taking your fences before you came to them,* and there was still a lot of noise up top, though not so close as it had been.

Olden, the L.T.O., came into the control room with his little pot and hydrometer to test the batteries and sound the sumps. We might well have cracked a cell hitting the bottom and if the acid mixed with any salt water in the sump it would give off chlorine. He put some soda into the sump in case, and went on forward to the other battery. Fortunately the battery had not shifted and he reported that all was well; it was a great relief. Every unnecessary light had been switched off; every amp in our battery might be required later when we got off to make our getaway—if we did get off.

All was very silent in the dimly-lit boat now. You missed the usual steady hum of machinery. As usual when being hunted conversation was in whispers. Everyone remained closed up at their diving stations, since it was always possible that we should get blown off by a depth charge. For the A/S operator alone it was business as

* As in fox hunting.

usual. The listening set was in the keel, which was half buried in the bottom, but it gave some result.

"H.E. closing starboard."

The swish-swish of the propellers of a hunter were heard closing, then passing overhead. They could be plainly heard throughout the boat. Breathless seconds followed; depth charges take some time to sink. If a hunter passed overhead it meant that he could have dropped them at the correct lethal moment. Waiting to see is not amusing. However, all was well, she had not picked us up and we breathed again; the depth charges by now had got more distant, the hunt had drawn away for the time being.

But then came another sound, far more menacing. We were used to depth charges, but this was something really chilling. We knew it, too—a rending crack followed by grinding noises; we had heard it before on occasions with satisfaction. It was a stricken ship breaking up, the great beams rending before she sinks.

Now it sounded right overhead, terribly close, and we were stuck on the bottom underneath. I looked at Dev, both he and I knew how close to the target line we must have been when we stuck.

I had blessed the gentle breeze when it sprang up to help us in the closing phases of the attack. Now it appeared that it was drifting a wreck down on top of us and we stood every chance of being entombed beneath thousands of tons of steel. If we blew ourselves off the bottom we were certain to buy it; the alternative of being buried was little more attractive. Conversation ceased. Anxious eyes glanced upwards.

Then came one of those things which is a typical example of how submarine crews went about their job. At my elbow I heard a quiet voice.

"Cup of tea, sir?"

It was Sutcliffe, our "wardroom flunkey," the able-seaman who amongst many other duties looked after the wardroom. He had been with the Chef, calmly brewing tea whilst the depth charges had been crashing round us; it was true we were quite used to depth-charging, but you never got to like it.

I never got to like submarine tea either, a dark, strong mixture made out of flat, distilled water, liberally laced with neat condensed milk and sickly sweet with much sugar, the whole drunk out of thick earthenware cups, crude to the lips. But at this moment, with those grinding noises overhead, I suddenly realized that I was still parched from the tense absorption of the attack. That was a drink that I shall always remember.

Time dragged on; it could only have been a few minutes, but it seemed an age before those grinding noises stopped. The wreck must have drifted on or sunk clear. A ripple of conversation indicated the relaxing of strain—one is apt to be a bit garrulous on such occasions—and the hunt was drawing off, apparently working a heel line to seaward. Anywhere away from us was satisfactory, but this did mean that they were between us and our escape route, though we had plenty of worries before that one had to be dealt with.

We had got escape sets of course, but they were useless at this depth after a longish dive. We should have been dead from carbon dioxide poisoning before we had flooded the boat enough to raise the internal pressure to get the escape hatches opened. I doubt if anyone gave them a thought. They were useful if you had a thick head in harbor the morning after, a whiff of oxygen works wonders, but otherwise they were an encumbrance in the deep Mediterranean. Just unnecessary bits of equipment which grandmotherly regulations made you carry.

The fore ends started reloading their torpedoes, others went about checking over their equipment and anyone whose immediate duties allowed it lay down; you use less air lying down. The trays of lithium were laid out and we settled down to wait till dark.

I climbed into my bunk; sleep is a precious commodity to take when you can and it looked like being a busy time ahead. However, I was not undisturbed for long. H.E. was reported closing again, the hunt was casting back and getting very close.

Suddenly there was a deafening roar, the boat jarred and shivered and all the lights in the fore ends went; a near miss for'ard.

Out of the darkness John McIntyre, the Torpedo Officer—he was to lose his life in a peacetime accident in *Truculent* seven years later—remarked:

"We may be only the secondary armament this end, but those chaps up top don't seem to realize it."

Torpedoes were, of course, the primary armament, but owing to my supposed predilection for the gun, McIntyre used to get his leg pulled about the unimportance of his torpedoes.

Someone asked for the score; both the fore and after ends used to keep a tally of depth charges, but, strangely enough, the count did not always agree. We were only in the sixties; we had done better than that.

This last lot was apparently only a pattern dropped at random and the hunt moved on. Some of the crew started playing Ukkers; the only sign of strain I heard was when someone cursed at the noise made by the dice.

The boat seemed strangely quiet. I wondered how many were thinking about getting off; or whether they just reckoned I would fix it. We had been stuck for six hours by then and it had been dark for some time. The Asdic set could no longer hear the hunters; there was no excuse for delaying finding out.

The familiar response to the order Diving Stations, the machinery starting up, brought back one's confidence. The end was an anticlimax—the boat came off without much trouble and No. 1 caught her with plenty to spare.

What was a surprise was a crashing pattern of depth charges; one of our hunters must have been lying stopped close by. We had no difficulty in throwing him off. At midnight we were clear and surfaced—God's open air again, the stars overhead, the start of another day. Paris brought me a signal, our recall. It was to be the last day of the patrol.

There was not time to go anywhere else, so I decided to go and see if either of our victims had been beached and beat up any salvage operations. Dev took us in through the familiar path in the minefields. Fuel-oil misted the periscope and it was hard to see under the cliffs, but presently we made out a ship, with two A/S boats patrolling to seaward. But it was the third ship, the elderly tramp. She must have lost heart at seeing her two predecessors going up, put her helm over and run aground. We worked round the motor anti-submarine boats and put two torpedoes into her to ensure that all her cargo was destroyed. Dev took a photo, through the periscope, of one of the torpedoes hitting; it was safe enough as we were well inshore of the patrols.

However, they did have a crack at us on the way out and, judging by the number and size of charges, called up some help. And so we came back to Algiers. Our bag was an armed liner, a tanker, an old tramp, a store ship severely damaged, an M/S trawler, and A/S brigantine and a trading schooner. We should have sunk that store ship.

Although I did not know it then, it was my last patrol. Barney Fawkes, our Captain (S), had been trying to persuade me to retire for some time. My experience was considered to be more valuable in training others.

17

FAREWELL SAFARI

It was a Sunday and I had been up in the mountains with the Bugatti, on one of those tours of gastronomical exploration which the inns of Algeria rendered so rewarding. I had dropped my companion and was feeling some regret, as I came over the side of *Maidstone,* that I should now be going into purdah in preparation for our next patrol in a couple of days' time.

The Quarter-master told me that the Captain (S) wanted to see me; it was after mignight, but the captain of a flotilla, like his boats, used to work a twenty-four hour day; I thought he probably wanted to ask me about some operating area.

Barney was at his desk and he motioned me to a whisky and soda; as I sank into one of his armchairs to enjoy his familiar hospitality, I looked at him enquiringly. He gave me a rather guilty look and then said:

"I am relieving you in *Safari;* she will not sail till Wednesday and Berkeley Lakin is taking her over."

Berkeley was the spare C.O.; he had already made his name in *Ursula* and I could not have wished for a better man to take over my boat. But Barney knew very well that I wanted to finish off the commission. We had argued this matter out before. There was an idea prevalent that successful C.O.s were apt to lose their boats on the last patrol of a commission; possibly, some thought, a slight easing of caution arising from familiarity; more probably just a case of the pitcher that goes once too often to the well. After all, if a boat gets enough depth charges hurled at it, whatever its experience and guile, the chances are that one day it will strike unlucky.

256

As I have said before, we had recently had a heavy spate of losses; fortunately it was to be the last run of severe losses in the submarine war, though inevitably there would continue to be some losses. With the turn of the tide they would be relatively light; with the fall of Tunis the end, though distant, was in sight. Our submarine effort was to swing to the Pacific. The Americans, whose submarine achievements in the Pacific were truly magnificent, had left the Japanese feeling pretty groggy. Japanese technique was easily dealt with by a service which we had learnt the hard way in Norway and the Mediterranean; we had very few losses indeed in the Pacific.

But at this time we were still feeling the recent loss of some of our most experienced boats: *Splendid, Sahib,* and *Saracen,* who had accompanied *Safari* to Malta, had just gone and so had Linton in *Turbulent.* I pointed out that this was no moment to relieve the last oldtimer. We had had all this out before. It was true that my experience, and there was not a lot of experience left now, would be of value for training, but I had set my heart on seeing out the commission. I knew it must be my last. I was getting too old for the game and anyhow now that the corner was turned there was not the same urge in it for me.

But Barney had known that all this was coming. The C.-in-C., he said, had given orders that I was to go sick. It would not look then as if I was being relieved specially. So I retired to my cabin and the P.M.O. sent up bottles of medicine; I do not know what they contained as I poured them away. I was allowed to rise from my bed to say goodbye to the crew before they sailed and, as I have said elsewhere, I was asked to leave my prayer book and sea-going cap in the boat.

Bill Harris was also being relieved; he was the doyen of submarine engineers, he should have gone before but we had stayed together. It was better that a younger Chief should serve with a C.O. not so much over half Bill's age.

We went up and stood by the rail together to see *Safari* sail, the first time she had been to sea without both of us on board. For once Silent Harris lived up to his ironic nickname. The boat probably meant even more to him than it did to me; he knew every nut of her; he had stood by her at the builders for months before I joined.

But for both of us it was the end of our submarining careers.

As *Safari* slid round the end of the breakwater, our eyes met. Without a word we turned and went down for a glass of gin.

EPILOGUE—
SAFARI'S PRAYER

A Prayer said every Sunday on patrol in H.M.S. *Safari* and which was called by some who served in her, *Safari's Prayer*, though she had no real claim to it, for it was written long before her day.

Lord of all power, and might, Who are the Author and Giver of all good things, mercifully grant us grace valiantly to fight in Thy cause.

Give us the sure conviction that Thou art ever by our side. Grant us in battle unflinching courage and an unconquerable spirit, so that no hurt nor obstacle may ever deter us from our duty.

And in victory, O Lord, grant us to be worthy of Thine everlasting love and to continue Thy faithful soldiers and servants unto our life's end; and this we beg for Jesus Christ, His sake.

Amen.

Special Offer
Buy a Bantam Book
for only 50¢.

Now you can have Bantam's catalog filled with hundreds of titles plus take advantage of our unique and exciting bonus book offer. A special offer which gives you the opportunity to purchase a Bantam book for only 50¢. Here's how!

By ordering any five books at the regular price per order, you can also choose any other single book listed (up to a $5.95 value) for just 50¢. Some restrictions do apply, but for further details why not send for Bantam's catalog of titles today!

Just send us your name and address and we will send you a catalog!